ENDING OUR
UNCIVIL WAR

A PATH TO POLITICAL RECOVERY & SPIRITUAL RENEWAL

JIM BROWN

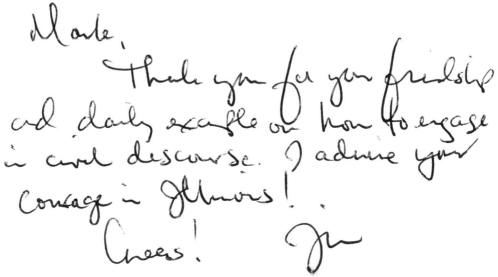

Mark,

Thank you for your friendship and daily example on how to engage in civil discourse. I admire your courage in Jefferson!

Cheers!

Jim

Published in Nashville, Tennessee, by Agape Publishing LLC
Edited by Chris Clancy

Library of Congress Cataloging-in-Publication Data
Library of Congress Control Number: 2017913996
Brown, Jim
Ending our uncivil war.

ISBN: 978-0-9993999-0-3
ISBN: 978-0-9993999-1-0
ISBN: 978-0-9993999-2-7

Printed in the United States of America

TO KATHRYN AND WILL, MY DEAR CHILDREN,

Thank you for supporting me while I wrote this book.

There were weekends we didn't get to hike or play.

I admire and appreciate your patience, love, and encouragement.

Much, much love. -DAD

TABLE OF CONTENTS

MY LIFE AND 'THE WHY'

I wanted to write this book for at least 20 years. Finally, I did.

Since graduating college, I've had "the writing bug." Initially, writing was mostly for fun or a release, like when I was in the Navy sending letters home. In 2000, it became a profession. I was hired as the business editor and a reporter for a start-up newspaper, *The City Paper*, in Nashville. I loved going to work, chasing stories in my hometown.

About that time, I began to write a book about reforming government, but, after a few months, I abandoned ship. There were too many holes below the waterline to count. There was much to learn about literary compartmentalization before any book could be seaworthy. My composition skills needed work.

A few years ago, I reread my old draft and recognized another problem. My presentation was quite firm. The book read like a recital, not unlike what you'd find in one of the many echo chambers on social media. Few sections presented multiple sides. It was clear I'd made the right decision to return to port. Then I heard a voice, "Hey, given what's happening in our country, and what you've learned since, maybe now is the time to go back to the Book Shipyard."

For at least 20 years, I also wanted to run a marathon. Every so often, I'd have a good race, maybe a 10-miler when I was in the Navy, or a 10K after I left. But a marathon was all talk, and deep down I knew it.

I doubted myself and did little research how to train properly for a half-marathon or marathon, much like my first attempt at a book.

I was missing focus. Then, focus came, but not the way I wanted.

My wife Dori was diagnosed with leukemia in 2007. We were devastated. Life went off cruise control. All hell broke loose, frankly. I needed a way to cope, so I started running more, a lot more. Over the next eight years, I ran a dozen half marathons and two full marathons. No more talk, no more try—just prepare properly and do it.

I started writing more, too. Another coping mechanism was my blog, *Run for Dori*. This was my space to share the journey of cancer as a spouse, caretaker and father. I began to write with more feeling and less judging. Mysticism began to overtake certitude. Dori invited paradox, and so did I. Our faith grew, and our trust deepened.

After her second relapse, Dori heard that the chemo didn't work. She accepted it with uncommon strength and grace. Before she died, she told our children, "When you say the Lord's Prayer, and those words 'Thy Will Be Done,' you either are saying them or you mean them."

Her love was agape, love at its deepest level. A few years ago, I felt compelled to write about agape, in a world that seems to have less of it at the moment. One reason I've written this book is in honor of her and what we learned together. The life she led continues to inspire.

The same year as Dori's diagnosis, I was promoted to state director for the National Federation of Independent Business (NFIB), an association representing thousands of small business owners. My role since has been to advocate on general interest issues for small business, such as workers' compensation, unemployment, tax, regulatory, healthcare, labor, tort and environmental. It's been an eye-opening education of how complex these matters are, unlike what we're reading in many social media feeds.

I've seen the good, bad and ugly in politics and policymaking. Some of what you will read, and especially in the last chapter, is how government functions better when power is divided among the political parties and three branches of government. Healthy friction may appear counterintuitive to some, which is another reason I've left the dock of unpublished authors.

Lastly, the preceding 10 years have been enlightening in another way. I made many new friendships once I left my old "comfort zone."

I believe becoming uncomfortable and changing routines is one of the most important things we can do to end our uncivil war. Before this transformation, I don't ever remember listening to a lesbian couple talk about being judged by family members, or how a black legislator feels about a statue of Nathan Bedford Forrest a few yards from her chair as a lawmaker.

I'm not seeking your agreement or consent when I share that. I am saying I hope you understand that I have more information than I used to have, and a better place from which to have a conversation.

I want to thank the leaders at NFIB for allowing me to pursue writing this book. Everything written is my opinion and perspective, and not NFIB's.

I appreciate the opportunity to engage a large audience on the importance of having fewer verbal takedowns, and instead take on issues that need our attention. There's a fine line between writing something constructively critical about someone's actions and something overly unfavorable about that person.

It's been a healthy exercise to live and breathe one of the main themes in my own book. I did my best, and appreciate their trust.

INTRODUCTION

"Don't believe everything you think."

—BUMPER STICKER

I'll never forget seeing that sticker in 2013.

On an early morning bike ride in my hometown Nashville, I arrived simultaneously at a stop sign with a small car. The driver had 30 stickers on the back. Some were a rant. Most were old.

One brand new sticker stood out.

I couldn't stop thinking about the sticker. What if I'm wrong, or not entirely right? Have I convinced myself that "my truth" is "the truth"? How good—or bad—have I been at staying open-minded or seeking information that might make me uncomfortable, or even change my mind? How can I process better? Am I listening enough?

My reflection felt right, like my car was getting a complete five-point inspection. Except this was self-introspection. I was in a unique repair shop.

I liked what was happening so much that I decided to talk about the sticker in professional speeches to civic groups. Audience members laughed every time, some nervously. Nice, I thought, that's how it started with me. Their own reflection was underway. People came up to talk about the sticker and its meaning in our hyper-certain world.

I thought, "This thing is resonating everywhere I go. Maybe I'll write a book about this."

Obviously, the sticker is a big inspiration for this book. So many seem so certain of their opinions and anger easily when there's disagreement, before even having a conversation or back-and-forth. The sticker appeared to me at a time when our civility clearly is declining and our political system is unraveling. Few feel good about the direction we're heading. We view fellow Americans as enemies. We're nervous for our kids.

Something isn't right. There's much to talk about.

———✳———

It was an election unlike any we'd seen.

Before and after the first two presidential debates in 2016, Facebook exploded. Your friends and mine went at it. And each other…

Before the third debate, I decided, tongue-in-cheek, to offer some levity and an alternative vision on my little corner of Facebook.

> *Exciting news about two new drugs for electile dysfunction right before the last debate…*
>
> *Have you been experiencing pre- and post-debate anxiety? Is this year's election resulting in sleepless-ness, despair and frequent mood swings, or rashes or cold sweats? Do political rants by good friends on social media cause anxiety? Are you afraid to witness it anymore?*
>
> *There's help. Nowatchia. A new drug from Jerck.*
>
> *Nowatchia has been proven to reduce over-affiliation with leading candidates from both major parties. Nowatchia, when combined with Informmeia, can lead to heightened awareness for term limits, ending redistricting, reduced gridlock, compromise, increased compassion, aversion to control by duopolies, balanced budgets, and respect for your fellow American.*

Possible side effects include scorn from highly partisan friends, the finger, defriending, and slight hypertension from a return to more independent thinking and sticking with your moral compass.

If you experience these side effects, don't call your doctor but vote your conscience immediately.

I did watch (survive?) some of the debate. The next morning, I returned to swirling activity on social media. My "friends" were busy:

"I'm done. I can't do Facebook anymore and I can't watch the news or check one-sided websites. Later!"

Others pecked away at their computers and phones, without a thought of pausing or self-editing.

"She's a liar! How could anyone sane vote for her?"

"He's a racist! How could anyone sane vote for him?"

"We're so screwed!"

———※———

The way many on the left and right are communicating is now beyond disconcerting.

The morning of June 14, 2017, started just as any other for Congressman Steve Scalise. The House Majority Whip from Louisiana had a full day ahead. Little did he know how full.

Around 7 a.m. that morning, Scalise and fellow Republicans were practicing for the next day's annual summer baseball game between Republicans and Democrats. Shots were fired. A House staff member for Rep. Roger Williams from Texas, a lobbyist and Scalise were struck. Two undercover Capitol Police returned fire. Other police arrived. The culprit, James T. Hodginkinson from Illinois, was shot and later died, but not before five people were wounded.

That day, the nation seemed quiet. Adversaries recognized each other's humanity. Congressmen Joe Barton and Mike Doyle, managers of the baseball teams, appeared at a press conference. They celebrated their longtime friendship, discussed the unraveling political climate and announced the game would be played as scheduled.

At the game, kneeling Democrats and Republicans prayed together on the field. The Democrats won, and handed the trophy to their opponents.

Elsewhere, the contrasts couldn't have been starker.

After Scalise was shot, GOP Rep. Claudia Tenney from New York received a threatening email with the subject line "One down, 216 to go…" The person emailing said: "Did you NOT expect this?"

Rep. Steve Stivers from Ohio received a voicemail that said, "We're coming to get every g*****n one of you and your families. Maybe the next one taken down will be your daughter. Huh? Or your wife. Or even you." Utah Rep. Jason Chaffetz received one, too: "I suggest you prepare for the battle m*********, and the apocalypse…Because we are going to hunt your a** down, wrap a rope around your neck, and hang you from a lamppost."

On my social media feed, a friend who is pro-gun control posted about a man near death: "Karma is a b****, Stevie."

Even before the shooting, things were out of hand. The previous month, Virginia Rep. Tom Garrett appeared at his town halls with a heavy police presence after he and his family received death threats. "This is how we're going to kill your wife," read one message.

In Arizona, GOP Rep. Martha McSally said a constituent left voicemails warning the Republican congresswoman's days were "numbered." In Tennessee, Congressman David Kustoff and his aide Marianne Dunavant survived an attempt by 35-year-old constituent Wendi Wright to run them off the road after a town hall about the GOP health care bill.

Some congressmen across the country from both parties showed up at their meetings to be berated by constituents. Many canceled events altogether.

Three days before the baseball event shootings, *Huffington Post* contributor Jason Fuller wrote that "Trump's impeachment and removal from office are no longer enough" and that "Trump and everyone assisting in his agenda" be charged with treason and (italics mine) "upon receiving guilty verdicts—*they must all be executed under the law.*" *HuffPost* pulled the piece quickly, but not before more damage to our declining state of discourse was done.

On Broadway, two sponsors, Delta Airlines and Bank of America pulled financial support for the play "Julius Caesar," during which actors brutally assassinate Donald Trump. A Delta spokesperson said, "Their artistic and creative direction crossed the line on the standards of good taste." Other sponsors dug in, defending the free speech of "murdering" a president.

The week prior, comedian Kathy Griffin posted a grotesque photo of herself holding the bloodied severed head of Donald Trump.

In Connecticut at Trinity College, Johnny Eric Williams, a sociology professor on race relations, recycled an article by Medium. com titled "Let Them F****** Die." Both the author and Williams were critical of Capitol Police Officer Crystal Griner, a lesbian black woman who helped defend Scalise and others in harm's way. Said Williams: "I'm fed the f*** up with self identified 'white's' [sic] daily violence directed at immigrants, Muslim, and sexual [sic] and racially oppressed people. The time is now to confront these inhuman a******* and end this now."

At what point does uncivil behavior explode into a civil war? One can argue that's already happening, with the baseball field shooting representing a crescendo of the many uncivil moments that led to it.

There are plenty of very disturbing right-against-left attacks, too. In the summer of 2017, Nashville Mayor Megan Barry, a Democrat, lost her son to a tragic drug overdose. She showed tremendous grace and openly talked about our out-of-control opioid crisis that must be addressed. The vast majority of Nashvillians, including many Republican Party leaders, expressed sympathy for her loss and thanked her for sharing her story, even as she was grieving.

Inconceivably however, some on the right couldn't help themselves, posting hard-to-believe comments from their Facebook bunkers.

Said one, "It's very sad. It's awful, in fact.... And I pray for her and her family, but she is the last person who should be lecturing on how to raise children to be drug-free.... At least wait awhile and not use his death for political reasons."

And another: "I hate to say it. But liberalism kills. It kills kids. It kills jobs. It will ultimately kill Nashville and America."

And another: "Read Romans 13. She disobeyed our president, and God did that to [redacted] when he disobeyed God."

And another: "Guess you reap what you sew."

Our uncivil war is very bipartisan.

This anger and lack of compassion for our fellow man, which has been growing behind computer screens, on extreme blogs and in chat rooms, is now on our streets. We've watched the murdering of innocent people, like the racist hate crime in Charleston, South Carolina; the chaotic race riots in Ferguson, Missouri, and Baltimore, Maryland; and white nationalists taking to the streets in Charlottesville, Virginia, where a woman was murdered in cold blood, as well.

———✳———

Perhaps you've heard the concern, disbelief and fear in friends' voices, or maybe your own.

> "*This country is going down the tubes.*"
> "*Yeah, what a mess.*"

> "*The election has come down to these two?*"
> "*I know. I can't do politics anymore with friends on social media.*"

> "*My vote or engagement doesn't really matter.*"
> "*Yeah, and no one is really talking about the important issues.*"

> "*I'm terrified for my kids and grandkids!*"
> "*Me, too.*"

Sound uplifting? Not really. Eeyore the Donkey would be proud!

Granted, the 2016 presidential campaign was enough to bring down even great optimists. The obvious flaws in both candidates consumed oxygen. The coverage and debates turned into discussions of deviant or corrupt behavior, with little mention of national challenges and opportunities.

On Election Day, Trump beat Hillary, in a shocking upset. Riots—staged and real—broke out. College students scurried to their safe places, and professors cancelled tests. The victorious gloated and prodded the losers. Empathy was in short supply as a shocked nation digested ever-growing polarization and the huge energy suck in our media, communities and even our inner circles.

Our National Mess didn't start during the 2016 elections. We started feeling like lobsters in a slow-boiling pot years ago. Now, we're feeling the full boil. How did it get like this, so out of hand? Today's war on each other took time to unfold, politically and culturally.

For many years, the two major parties have worked behind their curtains to retain and expand their power. They have done so not only with greater vigilance but also with disdain for their opponents and their bases of support. Just read the Wikileaks releases of Democrat Party operatives talking about minorities if you have doubts, or the Republican Party's confidential analysis of Trump during the primary. Control is the end game.

Both political parties have redrawn congressional districts, spent time inside the Beltway bubble raising ungodly sums of money, and researched the unseemly backgrounds of every third cousin of the opposing candidate. If they only had the same energy and focus to fix ticking time bombs: Social Security, Medicaid, immigration, decaying cities and the debt.

Both parties increasingly pander to dependably loyal sections of the electorate. The left glad-hands to minorities, delivering poor results while inner cities decay, while the right panders to evangelicals, enabling fearful rhetoric that somehow tax-paying, peaceful loving gay couples are the undoing of our culture. More misplaced energy and focus.

Political operatives are very smart. They know we live in an age of entitlement, wants and demands. Many of us believe we're entitled to something, or that we must not miss out since many government officials are amenable to requests. Crony capitalism has become commonplace, as corporations hold out their hands for tax cuts and kickbacks. Welfare and food stamps become a way of life rather than a way out for the dependent poor. Powerful interest groups request funding needs, and the political elite complies.

These same politicians, believing their role is critical to serve those who support them, become masters of those who seek the support. We become interdependent. The screeching irony is that people and groups with very different political viewpoints aren't really that different. Government coke is government coke, and too many of us are on it.

Over the last several decades, opportunities to pass reasonable solutions in bipartisan fashion have been missed. Take healthcare reform, a case study for today's dysfunctional political environment. Both the Democrat and Republican parties had opportunities to ignore controlling special interests like insurance companies and various uncompromising advocates and negotiate a plan that would have incorporated good ideas from both platforms. Imagine a health-care bill that would have had Republican ideas—allowing people and businesses to pool across state lines and purchase insurance, and expand use of health savings accounts that empower individuals and introduce market pressures. Imagine that same bill with Democrat ideas—ending restrictions based on pre-existing conditions, keeping young adults covered through age 26 and removing caps on benefits to ensure no one ever faces bankruptcy because of inadequate health insurance. The law wouldn't have been cheap, but it would have been affordable and productive, and bipartisan.

You know the rest of the story. What was rammed through Congress in 2009 without much time to read wasn't bipartisan, affordable or workable. Many lost their doctor, premiums soared and healthcare exchanges crumbled soon after launching. While millions benefited, millions more were worse off than before. Both sides dug in further, resistant to acknowledge benefits and problems with the law.

Fast forward to the early summer of 2017, when Republicans had control of Congress and the Oval Office. How did they craft legislation? Thirteen Republican senators drafted a bill behind closed doors and announced they had a good bill. They said no committee hearings were necessary, saying it would be a waste of time; instead, they would use a budget process called reconciliation because it would only require them to get 50 of the 52 Republican votes, not the 60 under regular procedures. You see, Obamacare wasn't bipartisan, so their bill didn't have to be, either.

We are in a time when proposals aren't debated and leaders don't meet with other leaders. Rather, they communicate like many of us—through social media. Like us, they've embraced this relatively new religion of technology. Their mismanagement and control endgame have contributed greatly to increasing anger and entrenchment in the electorate. So have our tweets and posts.

Our imperfect republic has worked historically because power by and large has been spread across the three branches of government—

executive, legislative and judicial. Alarmingly, that is not the case today. Congress has become weak and ineffective, which hurts and angers the people they represent.

We feel voiceless, so we have turned up the volume, and begun a lurch toward authoritarianism. Many now believe we don't have a choice but to fight our battles in the courts and through executive action, since Congress is punting.

This has the effect of putting the other branches into overdrive. More look to our Supreme Court and an increasingly imperial executive branch to win on their issues. The courts, the president and agency commissioners have been happy to fill this legislative vacuum. Many wonder, "Will our Republic hold?"

The division is increasing and resulting in dangerous decisions. People in right-leaning states and even counties have threatened secession. People in left-leaning states like California are organizing a proposition to secede. The state of California has banned state business travel to states that have passed laws with which they don't agree. My home state of Tennessee has called for all states to ban travel to California. And so on and so on...

It doesn't matter if you're a Republican, Democrat or Independent, you "get it" when you hear your friends talking about authoritarianism and nationalism. Most likely, you don't like or want either ism, if you're aware of history.

We have reached a critical point in our history. Big changes are needed. If you agree, this book is for you.

———❦———

Good news: More people are aware that something's wrong politically and culturally. They're engaging.

Bad news: Others also are aware something's not right in our country. But they're not engaging.

More bad news: Some are over-engaging and attacking their fellow American, rather than arguing civilly over ideas and solutions. It's become too personal.

Those who did engage in the 2016 election made sure it was not typical. It was a revolt against both parties. Voters showed up to express their displeasure of the parties' appetite for control and inability to fix problems.

Populists Donald Trump and Bernie Sanders recognized this, and openly mixed messaging based on fear, racial or class warfare, blame and distrust to generate energy for their campaigns. Post-modern leftists rose up against the Democrat Party, furious that it would anoint one candidate with her undemocratic super-delegates. Conservatives joined an unusual coalition of Rust Belt Democrats, minorities like Cuban-Americans and black pastors, union workers and others to tell the Republican Party, "I don't care what Trump says, I know he's an erratic nominee, but I'm fed up with you."

"Enough is enough. We're in charge, you're not."

Through a traditional lens, Bernie Sanders, from the socialist left, and Donald Trump, from atop Trump Tower, didn't appear to have much in common. They were similar candidates in one main sense, however. Both ran populist campaigns. They talked about trade, minimum wage, paid leave and breaking the establishment. While many of their proposed solutions were different, and certainly their tone and rhetoric were, both beat the drum about the haves and have nots, and ditched the traditional pitch of conservative vs. liberal.

So where do we go from here? Will our Union survive? Will states stay united? Can we find solutions to big issues?

Is it possible for people with very different viewpoints to decentralize the concentration of power and put some function back into a dysfunctional government?

What is happening in our culture, educational system and daily lives that we can address to get to a better place?

Can little ole me and you do anything about it? How?

Over the course of this book, I will offer critical points and action steps. At the end, I'll summarize into a Comprehensive Action Plan that will be available not only to you but also on a website you can share with your friends.

You are being invited, better yet empowered, to do something about the mess. I have a few simple requests before we embark.

CHECK YOUR POLITICAL BAGGAGE

"When you point your finger at someone, there's
always three pointing back at you."
—UNKNOWN

For more than a decade, I've been blessed to work as a professional
advocate at the state level, gaining knowledge of government systems
that work, and don't work. I've been on the front line as Tennessee
state director for the National Federation of Independent Business,
an association representing 7,000 small businesses in Tennessee and
more than 300,000 nationwide. I have seen how our federal system has
become warped, easily manipulated and corrosive.

I have seen also how states, by and large, have a much better
structure in place that stops or tempers much of the shenanigans we're
witnessing on the federal level.

I see a great American opportunity. There is a course to a functioning, representative government and society that people with
differing political and spiritual views can embrace and institute. I
believe there are non-partisan, bipartisan and multi-partisan fixes that
transcend any particular religion, faith or way of life. We have much
in common politically, which we can discuss, activate and implement.
We will help improve the tone and focus of our debates, help restructure
our government, and lift up each other in the process.

My invitation to you is to put aside your political views—conservative, liberal, some hybrid or none of the above—for the duration of
this literary journey. I promise you can have them back at the end. We
will talk about many issues, and I'm fairly confident you won't agree
with everything you read. I certainly hope you don't! File away our
different viewpoints, and move on. You might read something right
after that resonates and offers transformation opportunities.

This book is not an endeavor to ask you to change any specific
political or religious view or belief system. Rather, this journey is
dedicated to looking at the unfolding uncivil war from different
angles, making sense of the political and spiritual cacophony, and
working to make systemic and personal changes that reposition our
politics and culture.

This may sound idealistic to you. Right now, it is. I guess all I am saying is give peace a chance. If hippie tunes aren't your thing, think of your favorite peace song—country, rock, whatever—and bring it with you. Or whatever song makes your spirit move to deeper love.

We will develop a non-partisan playbook that will provide guardrails in our politics and dissolve gridlock. We will create a plan to stimulate healthier political engagements and deliver policy results.

We will teach our children that while perfection is impossible the imperfect works better and can be beautiful. We will achieve new empathy in our own lives that will spread through our ailing families and communities.

Another way to look at this is we'll be creating a new Energy Plan.

- We'll place emphasis on personal service to improve the energy in others' lives; importantly, this will improve our understanding of pain and suffering—and improve our lives, too.
- We'll generate more positive personal energy that will increase awareness of our common humanity; this will foster better civil engagement or help the disengaged to start engaging. (Some will be weaned off Nowatchia.)
- We'll promote *and* protect freedom of speech on college campuses; this will lead to more energy spent engaging civilly and celebrating diversity of ideas and reaching understanding.
- We'll produce focused political energy at the federal level by rewiring the system in bipartisan fashion; this will temper divisiveness that your favorite media outlets recycle and blast into your feeds that we in turn recycle, share and retweet.

Are you ready? It's time to take a really awesome trip. We're going to leave the tremendous ground turbulence and board a beautiful, state-of-the-art jet airplane, with legroom and five-star cabin service. We'll be flying on a spectacular day, experiencing a clear 30,000-foot view of a nation in turmoil.

There is only first class because you deserve it when you see everything you must do to get on this plane. Our in-flight service will include an exploration of four timely goal-oriented topics.

- Service Commitment
- Spiritual Renewal
- Scholastic Independence
- Systemic Government Reforms

Service commitment will spark greater interest in our fellow man. We'll identify and help the person in need who is different from us. Not unlike JFK's famous proclamation to do more for your country than for yourself, we'll become better citizens building better communities, and counter the runaway "selfie" culture. We will walk in the shoes of others, and gain meaningful understanding of their fear, pain and difficulties.

Spiritual renewal will enable us to find peace and love in one another, no matter our differences. We'll reject a reckless need to be right and to vanquish those with whom we disagree. We'll gain or regain a better understanding of loving our enemy, the Martin Luther King, Jr. Way, like so many of our streets are named. A renewed emphasis on empathy will create hope and optimism. We'll explore the meaning of separation of church and state, and make some sense of the tug-of-war between our minds and what media tells and doesn't tell us. Our uncivil blasting and bashing will wane.

Scholastic independence in our learning institutions will foster a greater depth of understanding of complex issues. Truths from differing viewpoints will be acknowledged, understood and incorporated. Disagreements will no longer be called "hate speech." We will teach children how to learn, not what to think. Victimization, shaming and blaming will become passé on college campuses and town halls. College administrators and their boards will hear us.

Systemic government reforms will reaffirm political accountability to the electorate. We're going to take requirements and structure many state governments have and apply them to the federal government We'll install guardrails that require elected officials to act on our behalf. They will be less inclined to spread or sell fear. In fact, they'll be quite a bit more attentive, as time goes on and they see unity among diverse constituencies. Power will be decentralized. Lifetime bureaucrats will be limited in what they can propose, implement and change. Bipartisan bills will pass. We will improve government functionality and representation.

Sound reasonable? Now the big things about this plane ride: our crew needs you to leave your political baggage behind. You won't need a carry-on.

We will be seating you next to a person whose views you neither trust nor like. You might even hate him or her. Who is that person? You must pick! Be honest, your stomach needs to be queasy when you select.

Are you a socialist? Consider picking a Wall Street capitalist. Are you pro-life? Maybe ride with a Planned Parenthood executive? As you settle in with your nemesis and take a look around the cabin, you'll notice other unusual seating arrangements.

A Muslim with a Jew.

A religious conservative with a protesting atheist. A college-educated liberal with an illiterate rural man. A CEO with five large houses next to a dishwasher on minimum wage.

A country club member with a gang member. A small business owner next to a regulator.

A Wall Street derivatives trader with an elderly woman with a small pension. A homeless woman next to a debutante.

An environmentalist adjacent to an unemployed coal miner.

And you and your new "friend."

We've been cleared for takeoff.

We're turning off everything that is contributing to fear and fire, including your portable electronic devices. We don't have Wi-Fi or TV, so there's no Fox News or MSNBC. HuffPost and Drudge Report will have to wait. You will be able to access the noise and turbulence when we're on the ground again. Trust me, it will be there when we land.

We're at 10,000 feet and climbing. It's a beautiful day!

JIM BROWN
Nashville, TN
August 2017

RECOGNITION: THE CALL TO SERVE

> "You never really know a man until you understand
> things from his point of view, until you climb into
> his skin and walk around in it."
> —HARPER LEE, **TO KILL A MOCKINGBIRD**

My seatmate on our plane is a homeless man.

Year after year, my Sundays went like many other Americans'
Day of Rest. Wake up, maybe go to church, and put some money in
the basket for the poor and less fortunate. Maybe I would turn on the
Sunday news shows and listen to politicians argue like they always do,
and then switch over to football. If the games were intriguing, I might
watch football all day.

This routine was comfortable. I could tell myself I was doing
something to help others, then retreating into my own world to be
entertained. The media was in control of me. I was in a big bubble, and
I didn't know it.

Underneath, the gnawing grew. What was it, specifically? Was
I doing enough? Was I consuming or producing? Who was I really
helping? What was I doing on that couch?

An internal argument was underway. My own whispers began. Whenever I heard them, I told myself I was doing good things. Yes, I served on various non-profit boards, all worthy causes—Prevent Blindness, Junior Achievement, Gilda's Club and others. My contributions to churches and various charities have some impact, I continued.

Then, another voice started talking. You're not getting your hands dirty. You're not in front of people who need help. Why are you avoiding connecting with the suffering and needy in front of you? Isn't that what your faith tells you to do? Who is this about, Jim, you or others who have it worse than you, much worse?

My internal arguing was most evident when I pulled up to street corners and saw the homeless. My hometown of Nashville, Tennessee, has been booming. Growth of all kinds has occurred. Jobs are everywhere. This growth, however, has included a spike in our homeless population. At ground level, this began to sink in. Most times when I pulled up to those street corners, a wrinkled, tired man would look at me, holding up his "I need your help" sign. I usually avoided eye contact. A sunburned woman would approach my car, holding up *The Contributor*, the newspaper that the homeless were selling for a measly dollar.

I told myself, "Heck, I'm doing a lot already contributing money to my church. And why is this same person on the street corner every year? Doesn't she know Nashville is booming and jobs are available?"

Some people I represented professionally complained often that they had jobs they can't fill. This added to my confusion.

One day on the street a homeless woman whom I bought a sandwich weeks ago approached me. I hardly ever gave money to someone on the street, thinking they would just go get drunk. "I really need money, not food," she said in frustration. I began to lecture her that Room in the Inn was a wonderful shelter and rehabilitation program supported by nearly 200 congregations. They could help her get off the street. I asked if she knew Father Charlie Strobel, who founded the program and helped people like her.

She looked at me like I was a nut job. And she was right.

Inner debate continued. My son came home one day during his sophomore year of high school saying he needed more service hours as part of a school requirement. I asked him what he wanted to do. He shrugged and said he didn't know. Out of my mouth, I blurted, "What about Room in the Inn?" He shrugged again.

I knew about Room in the Inn from friends, including a lobbyist, Anne, who invited me years ago to a fundraiser with city bigwigs. Father Strobel played softball with my dad in the 70s, and I knew he was a good man. I went to the fundraiser, gave some money and listened to one person after another praise Father Strobel and the mission. It was a seed planted, a seed that needed more sunlight, rain and better soil.

My friend Maureen told me how she and her two high school-age daughters went to the church once a week during the Inn's Winter Shelter Program that ran from November through March. She talked about how interacting with the homeless changed her daughters. She told me about her friend Amanda, who volunteered several times a week at the Inn's main facility, helping 450 people get off the streets on a cold winter's night into warm beds. My friend Michael told me that he loved going to Room in the Inn every Sunday with his son Sebastian. He encouraged Will and me to join them, so we did.

I could have chosen several plane companions, like an illiberal college administrator or a finger-wagging Christian. It was clear, though, that I needed to sit next to a homeless person. Buckle up, Jim! I didn't know it yet, but my uncomfortable self was taking charge of my comfortable persona.

Year One at Room in the Inn was awkward at first. The main facility is not in the best part of town. Will and I would arrive Sundays at 5 p.m., unsure of the process and what would unfold. Many of the homeless were exhausted and just wanting rest and to be left alone. A few looked very shady or angry. What are we getting into, I thought?

A few years before, only two miles down the street, a homeless man pinned me in my car and demanded money. I fought him off, called the police, and filed a report. The incident had an impact. I will never be so vulnerable again, I told myself and loved ones. They knew what I knew—that I had lost my wife to cancer a few years earlier, and I was the only parent left. I couldn't leave my children in such a way. I bought a gun, which I began to carry legally in concealed fashion.

The first few Sundays at the Inn, I entered on guard, carrying my concealed weapon. I channeled nervous energy and started engaging as many of the homeless as I could. It was sometimes awkward, not knowing what I would hear or what I should or shouldn't say.

One by one, I began to get to know them and remember their

names. Some told me stories, while some of their friends watched as we talked. More began to trust me, and I them.

One night at our church, just before Christmas, the kids and I made homemade pizza for 20 Inn guests who spent the night. Our first year of volunteering ended well. I started leaving my weapon at home, and started bringing more love. Will and I decided to go back for another year. He liked it, too.

During Year Two, I began to experience Room in the Inn in a deeper way. The volunteers and staff were a team, managing the chaos of getting hundreds of guests into buses, vans and small cars in 90 minutes. We got to know each other. We laughed a lot with each other and the guests we served.

My favorite job was to check in the guests and ask them what they needed that night—shower, clothing, laundry? Like a good lobbyist does, I remembered their names—Randy H., Winston W., Clarence S., Mary W., Ingrid H., and many more. As they would approach and start saying their names, I would say:

"Hello Clarence, how's it going?"

"How do you know my name?"

"I checked you in last week, do you need all three?'

"Yes, hey thanks, thanks a lot. Hey, is your name really Jim Brown, like James Brown?"

"It sure is, brother. Just like #32 for the Cleveland Browns and the Godfather of Soul. I stunk at football, but I've got smidge of rhythm! Let's catch up later."

"Hell, yeah!"

Later, Clarence and other guests would tell me about their problems:

- "It's just hard to get going."
- "My husband gambled it all away, and then we lost our house."
- "No one will hire me because of my (criminal) record. I really want to work."
- "I never got over the war. I don't really sleep."
- "I was abused sexually by my dad when I was young."
- "I can't seem to get to the career center on time, and I don't have a car."
- "My doctor says my cancer is advancing and probably because I couldn't get in to see him sooner."

- "I failed out of school because I partied way too much and wish I could go back."
- "I'm bipolar, and I keep losing everything."

Amid these difficulties, most managed a smile. Most said they had hope. Some asked me to pray with them. Some would come up and tell me something good that happened that week—a new job, a new home, and being reunited with family! Many of these people were much happier than some of the successful people I knew.

My heart was melting. Sunday nights at Room in the Inn became my favorite time of the week. Don't believe everything you think.

"No one will hire me because of my (criminal) record.
I really want to work."

I started noticing other things about myself. I started going to church more regularly. Dropping money into the church basket meant more. I started giving more. I was experiencing what great leaders like Gandhi had said: "The best way to find yourself is to lose yourself in the service of others."

I certainly wasn't going to find as much watching football or cable news all day. I already knew what was going to happen there: not much that meant much. Instead, I found humanity sitting next to me on the plane.

My friend Maureen said volunteering regularly with her daughters had a huge impact on their lives. "It's not what you say," she explained. "It's what you do. And it becomes who they are."

I hope that's true for my children. As parents and grandparents, we are their examples. I can go on and on about how important being charitable is, but until my children see action they're going to have a hard time taking me or anyone else seriously.

The end result is to change lives one by one, just like some good friends in the next chapter are doing.

CRITICAL POINT:

Don't believe everything you think, especially about the homeless man asking you for money. Judging or pontificating as I did distorts the ability to see other views. Regular service changes you, centers you and humanizes everyone around you.

ACTION STEP:

Discuss with your plane friend what volunteering means to her and to you. Reflect on how much time you spend *regularly* volunteering versus how much time you spend on social media. Look to adjust your schedule to include more time helping others on a consistent basis.

CONTEMPLATION:

"Humility isn't thinking less of yourself. It's thinking
  of yourself less."

- C.S. LEWIS

"You make a living by what you earn. You make a
  life by what you give."

—WINSTON CHURCHILL

ROLE MODELS

"The best way to cheer yourself is to try to cheer somebody else up."

—MARK TWAIN

"Hands that serve are holier than lips that pray."

—SAI BABA

I'll be candid again. I started volunteering at a younger age for less than altruistic reasons.

Volunteering looks good to employers. In fact, 82% of respondents to a 2016 Deloitte survey—which included hiring influencers from 13 major U.S. cities—reported they're more likely to choose a candidate with volunteer experience. However, only one in three résumés actually include volunteer work.

"Volunteer...experience speaks to a candidate's sense of purpose and passion for a cause, which are important qualities when seeking to fill positions," said Teresa Briggs, West region managing partner at Deloitte, noting volunteering also builds leadership skills and provides a marketability edge.

Often as a young man, I was told volunteering would help build my résumé. I was told I would meet people. I didn't hear much about changing lives. Whatever, right?

I volunteered as a younger man. I showed up early Saturday mornings to landscape a middle school or cut back brush from an elderly woman's home in the inner city. I certainly felt I was doing something worthwhile. But I didn't really understand at the time I was doing it more for me than for someone else.

Volunteering was an occasional occurrence, whenever "I had the time."

I didn't know it, but my sense of purpose trumped a greater sense of purpose. Volunteering wasn't a show, exactly, but it wasn't rooted. Once the roots grew, volunteering would become the gateway to growth opportunities in addressing my biases, fears and lack of understanding of some people and situations. It would help me understand people's situations better.

I want to share some role models who helped me get there, through their service. They include my mother Rachel, who planted the seed of service when I was a child and aforementioned friends who help the homeless regularly.

Many stand out, including the community leaders in my hometown who hold up the Mirror of Humanity every day of their walk.

CHARLIE AND "CORBS"

Good behavior, and bad, is modeled.

You've probably read books or heard a compelling speech about the critical role of fathers and mothers in our lives. President Obama gave such a speech on Father's Day in 2008 at a Chicago church about the critical role of a father.

Obama offered powerful observations, including: "Children who grow up without a father are five times more likely to live in poverty and commit crime, nine times more likely to drop out of schools, and 20 times more likely to end up in prison."

In that speech, Obama praised Reverend Arthur Brazier as a community leader who had grown his congregation to more than 20,000 strong. As a result, Obama said they were living with "less chaos," violence and crime. I suspect many of those 20,000 are role models for others.

I may not have had my awakening about the homeless unless another role model, Father Charlie Strobel, hadn't founded Room in the Inn. The successful concept in Nashville has been replicated in dozens of cities across the country. But it never would have happened if Father Strobel hadn't worked through tremendous suffering and stayed committed to service.

In 1986, Charlie started Room in the Inn with a mission "to provide programs that emphasize human development and recovery through education, self-help and work, centered in community and long-term support for those who call the streets of Nashville home." The organization's core values statement says, "Through the power of spirituality and the practice of love, we provide hospitality with a respect that offers hope in a community of non-violence."

Every one of those values—spirituality, love, hospitality, respect, hope and community—would be tested early. Only a few weeks after opening, Father Strobel experienced tragedy when his mother Mary Catherine went missing in early December. A few days later, her body was discovered in her car trunk. A demented prison escapee and several others were later charged with murder. More than 1,000 people attended her funeral.

Father Strobel said in his eulogy, "We know the answers are not easy and clear, but we still believe in the miracle of forgiveness....And we extend our arms in that embrace...There are still needs all around us, and we must attend to those needs."

I've reread that quote many times and wondered if I could get to such a place of peace.

Charlie Strobel says the first few years after his mom died were the darkest of times. "Looking back, I think that the homeless helped save my life," he told the *Nashville Scene* in 2004. "It's like when children get sick; the mother can't get sick, because she has to care for her children. I was so depressed, I would have stayed in bed if I hadn't heard them calling at the gate, 'Please, let me in.'"

And let them in he did. Today, Room in the Inn's network of 200 congregations in Middle Tennessee and more than 6,500 volunteers shelters 1,400 men and women during the cold months. Year round, the organization provides emergency services, transitional programs, and long-term solutions to help people rebuild broken lives.

The Inn outgrew its early spaces so that in 2010 the charity, which is privately supported and receives no government aid, opened a 45,000-square foot building, offering permanent supportive housing.

"We now can walk with people on their journey out of chaos, through periods of great change, and continue to support them as they rejoin the workforce, seek education, and work with partner agencies," a statement on the organization's website read. "We do this work with an emphasis on one-on-one relationships and a commitment to serving all those who call the streets of Nashville home."

Social activist Dorothy Day is a role model of Charlie's. When she died, he read a quote of hers that stayed with him forever. "I realized that I had failed to see [the man on the street] as my brother," he said. "I just needed to love him. Immediately, it all changed. He stopped ringing the doorbell, [and] he stopped cursing at me. It was a lesson I've never forgotten."

Charlie's view of our humanity, each life and our certain end is so different from the "live for me" culture we're in. "We are the only species who knows that we will die, that everything else will go on but that our time on this earth is short. So, what do you do with that time? Do you want to just get all you can while you are here, or do you want to make a difference to others, to leave the world a better place?"

I asked him what the word "service" means to him, after watching so many of Room in the Inn's volunteers serve. He believes that "service in love" is different than simple service.

"Service is important because our society is built on serving each other," he says. "We have important systems of service, such as government, education, housing, employment, medical, family and even religious. But we can serve and not have our hearts in it. The result is we become robotic and don't connect. We deliver results, but it doesn't feel compassionate or sensitive."

"More than ever, our society needs service in love—where matters of the heart are addressed," he continued, emphasizing the reciprocal nature of service. "The people you serve have no means to pay you, but they will repay you spiritually."

He said dramatic transformations occur during Room in the Inn's Winter Shelter Program.

"It becomes obvious from November to April," he says. "Any volunteer who walks through our doors leaves with a changed perspective of who the homeless are. The experience of being present with another changes attitudes. Volunteers enter with an opinion and leave with an understanding of the complexities people are dealing with."

Charlie had an "a-ha" moment the first year of the program when volunteers at various congregations said the homeless would get their evening meals and eat separately. He decided the meal needed to be a "communion meal," where volunteers and the homeless broke bread together.

"There is giving and receiving at these meals, and you can't tell the difference. The meal becomes one of love, not of service. It equalizes them as brothers and sisters."

I hear Charlie Strobel loud and clear. Volunteering can be about service hours or résumé-building, like it was to me for years. It can also be about doing good deeds and building our society, which are nice, important things. But volunteering regularly is about being connected. It softens the heart, transforms the mind, and centers the soul, all of which are much needed today.

These are major themes more good people are talking about, like my college buddy Jim Vernon, author of *Life On The Porch: From Comfort to Connection with God*. Ten years ago, Jim and his wife, Beth, received cancer diagnoses within six months of one another. Both came out of their cancer journeys with a different view of life. Jim recently left a very comfortable job to write a book about his transformation to being more uncomfortable. He talks a lot about service.

"[Service] may be our most important function on this planet," Jim says. "There are lots of ways to impact people's lives positively, but I believe when we serve others, we have the biggest effect. Plus, it fosters a caring, heartfelt connection with other people that the world can surely use more of."

Jim says the word "servant" has "a largely negative connotation in our society. It's counterintuitive to our Western world idea of freedom, independence and leadership. In my experience, however, the best leaders, employees and people I've been around definitely have that *servant's heart* that has been written and talked about so much.

"They are not afraid to do what is necessary to meet the needs of whomever and whatever the circumstance in front of them calls for. It could be as close as serving your immediate family, or as far away as those across the world you never knew existed. And this is serving in its purest form—when we don't do it because it's part of our job or some other similar situation."

"I'm talking about seeing a need, and caring enough about those involved that we throw off the blanket of 'comfortable' in our lives that's so easy to snuggle under."

Vanderbilt baseball coach Tim Corbin sees lots of needs. He is another role model—for me and for countless others. He's a great baseball coach, and one of the finest people I know.

Corbin took over the SEC's weakest baseball program in 2003. I'd never been to a game, despite being an alumnus. Fairly soon, the boys started to win a few games under Corbin's leadership. I started to hear about his impressive process and team values. I went to check them out.

When our National Anthem played, Corbin's coaches, players and team managers stood tall, feet pointed out properly at a 45-degree angle with heels together, ball caps off and over hearts. After the song, their opponents donned their caps and prepared to play, but no Vanderbilt player moved a muscle until the flag was off the field. It was respect and detail I had never seen during the ceremony.

His players also were having a lot of fun. Every few innings, players in the dugout would run to left field and begin a series of usually goofy calisthenics to keep their blood flowing and minds in the game. My young son especially loved the playfulness, imitating their moves. Again, I'd never seen anything like it from a sports team.

I wanted my children to see more of this, so we went to more games. Then we bought season tickets. Then we went to the SEC Tournament in Hoover, Alabama, to watch the team win the school's first SEC championship in baseball.

Then it all changed on June 15, 2007, when my wife, Dori, was diagnosed with leukemia. She entered Vanderbilt Hospital, where she would stay for more than two months without leaving. I didn't leave the hospital the first week. Dori said, "You need a break. Go get a beer with Al." I listened and did.

Two hours later, Dori called. She was very excited. "Guess who just left my room? Tim Corbin!"

"You're joking," I said.

"No, he stayed for 45 minutes, and we just talked baseball and life.

You'd love him, Jim."

"I already do, sweetie!" I said. "But that is ridiculous. Forty-five minutes?"

Coach "Corbs" continued the correspondence, checking in on Dori and our family. He would email. We'd text once in awhile with an update, or to congratulate him after a big win or encourage him after a tough loss. We'd stay once in a while after a game, and he would talk to my children and Dori, if she had the strength to attend.

One time, they hadn't seen each other in more than a year, after Dori relapsed. She weighed 105 pounds, straight out of the shower. That Sunday afternoon, she made the game and went to Coach on the infield and extended her hand. He went straight for a hug. Observing with Will in left field, I cried deeply, overwhelmed by this scene of love and mutual admiration. Both had grit and love, for each other and for life.

Our beautiful Dori died on June 7, 2011. That week, Vanderbilt was knocking on the door to get to its first College World Series in Omaha, Nebraska. Corbin had three or four teams that could or should have made it, most notably in 2007, but didn't. A monkey was on Corbin's back, and everyone knew it.

On the evening of June 10, the Commodores were scheduled to play Oregon State in a critical contest. With a win, they would advance to Omaha. That morning was Dori's funeral. As we greeted the 500 or so that walked through the doors of Cathedral of the Incarnation, in came a handsome couple —Tim and Maggie Corbin.

"Coach, what are you doing here? This is a huge day for you," I said.

"Jim, Maggie and I wouldn't miss this."

Later, we learned of another connection. Maggie's tennis partner is the wife of my good friend Deacon Mark Faulkner, who eulogized Dori beautifully. Corbin later said it was one of the best talks he had ever heard. Mark is another role model of mine, constantly giving and serving through his life as a father, husband, businessman, volunteer and deacon.

Dori's journey with cancer was hell on Earth for her. Tim Corbin, Mark Faulkner and many others saw what we saw in Dori—tenacity, grace, peace and love. She never turned on God, though she thought about it. Instead, she said cancer became "my opportunity to become a better person." I'll likely write about it all at some point. She'd like that.

After the funeral, the Corbins said they hoped we would go the game that night. We thought about it, and did. Dori would have insisted on it.

First baseman Aaron Westlake hit three towering home runs that might as well have been rainbows. Vanderbilt won, 9-3. The next morning, I told Coach we were thinking about going to Omaha. He said, "I want you to be our guests and sit with the players' families." He gave Will a jersey. We took it with us to Omaha.

In the hotel, after the Dores beat North Carolina 7-3 in Game 1, Coach texted me as I was falling asleep.

"What did you and the kids think of the game, Jim?"

"Incredible, Tim, just incredible. Thank you for thinking of my family." We stayed in Omaha for 11 wonderful days, as the team advanced before losing to the Florida Gators.

Through compassionate service, Tim Corbin was winning a lot more than ballgames. He was celebrating a life well lived and reminding my children and I not to forget we had lives to live as well—to their fullest. Dori wanted it that way, and so did he.

A year later at the annual pre-season banquet with players, families and fans, the kids and I were guests of honor of the Corbins. We sat at their front table. Unbeknownst to us, Coach Corbin was going to talk about Dori, a great Vanderbilt baseball fan, and boy did he. The whole room was moved.

In my mind, there never was a monkey on Tim Corbin's back. He was serving so many, including my family, out of love. Measuring any man on wins and losses in baseball games, or the number of championships and rings his teams won, is silly to me.

Tim Corbin and his extended family of players and coaches were champions already through compassionate service. He looks at people with respect, and people look back with respect. It is a simple, beautiful approach, but one that seems harder for some of us to achieve.

"HE BROUGHT OUT THE LIGHT IN ME."

Several years ago, I met a successful entrepreneur named Bill Lee. His third-generation company, The Lee Company, employs more than 1,000 electricians, plumbers, HVAC experts and staff in Middle Tennessee. (I want you to know at this writing that Bill is running for governor of Tennessee in 2018, and sharing this is in no way an endorsement of his candidacy. You will find mentions of other candidates for governor throughout this book; Tennessee is fortunate to have leaders from both political parties who possess great character.)

Bill lost his wife at a young age in a tragic accident. He picked up the pieces and raised four children on his own, remarried and continued to grow his company. He went on mission trips with his children to Haiti and Africa. He served in prison ministry for seven years.

But something was gnawing at him, too. Was this it? Was he here simply to build a business on a grand scale and be a role model to his kids? Sure, employing so many people and having a good family life were blessings, but something was missing.

He pondered, and began to look outside his family and business.

Bill served on several boards, including the YMCA of Middle Tennessee. There, he learned of opportunities to connect with disadvantaged youth, like a young African-American boy named Adam Smith. After they met, Bill decided to mentor Adam, who was living with his grandmother, who was struggling financially. Adam lived in "the projects," where violent crime was worst in inner city Nashville. It is not an easy place to visit, if you're used to a safe, secure home. Jim Vernon might say it's uncomfortable.

Each week, beginning in 2012, instead of turning for home Bill left the hustle and bustle of his CEO life to drive into the rough part of town to pick up Adam and began relating to him.

Bill asked Adam who his role model was. Adam stared blankly. He had no answer. He didn't have a role model. Bill was moved.

Bill helped Adam get into a better school, supported and encouraged him, and shared his faith and his own struggles. Adam began doing better in school. Bill went to his sports events, always showing up. He listened, and so did Adam. Gradually, life became more real, for both Adam and Bill. Adam saw possibility and opportunity, and Bill saw what's possible when that inherent love in all of us is taken to a deeper place.

Both experienced *agape*, the Greek word for deep, profound love, something Dr. Martin Luther King Jr. says we achieve when we "expect nothing in return and embrace its transformative power, that God loved each of us equally."

"If I hadn't met Bill, I probably wouldn't be thinking about my future today," said 16-year-old Adam in presenting Bill with the YMCA's highest volunteer honor, the Order of the Red Triangle. "I would be going to a low-performance school, I might not be in sports, and I probably would be in a lot of trouble. Bill brings out the light in people that others may not see. He brought out the light in me."

"Knowing him gives me hope. I hope one day I can get into a position to give back because I want to do the same thing."

Adam had certainly changed, but so did Bill, on just as large a scale.

"This is my 'why' story," said Bill. "I love Adam like my own kid. The cool thing about what we all do [when volunteering is] we really become the recipients not only of awards but of life-changing experiences. I've learned more about kids like Adam than I could have any other way....It has changed my desire to not only impact one kid's life, but makes me want to impact a lot of kids' lives."

We hear a lot today about white privilege. Some say it's real; others say it's too much of an excuse. I would say it may be a bit of both, but what's more important is, what are you and I going to do about the opportunities to make a difference in our communities? Are we going to argue about it, or are we going to act, and serve? Are we going to point fingers—blacks at whites, blacks at blacks, whites at blacks and whites at whites—or are we going to ask, "What can I do to make life better for people who need my help and support, regardless of my color or theirs?" This is not the message we're hearing from much of the media, including much of social media.

Like many of us, Bill knows the problem. More importantly, he's part of the solution. Odds are good that Adam will be, too. We have a responsibility not to create or add to the noise, but to join them in service of others.

I see similar characteristics of dedicated service from other gubernatorial candidates, like Randy Boyd, a Republican, and Karl Dean, a Democrat. Randy is a successful entrepreneur, and Karl was mayor of Nashville. Both are wealthy, like Bill. Their lives, however, aren't centered on keeping track of their investment accounts. They are public servants who generously and quietly give to and lead on various causes in their communities. Randy spearheaded a $14 million campaign for United Way in Knox County, for instance. When he was mayor, Karl took the bus and walked to work. Staying close to people led to unique experiences, like on the day Karl passed a man on a bus bench.

"Hey, Karl, remember me?'"

Dean, a former public defender, admitted he didn't.

"You represented me back in the 1980s," the man said. "I was accused of stealing stuff. You got me probation."

The man shared he had found a good job and experienced a complete turnaround. "You changed my life," he said.

'IN THE NAME OF LOVE'

In the summer of 2017, I made my first trip to Ireland. On my last night in that wonderful country, I heard one of my favorite bands, U2, play before 80,000 foot-stomping, singing Irish at Croke Park in Dublin. It was an overwhelming experience, but not just because the music was fantastic.

One of the most popular men in our world today is Bono. There's a reason. Millions around the globe admire his passion to serve.

Yes, Bono is talented. U2's music rocks. The band's songs also speak to a broken world with their calls for love of country and humanity ("In God's Country, "One") and social justice ("Pride: In the Name of Love," "Sunday, Bloody Sunday").

In a time when most bands don't stay together for very long, U2 has been together since they formed in 1976. Bono and his band mates have cultivated a family, staying loyal to and supporting each other through tough times, like when drummer Adam Clayton fought his alcoholism. Bono's mates stood by him battling terrible injuries, surgeries and his glaucoma.

Mostly, Bono is a servant. He is especially passionate about fighting H.I.V. /AIDS and helping the hungry and homeless, including in Africa. He spent time during the Dublin concert I attended talking about a charity he cofounded called ONE, thanking the eight million people who have donated. Through 2017, ONE, which is "strictly non-partisan," had secured $37.5 billion from the United States, Canada and European Union "to help fight corruption and ensure more money from oil and gas revenues in Africa is used to fight poverty."

Every time the band stopped playing, he would express gratitude.

He thanked many people by name responsible for putting on the worldwide Joshua Tree Tour the band was making. Through song, he celebrated historical and present day female achievers. I couldn't get enough of what Bono and his mates were offering.

Like many of today's musicians and actors (and us), Bono has been known to spout off about a politician whose actions he disliked. On occasion, he still does, like when President Trump proposed to cut AIDS funding. He said Trump supporters were welcome on the tour, but Trump could stay home. That's what liberal Bruce Springsteen used to say about center-right politician Chris Christie, governor of New Jersey, before The Boss made nice with The Guv. Maybe Bono will change his mind, invite Trump and sing to him one day, with love. I hope so.

That grumbling aside, Bono realized years ago he could do more for many by sharing big ideals, rather than dwell on anger about someone's actions. He changed his ways and tactics. To him, politics isn't about getting even; it's about getting resources to causes. He has found ways to obtain significant government and private resources over the years. He'll meet with politicians who are open to help. He is indeed one of today's greatest politicians.

Rather than judge, Bono lifts up others. He sees the humanity, dignity and hope in all of us. It is a central theme in his life and was a big part of his concert in Dublin.

While he sang, a video of a 15-year-old woman in a desolate part of Syria played on the giant screen behind his band. She shared her dream to be a lawyer. She smiled amid the rubble and despair. The crowd worked in unison to pass a massive banner of her image around the lower bowl of Croke Park.

That is his Christianity. It is open and accepting. That's why Bono is my favorite celebrity role model.

The positive impact of regular service in love cannot be understated. Charlie, Jim, Tim, Bill, Bono and others have different views on matters of the day. They identify differently in their politics, to varying degrees. They practice different religions and have their own perspectives on faith.

However, each is able to have a civil conversation about anything. None posts, tweets or re-tweets something uncivil. Their social media is uplifting and thought-provoking because they are living each day serving with love.

The last 10 years, I have witnessed uncommon commitment to service in contrast to the dehumanization we're seeing elsewhere in much of our politics, media, culture and entertainment offerings. Some of it is patently hateful, as we all know.

Tim Corbin, Charlie Strobel, Bill Lee and Bono won't give in to hate. It's too late, you see. They've made the practice of daily love a habit.

CRITICAL POINT:

Positive role models who serve can help us dig deeper and give more. They show us the incredibly positive impact of giving of ourselves. Daily service in love nurtures and centers our souls and tempers a human inclination to judge and be hurtful. Going outside your comfort zone allows for opportunities to make a difference to everyone involved. Love wins, and hate loses.

ACTION STEP:

Who are your role models, especially those known for service to others? Maybe some are the same as your plane mate's? Ask him or her, and ask what they respect most in their role models. Finding common ground in our humanity shouldn't be too hard. Ask each other if your social media needs adjusting. These are very important pillars that will help us in other places, like how we handle our politics. That won't be as easy!

---❖---

CHAPTER 1: SERVICE COMMITMENT

SCOUT OR SOLDIER?

"To handle yourself, use your head. To handle
others, use your heart."

—ELEANOR ROOSEVELT

"People don't care how much you know until they
know how much you care."

—TEDDY ROOSEVELT

How can we fight through our biases to elevate our appreciation
of humanity all around us?

Julia Galef, host of the podcast "Rationally Speaking," is exploring
such issues. Galef believes developing better "mental technologies" is
crucial to our future. In particular, given our human irrationality, how
can we improve recognizing and addressing our biases?

In a TED Talk given at Penn State University, "Why you think
you're right—even if you're wrong," Galef compares two mentalities:
the soldier's and the scout's. Are you a soldier, she asks, prone to
defending your viewpoint at all costs, or a scout, spurred by curiosity
and openness? The scout tries, she says, to get a more accurate picture
of reality, even when it's unpleasant or inconvenient.

Soldiers' emotions are rooted in defensiveness or tribalism, which isn't necessarily bad on one level. Coach Corbin and others, for instance, certainly rely on some level of tribalism when building their teams and families and teaching them to be resilient through tough times. I've got your back, and you've got mine.

When searching for truth or what's real, however, the soldier mentality can inhibit seeing humanity, admitting we're wrong or finding common ground. "Too much soldier" can lead to viewing any opposition as an enemy.

Scouts feel an itch to solve a puzzle, and are intrigued when they find something that contradicts their expectations. They believe it's virtuous to test their own beliefs. They don't believe changing one's mind conveys weakness or that their self-worth is tied up in being absolutely correct. They love bumper stickers that say, "Don't believe everything you think."

They might even put their baseball players in more positions to fail, so that they are ready when they are facing bigger tests under greater pressure. They might take the baseball away a little earlier from a star pitcher, so these things can happen. Coach Corbin did.

I watched Coach Corbin's reactions after his teams didn't make it to the College World Series on several occasions. Some of the losses were hard. He was devastated after some seasons, like in 2007. He talked about the devastation, which was the first step to a different place. His demeanor and body language seemed different to me. Maybe his players noticed, too. He seemed to be conveying that he would allow the World Series to happen, when it would happen—the Law of Attraction and the Power of Intention.

Vanderbilt didn't win the College World Series in 2011, but they did win it three years later. It was the school's first NCAA championship in a men's sport. Hundreds of his players have gone on to successful careers, and quite a few to the major leagues. Many more are experiencing tremendous success in their careers and personal lives. Tim Corbin developed winning soldier and scout mentalities, in himself and those around him.

"NOW SERVING?"

Soldier and scout mentalities are in our cultural institutions like sports, politics and even business. Two well-known companies, Chick-fil-A and Target, are good examples of having both strong soldier and scout mentalities in their leadership and company cultures.

Both companies are excellent at what they do—provide products with great service to every person who walks through their doors. Both have also jumped on to slippery slopes, getting away from simply serving to make strong political statements on controversial matters. Both paid a price.

Chick-fil-A has grown tremendously in recent years, largely because of its superior service, not just the magic combination of white pepper, peanut oil and breading on tender chicken. *QSR Magazine* noted Chick-fil-A employees said "thank you" or "my pleasure" in 95% of drive-thru encounters. Comparatively, KFC had a "thank you" rate of 85%, while McDonald's rate was 78%. Not surprisingly, in 2015, Chick-fil-A generated more revenue per restaurant than any other fast-food chain in the country, averaging nearly $4 million in sales per restaurant. The average KFC restaurant did about $1 million in sales.

Commitment to service to everyone goes a long way in life, and business. However, in 2012, Chick-fil-A hit a pothole of its own making when company President and CEO Dan Cathy spoke out against gay marriage. After his remarks, colleges like Johns Hopkins and cities like Denver banned Chick-fil-A from opening franchises. The mayors of New York City and Boston expressed outrage over Cathy's comments. Councilmembers across the country told the company not to come knocking on their doors.

All involved had a soldier mentality, defending their viewpoints at all costs, including chicken sales. Chick-fil-A lost a lot of potential business and opportunities to show it wasn't necessarily the company some were saying it was.

Two years later, Cathy went a-tweeting after the Supreme Court struck down the Defense of Marriage Act, saying, "Sad day for our nation; founding fathers would be ashamed of our gen. to abandon wisdom of the ages re: cornerstone of strong societies." He later deleted the tweet.

A spokesperson, displaying more of a scout mentality, and sticking to the mission of selling tasty chicken sandwiches to all guests, said,

"...His views didn't necessarily represent the views of all customers, restaurant owners and employees."

Give Cathy credit for being honest along the way.

"Every leader goes through different phases of maturity, growth and development and it helps by (recognizing) the mistakes that you make," Cathy said in an interview with the *Atlanta Journal-Constitution*. "And you learn from those mistakes. If not, you're just a fool. I'm thankful that I lived through it and I learned a lot from it....I know others feel very different from that and I respect their opinion and I hope that they would be respectful of mine....The wiser thing for us to do is to stay focused on customer service."

That's a great statement. Why not just sell chicken, to gays and straight people, and move on? Heck, Chick-Fil-A has gay managers and apparently no trouble with the Equal Employment Opportunity Commission. Their teams do incredible work in communities, like when several franchises in Orlando opened on a Sunday (against company policy) to feed volunteers after the massacre at Pulse, a gay nightclub, in June 2016. Chick-fil-A's actual practice of tolerance and outreach are great stories, but Cathy's statement in 2012—and again in 2014—became the narrative.

Target has also been in hot water regarding social justice issues, like its policies and responses around gender-neutral bathrooms. In 2016, the company posted on its website that "we welcome transgender team members and guests to use the restroom or fitting room facility that corresponds with their gender identity....Given the specific questions (several state) legislative proposals raised about how we manage our fitting rooms and restrooms, we felt it was important to state our position."

Christian and conservative groups responded just as liberal city mayors and colleges responded to Cathy's statements. They called for an all-out ban on shopping at Target, with moms expressing outrage and fear about what their children might see or experience. This reaction had a negative impact on the company's financial performance and stock.

Target responded. Later in 2016, Target announced it would build additional gender-neutral bathrooms in all 1,800 stores, seeking to mollify the negative publicity. The company invested $20 million, a paltry amount compared to the sales lost. The damage had already been done.

Increasingly, companies and some of their leaders appear more intent to pursue social change agendas instead of selling chicken tenders and bulk toilet paper. It's a shame and it's dangerous. It fuels our uncivil war. These endeavors may feel good or just from a soldier mentality's standpoint, but it doesn't bode well for attracting more people who love fried chicken sandwiches or need bathroom products. Nor does it show a scout mentality's openness to co-exist with differing viewpoints, respect our humanity and figure out who goes where to the bathroom.

Business owners with different political viewpoints are embracing a similar soldier mentality. Some, for example, have "Drain the Swamp" and "Make America Great Again" signs outside and inside their businesses. Others on the political spectrum are just as bold.

Honolulu's Café serves up "Radiatore Verde" and "Italian stir fry," but not to pro-Trump patrons. In 2016, the owner posted a bright yellow, handmade sign on the front door: "If you voted for Trump you cannot eat here! No Nazis."

Patrons celebrated on Facebook: "... The next time you're in Honolulu, eat lunch here, not only are they on the right side of things, the food is delicious and reasonable," said one poster.

Others were less amused, like Honolulu resident and Trump supporter Susan Roberts, who told FoxNews.com she found the sign in "extreme poor taste, ... childish and very unprofessional.... The restaurant owner doesn't have to worry...I will not be stepping foot in that establishment."

These pronouncements from businesses large and small are antithetical to what real service is about. Already, some companies—Target included—require their vendors to sign diversity statements not unlike what some universities are requiring. What's next? Conservative and liberal "think tanks" (pardon the expression) that send questionnaires to your neighborhood restaurants and other businesses to ask for their political and social opinions? Some think tanks that rate large businesses already exist.

Father Strobel talked about how simple service is important because it helps us build our society. Arguably, companies that get away from simple service and into political projecting are doing the opposite.

As the famous cartoon skunk Pepe Le Peu said, "Le Sigh."

"WILL YOU LET ME BE YOUR SERVANT?"

In America, we have important, long-standing service institutions, some of which are under attack. We must protect them, if we are to survive and thrive.

Take the military. Much of what's in that box is good. Sometimes, some of it isn't. I saw some of both during my service in the late 1980's and early 1990's.

As a naval officer during the time of Operation Desert Storm, I saw how rigid training and consistent values served us well during stressful or chaotic situations. I didn't like why my weekend liberty was taken away one weekend during Officer Candidate School in Newport, Rhode Island (allegedly, there was a wrinkle on my bed cover), but I vowed never to let it happen again. I ironed my bed, and slept on the floor for two months.

I learned precision. We drilled and studied, then studied and drilled. Ten percent of my classmates didn't make it. I advanced to Naval Supply School in Athens, Georgia, where we studied for seven months before going to our assignments. I learned teamwork and camaraderie in Athens, and we celebrated our service. I was assigned to the USS Bainbridge, a nuclear cruiser based in Norfolk, Virginia. I saw the world, drove the ship as junior officer of the deck, and ran four supply divisions. My tour was both boring and exciting, but mostly fulfilling.

I was doing my part to protect my country. I saw a world very different than my country. After four-and-a-half years, though, most of them at sea, I was eager to get home.

It almost didn't happen.

A few days from our homeport, after a seven-month cruise to the Persian Gulf, my superior officer told me our captain was going to the aircraft carrier to meet with the group commander. He wanted me to go with him, via helicopter. One of my roles was to manage helicopter operations with 20 enlisted working together to make sure they went safely. I had trained on a helo on land quite a few times, but never over the ocean, however.

That afternoon, the seas were bad. The captain said flight operations would continue, so we were going to the carrier. Because of the rough seas and rolling ship, we would have to be hoisted up via cable.

The ship was rocking hard side to side. Abandoning protocol, the captain said, "You go first." Sheesh, just like in *Raiders of the Lost Ark*.

As I put my left arm in the hoist, the ship took a major roll. I couldn't get my other arm in the hoist, and I had no choice but to run across the deck. I jumped over a safety net, like OJ Simpson in a Hertz commercial. I was dangling over the angry ocean, swinging wildly.

The pilot pulled up, seeking to stabilize me, a young naval pendulum just three days from his comfy bed in Virginia Beach. I looked up—now hundreds of feet above the ocean—as the ship sped away, and saw an airman whacking away at the cable apparatus. It was jammed. I swung, one-armed and three hundred feet above the Atlantic, for what seemed an eternity.

Finally, the airman unjammed the cable and I was pulled to safety. I was calm. Without incident, the captain joined us and said, "Are you OK? I'm sure glad that wasn't me!"

Right, sir.

Later, I knew I had been in survival mode and just trusted myself, and everyone involved, like I was trained. It worked. The ironed bed in Newport and practice evolutions in Virginia paid off. Discipline, preparation, trust and patience.

And a little luck. That night, I didn't sleep.

I look back on days like that, including when we churned through 35-foot seas in the North Atlantic, and again off Cape Horn south of the coast of Chile. I thought we might die on the latter mission, escorting ships carrying chemical weapons out of Germany after the Berlin Wall fell. The ship sounded like it was tearing apart during a relentless two-day storm.

I was proud of my service and what it meant to our country and to our world. I look at institutions like the military as necessary and good, but sometimes we participants aren't up to par. We should call out institutions when they fail us, not eliminate them or diminish their importance. The Tailhook scandal in Las Vegas in 1991, when 100 Navy and Marine Corps aviation officers allegedly sexually harassed 83 women and seven men, is an example. I experienced disappointment many times in Athens, including when a lieutenant told our class a very disgusting joke, one that made women out to be objects, in front of 25 ensigns, six of whom were women.

It's the same with businesses, like Enron's corrupt leaders, and my own Catholic religion, whose leaders sought to protect sexual offenders. The institution isn't necessarily bad. Sometimes, some of the people in charge are blinded by greed, or too quick to brush aside evil behavior.

My friend Marjorie K. Eastman knows this well. She was captain of an intelligence division of more than 100 people in Iraq and East Afghanistan. Along the way, she experienced bias simply for being a woman. She handled those situations beautifully, confronting them with information and strength. She could have expressed disgust and outrage, but that would have been giving her opposition too much credit.

Marjorie's book, *The Frontline Generation: How We Served Post 9/11*, is about the importance and impact of dedicated service. In Afghanistan, her company made a huge difference by finding weapons caches and proactively engaging the Afghan community in humanitarian endeavors. Eastman shows how proactive leadership, humility and service through difficult conditions build the character we need to overcome mounting obstacles in our nation. She argues about another 1% in our society—those who served in the military after 9/11 who will be part of that solution!

We've come a long way since the Tailhook sexual harassment scandal when I was a young man in service, but we have a ways to go. Leaders like Marjorie, who emphasize service, making great personal sacrifices and handling bias with grace, will help bring the Me Now generation along for a smoother ride. They are part of our Modern Greatest Generation.

You and I just need to tell folks, not holler at them, about the nobility of any kind of service to others—community, military, business or other. Scout and service mentalities help counter our uncivil war.

Let us not take offense when we cannot find common ground, or someone makes a mistake, or tweets something offensive. Help find common ground and love one another. Connect to people more, and the Internet less.

One of my favorite songs at church, "The Servant Song" by Richard Gillard, emphasizes service. If you're not Christian, insert your Creator, who you follow or even your belief system; it still works.

Will you let me be your servant
Let me be as Christ to you
Pray that I might have the grace
To let me be your servant too

We are pilgrims on the journey
We are brothers on the road
We are here to help each other
Walk the mile and bear the load

I will hold the Christ light for you
In the night time of your fear
I will hold my hand out to you
Speak the peace you long to hear.

I will weep when you are weeping
When you laugh, I'll laugh with you
I will share your joy and sorrow
Till we've seen this journey through.

When we sing to God in heaven
We shall find such harmony
Born to all we've known together
Of Christ's love and agony

CRITICAL POINT:

A scout mentality produces understanding, while a strict soldier mentality hardens the heart. Regular service and a curious mind generate understanding and compassion, which is in shorter supply in our country. American institutions and companies that deliver great service are taking some company values and projecting them more regularly on customers.

ACTION STEP:

Commit to regular service in your community. Seek a scout mentality in your actions to stay open and grounded. Find yourself by losing yourself in the service of others, and give until it hurts. Celebrate great service of all kinds, like business and military, while recognizing people and institutions aren't perfect.

RESOURCES:

www.EndingOurUncivilWar.com

CONTEMPLATION:

"Give, but give until it hurts."

—MOTHER TERESA

"If you want to be happy, practice compassion."

—DALAI LAMA

THE PATH TO AGAPE—
LOVING YOUR ENEMY

"Darkness cannot drive out darkness; only light can do
that. Hate cannot drive out hate; only love can do that."
—DR. MARTIN LUTHER KING JR.

"If you want to kiss the sky, better learn how to kneel."
—U2, "MYSTERIOUS WAYS"

An immigrant from India, Devji, wrote about Americans in 2004.
He shared "10 Noble Traits" about us. Astoundingly beautiful, they are:

1) GODLY: Almost all of us acknowledge that a power beyond us
    guides the swirling destinies of men; the Native Americans pray
    to a 'Great Spirit' and with a reverent heart tie it to the sacred
    earth and skies of America.
2) TOLERANT: European Christians settled this land and wrote its
    constitution. They then opened their arms wide and welcomed
    people from the rest of the world. Now mosques, synagogues and

temples pepper the landscape along with churches. Muslims can worship more freely here than in most Moslem countries. Sikhs wear turbans and Jews their yamakas.

3) VISIONARY: While we are an earthbound nation enjoying our material success, we are also an extraordinary visionary people. We dare to dream impossible dreams. We soar the skies searching the stars. We have landed on planets that lie shrouded in billions of years of silence. On earth, our vision in the healing arts will literally make the lame walk and the blind see.

4) PROSPEROUS: The capacity of Americans to work hard joyously is the stuff of which the wealth of this country is made. Our work ethic is unmatched. We are the richest country in the world, but our children start babysitting, bagging groceries and cutting lawns while they are still in school.

5) GENEROUS: There is possibly no country on earth [that] has not been touched by the generosity of Americans. We respond to earthquakes, floods and famines with compassionate hearts. We send money, medicines, clothes and prayers to victims of every color and creed, even our "enemies." We know that we are custodians of wealth, not its owners.

6) RESILIENT: Americans have an uncanny capacity to bounce back from adversity—accidents, bankruptcies, and divorces. They rebuild their bodies, businesses and lives. They do not sit in dark corners; they fight back.

7) COURAGEOUS: A four-year-old in my neighborhood comes around the corner wearing a helmet, riding a scooter, and my aunts in India still hold on to their 14-year-olds protectively! Americans seem to be born with an extra streak of courage. It seems to be seared within our soul. We teach the world the meaning of the word with our daring spirits and our exploits.

8) HUMOROUS: We love laughter and life. You can tell an American abroad because he is generally the one who has the biggest smile, sometimes the loudest voice and laughter, and is the most approachable. An American will fill a room with his infectious goodwill and just not treat anyone as a stranger.

9) SELF-INTROSPECTION: Occupying the unique position that we do in the world, we could be really arrogant and indifferent to

people's opinions, but we are childlike in our need for approval. We are a self-introspective people, we dissect our actions and thoughts, we form committees, and we discuss them in our newspapers, television, and town hall meetings.

10) SWEETNESS: Countries, like people, become dry and arid if the quality of sweetness is absent from the souls of their citizens. Americans have been blessed with a rare quality of sweetness of the soul.

I see many of these qualities in different kinds of people in my life. What about you? Do you have these qualities? Importantly, do you share any of these Noble Traits with your seatmate? I'm betting you do!

I'm also betting you're as concerned as I am about a decline in sweetness, tolerance and self-introspection, or you wouldn't be reading this book.

Some days, I wonder if Devji is right about America and its greatness. It seems harder to find inner strength, kindness and selflessness in abundance. Thirteen years after his observations, do you see a different, unraveling America—too divided, polarized, angry and vindictive? Is the more realistic assessment that we're at a point of no return? Is it just too late?

Could it be possible, however, that Devji is right and so is the alternative, less positive view? If both postulates are true, to what levels would you and your seatmate agree? More importantly, is it possible in today's exploding culture to acknowledge or agree to partial truths on any matter, including the one that brought you together on this plane?

Some friends post on social media that "love is the answer." I know many who scoff at such "idealism." To those engaged in uncivil war, such thought seems unsafe and even unwise. To them, it's safer to attack in full force. Others choose not to be exposed to what they fear. Each contributes to an unraveling society.

We have a blueprint. It's not idealistic. It's real and true. Great religions and philosophies teach that we can and *should* love one another. History, too, is a great teacher, not a passé account of what happened. We have seen our greatest leaders flirt with, and then reject, hateful approaches. Few lived this better than Dr. Martin Luther King Jr. We have a holiday every third Monday in January because King's spiritual, godly wisdom was so profoundly beautiful, transcending time and inspiring generation after generation.

King's earliest attempts to advance civil rights, ironically, were not rooted in love. He espoused aggression, physical contact and even violence to attempt to sway the minds of a restless nation. These attempts failed in his time, just as they fail today. King reflected. He pivoted. He prayed. He spoke up. He suffered, and so did many friends. He opened his heart. He lost battles, seemingly, and went to jail. He was mocked and persecuted, like many followers who were fire-hosed or bitten by dogs for daring to protest peacefully.

Again and again, he opened his heart, and encouraged others to do the same.

King's journey began to appear like Christ's, of whom he spoke often. His journey became a movement of love. He spoke about the least among us: the poor, the persecuted and the oppressed. His journey spawned followers and his word spread, just as Christ's did. Interestingly, some who admire him greatly dismiss his Christian rooting.

In the 1950s and 60s, King's rhetoric began to transform the people for whom he spoke, and even some who opposed him and who were engaged in oppressing minorities. He called on a higher power in all of us and around us to let light guide the way. Like the great prophets in all religions, King sought to reach our souls, calling on each man and woman to love one another.

Perhaps his greatest speech was delivered when his doctor told him he was too ill to speak. King summoned his strength on November 17, 1957, went to the pulpit at Dexter Avenue Baptist Church in Montgomery, Alabama, and encouraged us to embrace our enemies.

The eloquent and passionate King said we must do two things to overcome hate. First, we must look within and seek to find why we have difficulty loving our enemy. Maybe there is "something that we've done deep down in the past, some personality attribute that we possess... [something] within... that arouses the tragic hate response in the other individual."

Second, we must find the good in our enemies. We must "discover the element of good in [our enemy]... [and] realize that there is some good there and look at those good points which will over-balance the bad points."

This is a good time to pause and look at the person next to you, the one you don't trust or understand, maybe even hate. As King asked and Devji observed, are you able to look inwardly and find what causes your distrust, misunderstanding or ill will? Can you look next to you and see "some good there?"

King had to practice, like a great athlete does, to get there. He pled for love and inner peace in situations seemingly small, like a trip he took with his brother from Atlanta to Chattanooga. Both noticed many drivers were being very discourteous by not dimming their lights. Weary and angry, MLK's brother announced he would not dim his lights the next time a driver refused to dim theirs.

"Oh no, don't do that," the better King at that moment said. "There'd be too much light on this highway, and it will end up in mutual destruction for all. Somebody's got to have some sense on this highway. Somebody must have sense enough to dim the lights."

King translated this story to a greater level, arguing to the audience that if we don't have enough sense to "turn on the dim and beautiful and powerful lights of love in this world, the whole of our civilization will be plunged into the abyss of destruction. And we will all end up destroyed because nobody had any sense on the highway of history."

King called on his audience—and us—to embrace love's transformative power (italics mine):

> When the opportunity presents itself for you to defeat your enemy, that is the time which you must not do it," King said. "There will come a time, in many instances, when the person who hates you most, the person who has misused you most, the person who has gossiped about you most, the person who has spread false rumors about you most, there will come a time when you will have an opportunity to defeat that person. It might be in terms of a recommendation for a job; it might be in terms of helping that person to make some move in life. That's the time you must do it. That is the meaning of love.
>
> In the final analysis, love is not this sentimental something that we talk about. It's not merely an emotional something. Love is creative, understanding goodwill

for all men. It is the refusal to defeat any individual.
**When you rise to the level of love, of its great beauty
and power, you seek only to defeat evil systems.
Individuals who happen to be caught up in that
system, you love, but you seek to defeat the system.**

We know our political, social and cultural problems well, and
we know that our system of government and our culture are in peril.
Devji's view of America is beautiful, true and real, but it is under attack
on multiple fronts. So is Dr. King's.

RHETORIC OF RAGE

Politically, some candidates view elections as all-out wars against
opponents, rather than contests of ideas. Some have embraced the
rhetoric of front-running candidates who call Mexicans "rapists" and
conservatives "deplorables." These leaders either don't apologize, or do
so softly, so as not to appear weak to their bases. Rather than call out
both parties' candidates for such damaging grandiloquence, desensitized partisans merely point the finger at the other side, rather than
own the fact that love is absent and hate has taken root, on both sides.

The week before President Trump's inauguration, Georgia Congressman John Lewis told NBC's Chuck Todd he viewed the election results
as "illegitimate" because of alleged tampering by Russian hackers.
Lewis, a great friend of Dr. King and a courageous civil rights activist
who endured a tremendous beating during one march, unfortunately
said he would not be attending the inauguration. Other congressmen
announced they would sit out the peaceful transfer of power, a hallmark
moment every American should respect. This was a missed opportunity
for Lewis and fellow congressmen to love their enemy and remind all of
us of Dr. King's legacy. Then the president-elect made it worse.

Only two days before Martin Luther King Day, Trump tweeted
that Lewis "should spend more time on fixing and helping his district,
which is in horrible shape and falling apart, not to mention crime
infested rather than falsely complaining about the election results. All
talk, talk, talk—no action or results. Sad!"

Not only was much of the claim untrue, but Trump also did what
he almost always does, attack the accuser. One of the more courageous

and respected civil rights leaders was accused of being "all talk." Yet again, Trump reinforced his unsettling pattern to respond hatefully, attacking rather than loving, and not apologizing later. This has been evident in his business dealings, the presidential campaign, and his first year in office.

There have been missed opportunities from Trump's political opponents. We certainly saw this from Mrs. Clinton, who countered Trump's nasty personal attacks with her own, rather than let his wild assertions speak for themselves. No one could let anything go, and the national discourse followed along.

There was also disquieting rhetoric from others who sought the presidency. It is a softer form of ring fighting, but still damaging to the culture. Senator Bernie Sanders came off as one of the more honest of the candidates in the 2016 election. He talked about issues that interested people of diverse political views, like rampant greed and crony capitalism, tapping into the growing belief we are a nation of haves and have nots.

I respect Senator Sanders for this elevation of issues. To many I know, he was the most believable candidate, authentic and real. We do have greed. Our narcissistic tendencies seem to be advancing. Many corporations certainly have their hands out, and are getting hand outs, from both political parties.

But is it fair to classify the 1% that Sanders rails against as *all greedy*? This may not be his intent, but it comes across as broad-brushed and bombastic to some. Many very wealthy people are quietly donating significantly to charities and causes that lift up the poor and less fortunate. Sanders' claims sound reasonable to those who believe his blanket statement, but they are offensive to many one-percenters who are quietly giving away their fortunes to help the less fortunate or people in need. Americans gave $358 billion to philanthropics in 2014. In 2015, it was $373 billion, with $265 billion, or 71%, coming from individuals. This is the generosity Devji noted.

Rather than recognize a positive trend and opportunity to do more, we don't question the rhetoric and spin from today's leaders. We regurgitate Bernie's and Trump's and Hillary's "tough talk" into our own circles, and it has a big impact how we engage socially.

On Twitter, Facebook and elsewhere, virtually every American has

his or her own platform that's become a War Room behind their computer or smartphone. Feeling protected and often armed with only one
view pulled from a favorite hyper-partisan website, we battle each other
daily, entrenched in our cyber-bunkers, firing off hateful responses.

Love and information are absent.

Culturally, we have a media that frequently sets us up to hate with
news and reporting that lacks depth, perspective and diverse opinions.
Cable TV and talk radio hosts frequently only offer, in bombastic fashion, hardened views, presenting guests who agree with them. Some
bring on and eviscerate those who have an alternative view. The left
and right in media know this is good for ratings, and truth be damned.

Again, love and information are absent.

Is this the daily bread we ask for in our Lord's Prayer?

So I ask...Will you be a change agent that King, Gandhi, Christ,
the Buddha and all the great prophets ask you and me to be?

What have these great spiritual leaders said to us that can help us
bring peace to our political, spiritual and cultural systems?

How we can start the day right, with good daily bread?

I have my own dream.

LOVE STARTS AT SUNRISE!

> "We ought always to thank God for you, brothers
> and sisters, and rightly so, because your faith is
> growing more and more, and the love all of you
> have for one another is increasing."
> —2 THESSALONIANS 1:3

How do you start your morning? What is the first thing you do
when you wake up, when physical consciousness begins?

What do you think? Do you pray or reflect? Do you start a routine?

Or is it less structured? Do you turn on the computer, TV or radio
to get the news? Do you head straight to the kitchen to begin making
breakfast for your children or family, without reflecting on the gift of a
new day?

Do you head to your phone to see who has posted what about
their social selves?

Are you more interested in what people are doing or thinking, than what you are doing and thinking?

Love must start from the moment we begin each and every day. Whether you are religious or not, this seems to be an accepted theme from many philosophers, counselors and therapists. Unfortunately, it's in poor practice today.

We're more in touch with social media than ourselves, something I heard loud and clear during a homily in May 2017, given by Father Peter Wojcik at St. Clement Church in Chicago. The theme of the Mass was "The Lord Is My Shepherd," to which Father Wojcik offered a different take with the following reflection.

> *The Internet is my shepherd I shall not want,*
> *It makes me to lie down on the sofa.*
> *It leads me away from the faith,*
> *It slowly destroys my soul.*
> *It leads me to the path of self-focused and self-*
> *righteousness for the advertiser's sake.*
> *Even though I walk in the shadow of Christian*
> *responsibilities,*
> *There will be no interruption, for the Internet is with me.*
> *Its Wi-Fi and remote ability, they comfort me*
> *It prepares a commercial for me in the midst of my*
> *worldliness*
> *And anoints my head with secular humanism and*
> *consumerism.*
> *My greed runs over;*
> *Surely ignorance and laziness shall follow me all the*
> *days of my life,*
> *And I shall dwell in the house of desolation searching*
> *my Internet forever.*

Wojcik is saying what we know in our hearts and minds...technology is a false religion. The gospel, he said, is our solution. If you're not Christian, it is some other good word.

The constancy of media is a threat to being a better person, and my own well-being. I started thinking. I fall short often. I can spend too much time on social media or watching TV, thinking less and absorbing more than I need to be. Maybe this is one reason I can be short with my family at times.

Wojcik pointed to that day's reading for guidance.

> *But how is it to your credit if you receive a beating for doing wrong and endure it? But if you suffer for doing good and you endure it, this is commendable before God. To this you were called, because Christ suffered for you, leaving you an example that you should follow in his steps.*
>
> *He committed no sin,*
> *and no deceit was found in his mouth.*
>
> *When they hurled their insults at him, he did not retaliate; when he suffered, he made no threats. Instead, he entrusted himself to him who judges justly. "He himself bore our sins" in his body on the cross, so that we might die to sins and live for righteousness; "by his wounds you have been healed." For "you were like sheep going astray," but now you have returned to the Shepherd and Overseer of your souls." —1 Peter 2:20-25*

What a choice we have.

Redemptive passages aren't exclusive to Christianity. Other religions interpret love and offer a meaningful path to a loving life. The great religious and spiritual teachers knew and lived it. Some even accepted it across other religions. The concept of the power of love permeates all religions, at least in its most holy form.

The Dalai Lama said it very well, "The essence of all religions is love, compassion, and tolerance. Kindness is my true religion."

Christ, who spent much of his time around the least among Him, also said it well: "I'm giving you a new commandment so you'll know where I am, and who I am: 'You must love one another.'"

Perhaps the most quoted biblical scripture on the matter in 1 Corinthians 13 seeks to offer a larger understanding of the mystery and simplistic beauty of deep, infinite love (italics mine): "Love is patient,

Love is kind, Love is not jealous, *Love is never boastful or conceited,
Love is not rude, nor does it take offense. It takes no pleasure in other
peoples' faults. It is always ready to excuse, to trust, to hope, and to
endure.* Love does not come to an end."

Many of us hear this on Saturday or Sunday, and nod approval.
Then we go home, to work and to play, and fail to clear the bar.

The great religions define love similarly and differently. However,
there is an apparent commonality among these creeds that invites us—
yes, all on this plane—to an exceptional bond that can lead to the path
of light Dr. King offered in the 1950s and 60s.

Buddhism, for instance, looks at love in parts. There is sensuous
love, *kama*, which many Buddhists believe is an obstacle to selflessness. *Karuna* is compassion and mercy; it reduces suffering, com-
plements wisdom and leads to enlightenment. *Advesa* and *metta* are
benevolent and unconditional love that promotes self-acceptance and
avoids self-interested pursuits. This detachment leads to a state of
grace, much like Christ taught.

Hinduism *kama* is pleasurable love, similar to the Buddhist
notion, while *prem* refers to elevated love. This love is a sacrament
that preaches that one gives up selfishness in love, expecting nothing
in return, and that God is love, exemplified in the deity Krishna with
Radha and other milkmaids.

Muslims are directed to become close to Allah with ways to earn
that love, by "doing good, being pure and clean, acting rightly, being
patient and persevering," among several pursuits. Islam teaches many
of the same principles taught by the other religions, like love and compassion. The Quran even says that Allah loved Moses.

The Quran and Old Testament can also be, at times, patriarchal and
judgmental, and leave little room for nuance. They were a product of their
times. There are also a few sections of the Quran that are not only negative
but dangerous, in particular how Allah withholds love from those who
practice certain deeds, for example, for the *kafireen*, or non-believers.

This is the current struggle we are witnessing in parts of our
world, but it is unfair or unwise to label that struggle as the pervasive
view of Islam. It's the distorted view. Much like many Christians are
fighting each other or have in the past, many Muslims are doing the
same (Shiite and Sunni, for example, in Iraq and Saudi Arabia). All

religions have dogmatic interpretations that are a blight on love. Being religious doesn't mean you're loving; in fact, it can mean the opposite.

The Jewish faith addresses love in various ways. *Ahava* is a term for both interpersonal love of family and love of God. *Chen* (grace, good will, kindness) and *chesed* (kindness, love) is similar to our modern view of "steadfast love."

Christianity, the largest religion in America, shares much in common with other religions. Not dissimilar to Buddhism, the apostles noted Christ's teachings emphasize that the two greatest commandments are the first two:

"Thou shalt love the Lord thy God with all thy heart, and with all thy soul, and with all thy mind, and with all thy strength" and "thou shalt love thy neighbor as thyself."

There are only two words about love in the New Testament, which was written in Greek—*agape* and *philia*. Two other Greek words for love—*eros* and *storge*—are not to be found. Eros, which conveys passionate or romantic love, is in the Old Testament. Storge depicts familial love, or love of one's offspring. It's agape and philia that deserve further scrutiny, as they run in strong currents with other great religions and teachings.

Agape is the love God has for all Christians, who "so loved the world, that he gave his only begotten Son, that whosoever believeth in him should not perish, but have everlasting life. For God sent not his Son into the world to condemn the world; but that the world through him might be saved." Philia imparts a love of mutual respect, or love like among brothers, hence Philadelphia being known as the "City of Brotherly Love."

In his "Loving Your Enemies" speech in 1957, Dr. King engaged the congregation on the Greek definitions of love. He called eros "a sort of aesthetic love...a sort of romantic love, though it's a beautiful love." Philia, he said, is "another type of love that's also beautiful...a sort of intimate affection between personal friends...the type of love that you have for those persons that you're friendly with...It's a sort of reciprocal love. On this level, you like a person because that person likes you. You love on this level, because you are loved. You love on this level, because there's something about the person you love that is likeable to you."

The first two, eros and philia, are easier to give and receive. Both are important. But it is agape, Dr. King said, where we have much difficulty, because we must expect nothing in return and embrace its transformative power, that God loved each of us equally, sinners included (italics mine):

> *Agape is more than eros; agape is more than philia; agape is something of the understanding, creative, redemptive goodwill for all men. It is a love that seeks nothing in return. It is an overflowing love; it's what theologians would call the love of God working in the lives of men. And when you rise to love on this level, you begin to love men, not because they are likeable, but because God loves them. You look at every man, and you love him because you know God loves him.*

> **And he might be the worst person you've ever seen.**

This journey to redemptive love is a theme that has troubled man for the ages. The early Christian author Tertullian wrote about loving our enemies: "Our individual, extraordinary, and perfect goodness consists in loving our enemies. To love one's friends is common practice, to love one's enemies only among Christians."

If this has been and is our guidance, from Christ and his supporters like Dr. King, why are many Christians struggling to translate their firmly held religious views of a loving God into daily practice? To a gay man, an abortion doctor (that one is hard for me), an atheist or a Muslim neighbor?

I'll share a few personal experiences as well as another that caught national attention.

The day after the presidential election, as I drove to a business meeting, my cell phone started receiving messages. All came from Christians like me. Some were gleeful about Trump winning; others were in deep despair.

One Trump supporter told me he couldn't "stop grinning," and sent several doctored photos. One said, with a picture of Trump talking on a phone, "Hey Rosie (O'Donnell), when you finish packing your s***, head over and help Al Sharpton pack his," alluding to their threats to move to another country if Trump won the election.

I responded that some empathy would be welcomed as many adjusted to the new direction all Americans, who have much more in common than not, were processing. My friend doubled down, responding, "Empathy? Yes, but to those who were deep in the foxholes with me fighting, I'm gloating. I will, however, remain humble and graceful in public."

After some reflection, I offered my friend another way to view himself in the Mirror of Love. I texted: "'Do unto others as they have done to you'? 'Turn the other cheek'? 'Faith, hope and love'? Fill your heart mind and thoughts with such things, and you will have peace, whatever any election result. Gloating is not Christ-like, publicly or privately."

My friend looked in the mirror and owned it. I appreciated his response as he thanked me for a "reality check." I ended with "Love you, my friend."

I had similar exchanges with friends who thought the end of the world was close at hand after Election Day. One good friend, a woman who married her partner after the Supreme Court legalized gay marriage, wondered with much despair if her new union would stand. Very likely, I thought, given Trump's longtime personal views on the matter, not his campaign rhetoric. Why jump to despair, knowing that fact and knowing that bridge wasn't anywhere near, anyway? I was encouraged to see my friend recognize this and express more peace about the situation.

Several months later, a close friend texted that "Trump is an abomination of a human being." OK, I found some of his words and actions were abominations. I texted back, "He is a human being, though. At least that's what St. Francis, the Buddha and Christ are teaching me, right?" My friend: "Screw em all. Just kidding yer right."

I recall another conversation with a political operative who holds Dr. King in high regard but said agape is really not possible in today's political environment. Really, I asked? What about the families who forgave Dylann Roof after he gunned down loved ones in the Charleston church? What about President Obama, who sang "Amazing Grace," at their funeral? What about Louie Zamperini, who forgave the Japanese prison guard who tortured him and years later carried the Olympic torch not far from the POW camp where he had been confined and beaten repeatedly? What about Father Strobel, after his mother was murdered?

Another illuminating post-election moment occurred shortly after the New Year. Atlanta pastor Louie Giglio invited country music superstar Carrie Underwood, a Christian who supports gay marriage, to perform at his evangelical conference at the Georgia Dome. This did not sit well with Wesley Wildmon, the outreach director for the American Family Association (AFA), a Christian non-profit.

Said Wildmon, in a letter published on the AFA's website: "I was very frustrated that you would allow [Carrie Underwood] to help lead thousands of people in worship. My frustration quickly turned to disappointment and then to sadness. Carrie Underwood encourages and supports homosexual marriage which the Word of God does not."

Wildmon ended with a threat, even claiming the Lord's judgment (italics mine): "It is God who has blessed you with this platform and *it is God who can remove His hand of blessing if you become careless with His principles.*"

That is ridiculous, not redemptive. It's almost like Christianity, to some, has become two very different religions. It understandably confuses people and causes some to resent religion.

Your heart and mind, if you are for or against gay marriage, likely are racing right now. The point here isn't to debate anyone's position on gay marriage. It's to draw attention to the lack of tolerance, and the love that was missing in Wildmon's letter. Whether you agree with him or not, his words did not reflect the overriding teaching and principles from the "Word of God" and "His hand of blessing." Maybe on that, we can agree, whatever you believe regarding the debate of whether Carrie Underwood should have appeared or not. (I'm glad she did.) If you don't agree, maybe remember that Jesus spent a lot of time with the oppressed, and that there are none without sin, except Him.

I don't know how my friends who were gloating or in despair started the beginning of the day after the election, but I know how I started mine. My very human condition lends itself to being vulnerable to our many sins—vanity, pride, absolute certainty, denial, lust and selfishness, just to name a few. Even hate.

I know, also, I am less prone to committing these acts if I start my day first thing with prayer and meditation. Maybe for you it isn't prayer, but simply sitting quietly for 10 minutes. I wake up at dawn and offer my day to humility, service and compassion. I read short reflections from prayer books I like. I remember those who have asked for prayers. I also ask for the grace to get up quickly when I stumble, because I will stumble. Then, it's out the door...

It took awhile to realize the importance of this spiritual routine. The Spirit had to hit me over my stubborn head to move me into a better place of peace and protection from negative thoughts. It is an ongoing struggle, but one that is easier if I keep my morning repetitions.

Almost every book I've read that talks about religion or spiritual growth avows that beginning one's morning in prayer is essential to living in love and shunning hate. Two authors I've read stand out, among a choir of spiritualists who are seeking to lead more of us to a reflective, not reactive, beginning to our days.

Father Richard Rohr, a Franciscan priest who runs the Center for Action and Contemplation in Albuquerque, New Mexico, is a believer. This is what he says about the benefits of morning prayer:

> Love, like forgiveness, is a decision. It's a decision in your mind and in your heart. And you'd better make it early in the day, because once you're a few hours into resentment, it's too late. Already you're angry at your husband or wife, and you're upset because the paper boy didn't deliver your newspaper. You see, when you're not in love, you'll use any excuse you can to be unhappy. You'll use any excuse to be irritated. But you were unhappy before your husband or wife did anything or didn't do anything, before the paper-boy came or didn't come. You were already unhappy, and they just occasioned it. The exact object for your unhappiness is actually arbitrary and illogical. Un-happiness just needs an object—and so does happiness and love. You have to recognize ahead of time when you are not living in love.

> This is surely why morning prayer is so important.

Rohr wants us to experience agape. So does an Australian, Matthew Kelly, author of *Resisting Happiness*, who encourages every person to begin each morning with 10 minutes of prayer.

> *Resistance loves keeping us busy with anything but the one thing that will most help us grow. Our lives change when our habits change. New habits bring new life.*

Kelly says people are better off when they invite God's love to take root. That love then grows daily with proper water, sunlight and fertilizer. Like it does for Father Strobel, Coach Corbin, Bill Lee and Bono.

Prayer is that "divine love that is God's Self in an absolute open-heartedness," adds Rohr, author of *Falling Upward* and *The Divine Dance*. "When you're in that space, your energy flows outward and even expands. When you're not in that space, your energy sucks in. It's all about who did me wrong and why I don't like those people and how my aunt never talks to me and why so-and-so is a jerk. It doesn't help that our brains have evolved to hold onto negative thoughts (like Velcro) and let the positive thoughts slip off (like Teflon).... You have to deliberately, consciously choose to love and not hate. Because people haven't been taught that, we have even decent people in our country, in political parties, and even in leadership positions in our churches who are much more at home with hate than they are with love. And they do not even know it."

We are at a crossroads. Many have woken up politically. Many are also awakening spiritually. There are not dissimilarities in these awakenings and movements. People feel empty, and they don't like how it feels. Just as we have spiraled downward politically and spiritually, we will rise again, and lift up each other.

Will people on our plane—the Muslim and Jew, the atheist and Christian, and even the Christian fighting with the Christian—realize this? I believe we will. I pray daily for this. This prayer for peace is always the last prayer at the Sunday Mass I attend. I invite your daily engagement, whether through prayer, reflection or meditation.

Rohr says "routine is essential, we must commit to daily, constant work because [our] ego and the events of life want to close it down.

The voices in the dominant culture tell you to judge, dismiss, hate, and fear.... You have to work to live in love, to develop a generosity of spirit, a readiness to smile, a willingness to serve instead of to take. Each morning you take your inner temperature, observing if your energy is loving and flowing outward or negative and sucking in. Contemplative prayer helps us witness and recognize these outer flows and inner suckings."

Change is happening. The great philosopher Yoda from Star Wars is an iconic figure in our culture, not because of his cute ugliness and unique gravelly voice, but because he teaches us about The Force, and how we can achieve this heightened Spiritual State:

> *"You must unlearn what you have learned. Do, or do not. There is no try."*

I encourage you to do (not try) daily prayer, meditation or simply silence (or whatever works for you), early and often, when we deplane, and to invite others in your life to do so, too.

CRITICAL POINT:

Certitude, ritual and dogma in religion and politics have redefined our spirituality, often making
it harder to love one another. A commitment to
selfless love in our daily lives is essential to political
recovery and spiritual renewal.

ACTION STEP:

Embrace uncertainty. Commit to *agape*, a deeply
reflective and selfless love. Start each day with loving
prayer, at least 10 minutes first thing in your morning. Do not confuse predictable temporal cacophony
with everlasting spiritual grace and peace. Whenever you feel yourself abandoning love on this planet,
find time for prayer to stay away from the hate and
certitude that is tearing our culture apart, and away
from the promise of peace.

Find and practice a centering repetition to peace
and understanding that works for you. Is it:

- Simple meditation?
- The Hindu practice of Om?
- The Gregorian, Native American or West African
  practices of melody, drumming or polyrhythmic
  chants, respectively?
- Bowing to Mecca?
- Walking the Camino in Spain or some other
  pilgrimage?
- Praying the rosary?

Whatever helps your negative thoughts and sen-
sations disappear, do it with repetition. Find what
works for you, and may God be with you always.
Strive to live Devji's 10 Noble Traits!

Before we move on, I share this prayer, now part of my morning routine, from a booklet on a daylong pilgrimage up and down Croagh Patrick, Ireland's Holy Mountain. It was intended to be read "along the path" up the mountain. It is an excellent daily reminder for my own path, and maybe yours.

Breathe...
Feel the air in your lungs.
Breathe in peace, breathe out anxiety.
Breathe in beauty, breathe out hurt.
Breathe in love, breathe out fear.
Become aware of God's Spirit sustaining you.
Be inspired as you stop and stare.

As I resume my journey up this incline,
I ask for the grace, Lord,
To remain compassionate towards myself,
Steadfast despite setbacks,
And mindful of the fact
That mist and cloud eventually lift.
I continue in your name.
Go raibh liomsa innui, Triur ar shilabh
Athair, Mac is Spiorad Naomh.
(In the name of the Father, and the Son,
And of the Holy Spirit. Amen.)

HELPFUL LINKS AND RESOURCES:

www.cac.org (Center for Action and Contemplation website)
www.dynamiccatholic.com
Falling Upward and *The Divine Dance*, by Richard Rohr
www.EndingOurUncivilWar.com

COUNTERING CERTITUDE AND FEAR

"Teach thy tongue to say 'I do not know,' and thou
 shalt progress."
                                                    —MAIMONIDES

"The wind of anger blows out the lamp of intelligence."
                                                    —ANONYMOUS

"Extremism, so far, is the great problem of the 21st
 [Century]....Extremism is a powerful alliance of
 fear and certitude. Complexity and humility are its
 natural foes."
            —JON MEACHAM, AMERICAN GOSPEL: GOD, THE
            FOUNDING FATHERS AND THE MAKING OF A NATION

Why are many people acting so afraid today? And why are many
people so certain about things, especially their opinions?

A few years ago, when I came upon that bumper sticker "Don't
believe everything you think," I thought of all the fear and anxiety,
and certitude and finger-pointing, on and in our social and traditional
media, respectively.

I thought of the Buddha, who said, "The mind is everything. What you think you become."

I thought of Oprah Winfrey as well, when she said, "You become what you believe." We do indeed, whether it's positive, negative, or some combination of energy that our powerful brain generates. There is a lot to be said about the law of attraction and power of intention, conscious or subconscious.

I was born in 1965, so I don't remember the raucous 1960s, but those who were there say today's time isn't dissimilar. There was rioting over racial, political and social issues then, as there is today. We were at war with each other then and now over many of the same issues—foreign policy (Vietnam and communism/terrorism and Middle East instability), civil rights (racial equality and women's rights/the same), social and domestic issues (entitlement programs/socialism, spending and immigration). Then and now, we disagreed over the extent of government's role on many of these questions.

You know the story on social media. A leader tweets or makes a racist, sexist or hateful comment. Many respond similarly and firmly, without thinking hate often begets hate, increasing the heat. Some who are self-assuredly religious support or rationalize what's been said, knowingly or unknowingly accepting the hate. Some of these same deeply religious people later will roll out excerpts from Scripture, blind to the fact that many other available scriptures overwhelmingly are in conflict with their dogma.

We have to be right!

President Trump's continually active Twitter account (often most active in the wee hours of the morning) is a well-known example. Many like what he's doing—going around the mainstream media— even when they don't like what he's saying. There is a fair argument that he's controlling his message in this way.

Here's a different view. Any issue becomes more challenging to solve, or message becomes harder to hear, when we flash the rhetorical middle finger, rather than begin by extending a handshake, an ear and an open mind. With a one-gun salute, political enemies become significantly more energized. Potential allies run for cover. Ad hominem attacks make it less likely to keep the opposition (and as we saw later, his inner circle) at bay, instead fueling easily stoked fire. Even the conservative *Wall Street*

Journal concluded in a mid-year 2017 editorial that Trump became his own worst enemy with his unhinged social media missives.

None of this certitude is surprising. On a 2016 *Frontline* special profiling the candidates, a friend recalled how Trump's father drilled into his son that the end game isn't just to win in business, but to "kill" the opponent. This explains much of his dehumanizing behavior.

These rants and outbreaks can be successful for a period, in some instances, if the end game is to run over your opposition. It's an obvious strong-armed authoritarianism.

Why are more personalities today behaving like this? Why are many friends tolerating the political rough-housing? Have we changed so much as a nation that this is the "new us"? When did this happen?

The author Susan Cain points to specific changes in our nation that began about 100 years ago. In her book *Quiet: The Power of Introverts in a World That Can't Stop Talking*, she argues that we've been experiencing a rise of the Extrovert Ideal. Cain says the famous journey of Dale Carnegie, who authored *Public Speaking and Influencing Men in 1913*, occurred at the beginning of that shift.

"Carnegie's journey reflected a cultural evolution that… [changed] forever who we are and whom we admire, how we act at job interviews and what we look for in an employee, and how we court our mates and raise our children," she says.

"America has shifted from what the influential cultural historian Warren Sussman called a Culture of Character in the 19th century to a Culture of Personality, and opened up a Pandora's Box of personal anxieties from which we would never quite recover. In the Culture of Character, the ideal self was serious, disciplined, and honorable."

Over time, Sussman would say, "Every American was to become a performing self."

Cain says Carnegie and his disciples started convincing Americans that how others perceived you was more important than how you behaved privately. These coaches and speakers heralded the importance of perception, according to Sussman.

After World War I, advertisers began to pitch products differently, not as solutions to our aches and problems but to build a more confident and likeable you. In the 1920s and 30s, we began to identify with movie stars who were, like Carnegie said we should be, "magnetic, fascinating, stunning, attractive, dominant, forceful and energetic."

We've gone to new extremes in this generation, with narcissistic selfie photos on social media, with children on smart phones a year or two out of their cribs, and with continual dawn-to-dusk opining and denigration of that opining.

We've been given the gift of technology, and it's a damning curse.

Cain is not alone in believing that our sensitivity to each other has been in decline as our conscious selves have been in retreat. In 2010, the University of Michigan published a study that showed college students are 40% less empathetic than they were 30 years ago. Maybe you're surprised it wasn't higher. In 2017, it probably is. We'll explore later, in detail, the growing intolerance and declining civility at many universities and how it's contributing to polarization and growing spiritual emptiness.

The Pandora's Box of technology may be opened forever, but it's not impossible to incorporate and manage it. Sure, you can unfriend or unfollow an annoying friend. But where does that get you? Following only people you agree with, if you take it to its extreme. You've created your own safe space, not unlike the one you criticize some college kids for demanding.

There are other ways to cope and thrive. Some schools are adapting to the times in positive ways. At Liberty University in Lynchburg, Virginia, Dr. Sylvia Frejd has founded the Center for Digital Wellness. Her mottos are "Thrive in Real Life" and "Look Up!" The Center contains a fireplace in the middle of a comfortable living room and a kitchen table for conversation. Frejd holds a "digital detox day when students are expected to leave their digital devices at home."

"Life is about relationships with our parents, spouses, friends, kids, and bosses, and we cannot allow technology to erode them," she told The College Fix, a media outlet that monitors free speech impediments on campuses across the country.

Frejd notes the therapy isn't just for Christians at her conservative school. It is critical for every person to maintain the "silence and solitude needed to reflect and focus," she asserts. "Every religion and spirituality requires this in some form. If we become addicted to technology, the distraction it brings will rewire our brain to the point that we lose our capacity to contemplate God."

Digital detox. Count me in. One of the best feelings I have each year is when my children and I find a remote area with no wireless or phone capability, like Charit Creek Lodge in the Big South Fork National River & Recreation Area in Tennessee. For the duration of our getaway, the constant whirring of bells, whistles, dings and other phone alerts are replaced by the sounds of slow-moving streams, wind rushing through the trees and valley, and conversation. There is no electricity at the lodge. At community dinners, we meet people from all over the country. It's our outdoor Center for Digital Wellness.

Leaving the park can be jarring, as phones power back up, Spotify and Pandora reappear, and the snap-chatting, texting and posting kick into high gear. You go from 0 to 60 in far fewer seconds.

Back in civilization, it's important to have time to myself every day, to have my phone off for periods, and not to have it next to my bed at night. Reading regularly is important. Writing this book has been huge.

It's very good to have face-to-face time with others to discuss what's going on. I meet regularly, because of my job, with people who hold diverse views. I love what it does for my perspective. I'm constantly challenging myself not to believe everything I think, just like the bumper sticker warns. It's not easy, but it's made easier with this routine.

I continue to seek new ways of staying connected to people, not my phone. I've been meeting for the last year with a group of a dozen people. We call it En Masse Circle. The group meets every few months in a peaceful room with candles lit. We remove our shoes, close our eyes at times and meditate, offering unifying thoughts. We breathe slowly and talk slower. We're honest, raw, exposed. We talk about what's concerning us in politics, our culture and our lives. Several in the circle talk about how they're are afraid to engage elsewhere because of the unloading they may receive from a friend, spouse, co-worker, or really anyone. No one interrupts—it's just you engaging a circle of non-judgmental friends, allowed to speak whatever is on your mind. It's crazy cool!

What I like about En Masse Circle is that it reinforces traits that I need—that we all need—to practice more often, such as slower or no responses and just listening, and finding where someone is coming from especially if I disagree with them.

Rohr, the provocative Franciscan priest from Albuquerque, offers another kind of reflective examination. Perky yet peaceful, Rohr has invested in helping how each individual can find goodwill amidst the chaos. Rohr's emphasis on oneness with our universe is prevalent in his works, like *Falling Upward* and *The Divine Dance*.

In *Falling Upward*, Rohr talks of our "spirituality for the two halves" of our lives, the first where we learn the necessary rules for life and the latter we can learn from our failings and adjustments. How often have you heard that failure is the greatest teacher? Unfortunately, that is not what our "modern" Culture of Personality would have us accept.

"You need a very strong container to hold the contents and contradictions that arrive later in life," says Rohr. "You ironically need a very strong ego to let go of your ego. You need to struggle with the rules more than a bit before you throw them out."

Our first-half-in-life container is "constructed through impulse controls, traditions, group symbols, family loyalties, basic respect for authority, civil and church laws, and a sense of goodness, value and special importance of your country, ethnicity and religion," says the Franciscan. These are not bad things, but necessary things. The Ten Commandments are excellent teachings, for example; life would be "pretty pathetic" without them.

But we all fall off the bike, right? That's when you get back up. When we're off balance, we learn to find it. Why don't we do the same in life?

The lack of acceptance of failure, and the wisdom that comes from it, is limiting many and destroying others. You've probably seen it close up, with a friend, family member or even yourself. I watched someone dear to me suffer tremendously, until he finally accepted failure. Just as Rohr says, it centered and freed his lovely soul. His favorite book happens to be...*Falling Upward*.

"We are not helping our children by always preventing them from what might be necessary falling," Rohr says, "*because you learn how to recover from falling by falling!*"

There is a growing number of scholars like Rohr who are teaching alternative ways to view and process what concerns us, starting with an embrace of mysticism instead of the literalism we get from our media, politicians and, increasingly, many college professors. It is unfortunate so many universities have taken out the "liberal" in liberal arts, but I'll tap the brakes until the next chapter.

Rohr encourages each man and woman to "live in the flow" and let go of our limiting ego, which generates sin, like hate and intolerance, and resists happiness, which come from acceptance and understanding. The work I need to do is work for me to do, the work you need to do is for you, and so on.

Rohr is especially adept in communicating the importance of avoiding binaries, dualistic viewing and certitude, which he believes in part explains the rise in spiritual emptiness and apathy, as well as atheism, agnosticism and fundamentalism. This is profound!

"Mature people are not *either-or* thinkers, but they bathe in the ocean of *both-and*," says Rohr. "Think Gandhi, Anne Frank, Martin Luther King Jr., Mother Teresa, Nelson Mandela and the like.... As Albert Einstein said, 'No problem can be solved by the same consciousness that caused it in the first place.'"

Let's ponder through a prism of what issue or person bothers, disturbs or ails you most. I'm encouraging your plane mate to do the same. It's hard, at least for me, to think I'm getting anywhere or moving the needle unless I approach the frustrating issue or annoying person with a different, healthier state of being, knowing and accepting. I suspect this may be true for you and your adversary as well.

Rohr takes it to deeper levels with a critique of religion in general and certain religions in particular: Western Christianity, under which he says "very few Christians have been taught how to live both law and freedom at the same time. Our Western dualistic minds do not process paradoxes very well." More Jews, Hindus and Buddhists are able to hold creative tensions through a more contemplative mind, he says. It's hard to disagree with him, if you're on Facebook these days.

Here's a big quote: "In the Western World, it seems we cannot build prisons fast enough or have enough recovery groups, therapists or re-parenting classes for all the walking wounded in this very educated, religious and sophisticated society, which has little respect for limitations and a huge sense of entitlement."

I would add "safe spaces" on college campuses to round out what otherwise says much about our society today.

Religion, of course, has a huge place for us, and should. The great religions are instructive, and in their best and undistorted forms, able to help us center our spirits and foster the faith, hope, love and peace this world needs to survive. The founding principles in the great religions are very similar. Understanding this, some of which we visited in the previous chapter, enables us to view our universe holistically, which generates compassion and understanding of what previously was difficult to accept or comprehend.

SAT, CHIT, ANANDA

In Latin, *omne trium perfectum* means anything in threes is perfect or conveys the same idea as the rule of three.

So what's up with this three thing? I keep seeing it everywhere. Don't put two pillows or candles together, I'm told. Make it three.

In writing, the principle of the "rule of three" suggests events or characters introduced in this fashion are more humorous, satisfying, or effective in the story's execution. Information conveyed is easier to remember since three entities combine brevity and rhythm and smaller amount of information to create a pattern.

How do religions and spiritualists view three? Rohr not only makes the case how the Trinity can work in our lives but also draws the parallel of three in Hinduism: "Our Christian God isn't a Man, on a throne, with a beard, observing, judging and damning us. Instead, God is the Creator. He is Silence and Knowing. His Son, Jesus, is the Living Manifestation of His Omnipresence; he is alongside us with his teaching and examples. The Holy Spirit is Dynamism Within and Between. His Spirit is Implanted Hope, Inner Momentum and *Élan Vital* (vital impetus)."

Hinduism, the world's oldest religion, dating back five millennia, also shares three qualities of God—*Sat, Chit* and *Ananda*, or Being, Knowledge and Happiness. *Sat* is God being itself, just as Paul told the Athenians on Mars Hill when he called God our "Universal Being, the Source of all Being." *Chit* is consciousness or knowledge, similar to the Christian view of *logos*. *Ananda* is happiness or bliss, just as Christians express joy in the Holy Spirit. Rohr summarizes in threes:

> *Sat-Chit-Ananda.*
> Being-knowledge-happiness.
> Father-Son-Spirit.
> Truth is one, and universal.

Dante, author of *The Divine Comedy*, described the Trinity another way: "In the profound and clear substance of light, three circles appeared to me—of three different colors and one single dimension."

Dante doesn't describe the colors, but calls this unity Knower, Known and Knowing, and Love, Loved, and Loving. God is One, and you pick which colors (or path that is right for you). This is beautiful religion—you get to pick, but be careful not to pick for others. Greater certitude leads to greater conflict, as we are witnessing.

So we must step back. We must reflect. We must breathe more and talk less. I work on this constantly, and encourage another discussion with your seatmate. I continually seek to experience grace and love, whatever the outcome of any legislation, executive order, and judicial decision, or meaningless "fake news" I've read or projection my buddy emailed me.

The best teachings advise that peace and understanding will pervade our souls through contemplation and less reaction. Our restful, clear minds then allow us to engage nobly and civilly in this short temporal, and very noisy, universe.

An embrace of mysticism—whatever religious or spiritual compass is guiding us—nurtures our souls. The great mystics are saying an awareness of a spiritual trifecta, whatever our predilection, can help us stay true to the path of being, knowledge and happiness in any personal or societal storm.

CRITICAL POINT:

Our minds are powerful muscles that, like our bodies, need proper exercise to remain healthy. Dualistic thinking is counterproductive to achieving happiness in our spiritual lives and in our politics. Certitude and fear are inhibitors, not contributors.

ACTION STEP:

Commit to repetitive spiritual practices that enable you to be happy, maintain peace amidst the chaos and be the change agent you wish in this world. Be a walking, humble example in the renewal of our Culture of Character. Think, act and expect more of yourself, not less; be an example for others on the high road and others' projections won't hurt you.

RESOURCES:

www.QuietRev.com (Susan Cain's website The Quiet Revolution)
www.EndingOurUncivilWar.com

CONTEMPLATION:

"Be the change you wish to see in the world."
                                        —MAHATMA GANDHI

"No one can make you feel inferior without your consent."
                                        —ELEANOR ROOSEVELT

"The quieter you become, the more you can hear."
                                        —RAM DASS

"Be not ashamed of mistakes and thus make
them crimes."

—CONFUCIUS

"Our culture made a virtue of living only as extroverts.
We discouraged the inner journey, the quest for center.
So we lost our center and have to find it again."

—ANAÏS NIN

"Breathe in the Spirit, and breathe out your humanity."

—MAUREEN DOYLE, AUTHOR AND LIFE COACH

THE TRUTH—AND MYTH— OF SEPARATION OF CHURCH AND STATE

Are church and state meant to be separate, as many Americans have come to believe? By separate, does that mean completely? These are important questions, since freedom of religion is a big part of the Bill of Rights in our Constitution.

The answer to the first question, I will argue for your contemplation, is yes and no. The answer to the second question is no, not completely as some would like you to believe.

Our Founders were very careful on the subject. They were also quite clear. They chose to establish a framework where it would be difficult if not impossible to promote one religion over another. They avoided using or choosing one term of God, from any specific religion, in our founding documents.

Their view of religion is that we would have a "public religion," which many believed was or should be inherently understood. Wisely, some during that time thought otherwise and insisted the protection of religion should be coded in a proper and general way, hence the adoption of the First Amendment of the U.S. Constitution with no mention of a specific God or particular religion.

Thirteen years prior, in the Declaration of Independence, there was no mention made of Jesus, the Father or Trinity, Yahweh, Allah or any other religious term for a higher authority. The Declaration's author Thomas Jefferson described a common God in more general terms, like the "Creator" and "Nature's God." Ironically, Jefferson's "separation of church and state" statement would several decades later become a rallying cry for secularists to diminish the understanding of our "Creator's" role in our way of life. They want any mention of our Creator, your Creator or a Creator eliminated.

In 1776, Jefferson wrote that human beings are made in the image of God, with sacred rights to life, liberty and the pursuit of happiness. Jefferson and the document's signatories, however, carefully avoided enshrining a Christian God, or any other, for important reasons.

"Properly understood, the God of public religion is not the God of Abraham or God the Father or the Holy Trinity," writes Jon Meacham in *American Gospel: God, The Founding Fathers and the Making of a Nation* (2006). "[But the Founders also] were not absolute secularists." Meacham says the Founders struggled mightily in Philadelphia at the Convention in 1787 over the topic of religion, just as we do today, but settled on having God as part of public life. They did so in a way that distinguishes between private and public religion in their drafts and in adopting the First Amendment.

"Public religion is not a substitute for private religion, nor is it a Trojan Horse filled with evangelicals threatening the walls of secular religion," Meacham says in honor of their work. "It is rather a habit of mind and of heart that enables Americans to be tolerant and rever-ent—two virtues of relevance to all, for the Founders' public religion is consummately democratic. When a president says "God bless America" or when we sing "America! America! God shed his grace on thee," each American is free to define God in whatever way he chooses. A Christian's mind may summon God the Father; a Jew's, Yahweh; a Muslim's, Allah; an atheist's, no one, or no thing."

Though most of the nation was decidedly Christian at the time (and still is), the Founders "were not interested in establishing yet another earthly government with official ties to a state church." After all, that was part of what they were separating from. Church and state would both be more authentic and powerful, if they were not together in some private contract with one religion.

"The magistrate is to govern the *state*, and Christ is to govern the *church*," said Reverend Samuel Stillman in 1779 before the Massachusetts Supreme Court. In this way, the two would not be one. Both would be better in the 13 states that would convene, eight years later, uniting in 1789.

Fifty years after that, Alexis de Tocqueville made observations that showed how well such a system was working. Religion was nurturing a moral society with virtuous people, he said, without going too far or not far enough. The right balance had been struck.

"I do not know if all Americans have faith in their religion," said the famous French visitor who penned *Democracy in America*. "But I am sure they believe it is necessary to the maintenance of public institutions."

Conversely, he found that, in Europe, Christianity had become "intimately united with the powers of the earth. Today these powers are falling and it is almost buried under their debris." Tocqueville appears to be saying that a dilution of the influence of a separated church can harm the state. He said the way in which America devised and respected such boundaries was a great achievement.

Meacham, a graduate of the University of the South in my home state of Tennessee, editor of *Newsweek* and contributor on several news programs, agrees: "The great good news about America—the American gospel if you will—is that religion shapes the life of a nation without strangling it.... Faith is a matter of choice, not coercion, and the legacy of the Founding is that the sensible center holds.... The balance between the promise of the Declaration of Independence, with its evocation of divine origins and destiny, and the practicalities of the Constitution, with its checks on extremism, remains perhaps the most brilliant American success."

This practical idealism, the protection of religious freedom and the rejection of radical fundamentalism in certain religions are and will always be important to the protection of our union and promotion of a civil society with guaranteed civil rights. Unfortunately, all are under heavy attack from the left, the right and elsewhere. Unknowingly or otherwise, we are enabling fundamentalism to grow in America.

Let's look at when Meacham's "sensible center" was first challenged and when the ongoing debate of "separation of church and state" began. In October 1801, the Danbury Baptist Association of Connecticut wrote to President Thomas Jefferson, asserting "our Constitution is not specific" on the matter of religious practice, that "religion is considered as the first object of legislation," and that the "religious privileges we enjoy we enjoy as favors granted and not as inalienable rights." Further, said the Baptists:

"It is not to be wondered...if those who seek after power and gain under the pretense of government and religion should reproach their fellow man-should reproach their Chief magistrate, as an enemy of religion, law and good order because he will not, dare not assume the prerogative of Jehovah and make laws to govern the kingdom of Christ."

Jefferson, measured in his reply, knew such attempts were forthcoming when he and fellow Founders deliberately left out any reference to a specific religion's term for God. On January 1, 1802, Jefferson penned the following response (italics mine):

> *"Believing with you that religion is a matter which lies solely between Man & his God, that he owes account to none other for his faith or his worship, that the legitimate powers of government reach actions only, & not opinions, I contemplate with sovereign reverence that act of the whole American people which declared that their legislature should "make no law respecting an establishment of religion, or prohibiting the free exercise thereof,"* **thus building a wall of separation between Church & State** *....I reciprocate your kind prayers for the protection & blessing of the common father and creator of man, and tender you for yourselves & your religious association, assurances of my high respect & esteem."*

Jefferson knew that many wars had started, and would start again, when a government, in the name of their adopted religion and distorted by politicians and their clergy, pressed resources coercively into battle. His masterful reinforcement and defense of public religion was well received by many, but not all. The devoutly religious questioned Jefferson, declaring him to be a secularist. Conversely, emboldened secularists took the Virginian's words as proof their view was right—that religion had little or no place in American life.

What has transpired since then has been a constitutional battle about the limits and expansion of God in our public life. As progressives grew stronger in the late 19th century, the U.S. Supreme Court unanimously decided to slow their advance, declaring in a poor 1892 decision that "everywhere [is] a clear recognition of the same truth…this is a Christian nation." This is a hard view that would have been concerning to the Founders. The court's stance in 1892 began to moderate during the progressive movement, as the pendulum swung. Then came a new era of judicial interpretation, which would lead to greater activism that would ignite and remain to this day.

After World War II, Americans concerned about "godless Communism" began to approve including "God" increasingly into government terminology. Congress voted for "In God We Trust" as the national motto, and "under God" was added to the Pledge of Allegiance. These were signs that Americans were once again warming to public religion. The pendulum was swinging the other way.

Then came a Supreme Court decision that sparked the same debate once had by Jefferson, the Connecticut Baptists and others. In 1947, the same year that Americans United for Separation of Church & State formed, Judge Hugo Black dusted off Jefferson's famous phrase, and reshaped it into something that would set the stage for new interpretations.

In *Everson v. the Board of Education of the Township of Ewing, New Jersey*, Black opined (italics mine), "In the words of Jefferson, the clause against establishment of religion by law was *intended* to erect a wall of separation between Church and State…. The First Amendment has erected a wall between church and state. *The wall must be kept high and impregnable. We could not approve the slightest breach.*"

There is a hint of activism in Black's interpretation. To Jefferson, the wall was already built and it needed to be defended, as Black opines. Black took Jefferson's words, however, to another level. The courts, with more liberal appointees from President Franklin D. Roosevelt, now began to reverse the pendulum, but with more energy than at the turn of the century.

A year after *Everson*, an atheist argued successfully in *McCollum v. Board of Education* against allowing religious teachers to enter public schools to teach religion, a breach of "the wall."

In 1940 in Champaign, Illinois, members of Protestant, Jewish and Catholic faiths formed the Champaign Council on religious Education. The local school board granted the diverse group permission to offer *voluntary* religious education classes for children in grades four through nine.

Vashti McCollum objected to the classes because she said her son James was ostracized for not attending them. Notably, her son was never compelled to attend, which was her choice and her young son's, despite assertions to the contrary. The case thus would test the principle of "released time" under which public schools had set aside class time for religious instruction, a common practice in the 1940s. Some 2,000 communities across the country had similar programs impacting 1.5 million children.

McCollum's mother sued the Board of Education under the pretense that religious instruction in public schools violated the Establishment Clause of the First Amendment, the principle of separation of church and state, and the Equal Protection Clause of the Fourteenth Amendment. Principal assertions included that certain Protestant groups exercised an advantage over other Protestant denominations, the program was "voluntary" in name only because school officials coerced participation, and the Champaign Council was able to select its instructors with limited oversight from the school superintendent.

McCollum sought to ensure the Board of Education be ordered to "adopt and enforce rules and regulations prohibiting all instruction in and teaching of all religious education in all public schools in [the district], and in all public-school houses and buildings in said district when occupied by public schools."

The Circuit Court ruled in favor of the school district in January 1946, and the state Supreme Court upheld the ruling. The U.S. Supreme

Court found otherwise. Judge Black opined against the defendants who had asserted "historically the First Amendment was intended to forbid only government preference of one religion over another, not an impartial governmental assistance of all religions. In addition they ask that we distinguish or overrule our holding in the *Everson* case that the Fourteenth Amendment made the 'establishment of religion' clause of the First Amendment applicable as a prohibition against the States."

Black rejected defense arguments and went well beyond *Everson* to say "the state's tax-supported public school buildings [cannot be] used for the dissemination of religious doctrines" and the state cannot afford "sectarian groups an invaluable aid to [help] to provide pupils for their religious classes through use of the state's compulsory public school machinery.

"This is not separation of Church and State."

The lone dissenting justice Stanley Forman Reed objected to the breadth of the majority's interpretation of the Establishment Clause, noting an incidental support of religion should have been permissible with a more narrow reading of the First Amendment.

In 1952, the high court revisited the issue of religious instruction in *Zorach v. Clauson*. In a 6-3 ruling, the court said religious education during the school day was permissible since neither public school facilities nor public funds were used. More on that importantly grounded decision later.

We all have a view of religious instruction, depending on how we did or didn't experience it. My religious education at St. Henry's in third through sixth grades was required, rigid and regular. We would attend Mass during the week as students. The Dominican nuns engaged us often through the prism of religion. I can say I took positives and negatives from the experience, but it was easy to get turned off to Catholicism when it seemed like unquestioned dogma, or felt force-fed. In this way, I can understand Vashti McCollum's positions.

I can also say I had a very different and generally more positive Catholic experience at St. Bernard Academy, where my children attended school from kindergarten through eighth grade. The school's tradition of incorporating the Sisters of Mercy's mission of helping the poor and their aversion from strict interpretation resonated with my children and their parents.

In later schooling at the all-boys Montgomery Bell Academy, the approach to the subject of religion was less regular but much more open, the *both-and* approach the Catholic scholar Rohr encourages us to experience. Our faculty introduced us to speakers from many religions—a rabbi one month, an Episcopalian priest the next, a Bible-thumping Southern Baptist and others.

As a Catholic, I found the introductions highly informative and enlightening. I agreed with much of what they shared, fascinated by the commonality in the religions. Some statements were intriguing, as were the varying tones in presentations. Some offerings were contrary to my beliefs, but it was good to know what was being said, straight from the people saying them. I still attend diverse religious gatherings, always open-minded to what I'm hearing, whether or not I believe in everything being said. I am free to leave whenever I want, which should be a big part of any religious engagement.

This is where I disagree with *McCollum*, Black's court and those who want all religion eradicated from state-sponsored functions. For the Founders, there was allowance for religious expression, as long as it was not specific. If McCollum had sought to include other religions (Buddhism, Hinduism, etc.) that wanted to be a part of the education course, she would have had my full support. If she had proven her son was forced to attend the classes, she would have had my full support, as well, to have equal protections that students attending the classes had. Two-way streets are easier for all; driving crowded and noisy one-way streets is no fun.

Instead, Black's court went in a different direction and created a one-way road. The court equated religious educational opportunities, however imperfect, to an infringement of constitutional rights. With the stroke of the pen, voluntary educational opportunities in publicly funded schools were stopped. One can argue the court's closure and repudiation has contributed greatly to our march to being a highly intolerant people and the hardening and distrusting viewpoints from the left and the right, the religious and non-religious.

The *McCollum* decision, in my mind, has done much more harm than good. It was an abrupt bend of Jefferson's view on separation of church and state. Jefferson's view on "separation" was to hold firm against the Connecticut Baptists' desire to impose their views on others. One would think he would have celebrated liberal arts—the teaching of religion in general through voluntary, diverse instruction—as long as the choice of worship and faith, or no worship and no faith, was left to the individual. Compelling doctrine is much different than offering views of a doctrine, the Founders might have said. Was the Illinois course telling the student would be damned if he didn't go to church or the synagogue, or that certain Protestants, Catholics or Jews believed this?

The kind of open engagement on religion I received at a private high school was similar to the kind Champaign district students and 2,000 other communities experienced before *McCollum* ended it. It is classic liberal arts instruction in its finest form, something secularists have been working diligently to eliminate in our public schools and universities. They've been quite successful, which I believe has hardened views against religion, conversely, by creating an ever-higher "wall" around it. Some hardliners in certain religious communities, however, aren't doing religion any favors when they become increasing dogmatic in their views and statements.

Liberal arts can include religion, if it remains within the framework of its true definition. Religion, as Jefferson and the Founders were aware, could be explosive, corrosive and corruptive, when used selectively or distortedly for the purpose of war or oppression.

Liberal arts, as defined by Merriam-Webster, means "college or university studies (such as language, philosophy, literature, abstract science) intended to provide chiefly general knowledge and to develop general intellectual capacities (such as reason and judgment) as opposed to professional or vocational skills." We could apply a liberal arts philosophy to the teaching of religion, as many private schools still do, with the goal of learning about religions and their astonishing commonality and differences rather than what you must believe.

Religious fundamentalism, secularism and religious liberalism can be contentious, depending on one's point of view. The emergence of religious liberalism is seeking to reconcile pre-modern religious tradition with modernity, which is a controversial philosophy and by nature antagonistic to the other two philosophies. Religious fundamentalists are seeking to protect religious tradition, while secularists are seeking to eliminate religion altogether.

Exposing more people to the concepts of religious fundamentalism, secularism and religious liberalism will undo much of the growing hatred and distrust. Most of us are weary or skeptical of the never-ending battle between hardliners from all three camps, but there can be room for everyone.

The walls that have been erected have not been very good for society and civil engagement. So is not obeying, enforcing or respecting the true intent of our laws to include allowing the practice of public religion. It's a path to anarchy, and a big reason I'm engaging you and others. When you remove something big, a vacuum ensues. That vacuum is filling and will fill further with something else, much of it antithetical to healthy religious tolerance and teachings. It's led to quite a few head-scratchers recently.

Should "the wall" mean that a coach shouldn't be allowed to kneel and pray with his players at a public school to offer thanks and seek protection and guidance? Many school boards, which once protected such a freedom of expression and now condemn it, seem to think so. But should a player who is a Muslim or Jew have to hear a coach's prayer only to Christ our Savior?

It is an intriguing question that I believe Jefferson already answered in 1802. Pray as you like. Leave if you like. But don't make me say or agree with your prayer. I may want to say my own, or not say it at all.

At a private Christian school, or any other religiously affiliated school, there are no issues. Pray as you'd like to whatever God or idol you like. But we do have modern-day Danbury Baptists among us. If some religious hardliners would be less assertive in such situations at public gatherings and respectful of those among us, the secularists would have less of an argument and more room to breathe.

Praying to God in general in a public setting, as most presidents have done, makes sense and should always be protected. "So help me God," started with George Washington; no president, I believe, has since said, "So help me Christ." I don't know of an instance at a public setting or in a public school where a Jewish coach has called specifically on Yahweh. Maybe it exists...

Freedom of speech and religion are in the same amendment for a reason. One of the most notable cases of our time is still unfolding in Oregon. Just ask two bakers in that state who have been through it with the Oregon Department of Labor. Aaron and Melissa Klein, an Oregon couple, have been ordered to pay a $135,000 fine, through a state administrative proceeding, after refusing to bake a cake for a same-sex wedding. Never mind the two had served gays happily for many years. The case likely won't be resolved for at least a year, as it has advanced from an administrative proceeding into state court.

As you may have picked up in my introduction, I believe fully in the rights of lesbians and gays to marry. How that was decided in the courts and whether the government should be involved in matrimonies at all are two topics (states' rights and a more libertarian approach to marriage) for another day. I further believe that the same-sex couple in Oregon has every right to purchase a wedding cake, so long as they are not infringing on the protected rights of others.

There's a lot to mention here. First, there are quite a few bakers in Oregon, so the couple clearly had options for their wedding cake. Also, the Kleins run a private enterprise with no government funding; they should be able to run their business as they choose, while adhering to federal, state and local laws. There are no laws compelling the Kleins to serve customers they choose not to serve. No shoes, no shirts, no service would apply, as would any other house rule, however objectionable to some. If it were an extreme rule or something the community objected to, they'd be out of business pretty fast. Also, if their city council, the Oregon legislature or Congress had passed a law requiring their private business to make a wedding cake for the couple, they would be in violation. But no such law exists.

A high-ranking government bureaucrat, Commissioner of Labor Brad Avakian, didn't see it that way, making the sweeping decision to impose a breathtaking fine on the Kleins. It was later learned this action was taken in close concert with an advocacy group looking for test cases. Red flags went up. Then, the people of Oregon spoke. Avakian, who ran for Secretary of State as a Democrat in a state where no Republican has held a statewide office in two decades, was defeated in November 2016. Next, we'll see what the courts decide about this case and related cases.

We'll take a deep dive on freedom of speech in the next chapter, but on the related subject of religious freedom, the question remains: Where do we go from here? For 70 years, Justice Black and others, like Americans United for Separation of Church & State and the ACLU have built what they see as a necessary, impregnable and high wall.

We have helpful guidance from a number of justices to help us

keep the wall but ensure it looks more like Jefferson's. Justice Sandra
Day O'Connor is one of those scholars who understood the Jeffersonian
construct of religious freedom and protection.

"Reasonable minds can disagree about how to apply the Religion
Clauses in a given case, but the goal of the Clauses is clear: to carry out
the Founders' plan of preserving religious liberty to the fullest extent
in a pluralistic society," she wrote. "By enforcing the Clauses, we have
kept religion a matter for the individual conscience, not for the prose-
cutor or the bureaucrat."

Then she adds caution to the other side: "At a time when we see
around the world the violent consequences of the assumption of religious
authority by government, Americans may count themselves fortunate:
Our regard for constitutional boundaries has protected us from similar travails, while allowing private religious exercise to flourish."

O'Connor is saying a lot. The court's job is to uphold the law,
not make it. She also might as well have been saying, "Go seek your
remedy through the legislative process and let the people of Oregon or
our country speak on the matter." Lastly, personal religion is a private
matter, and it must remain so, for the good of all.

Justice William O. Douglas wrote similar words in the aforementioned 1952 opinion, *Zorach v. Clauson*, one of the great reflections of
the Founders intent to strike a balance near the middle. While defending
separation of church and state, he opined:

> *The First Amendment, however, does not say that,*
> *in every and all respects there shall be a separation*
> *of Church and State. Rather, it studiously defines the*
> *manner, the specific ways, in which there shall be no*
> *concert or union or dependency one on the other.*
>
> *Otherwise the state and religion would be aliens to*
> *each other—hostile, suspicious, and even unfriendly....*
> *Municipalities would not be permitted to render police*
> *or fire protection to religious groups. Policemen who*
> *helped parishioners into their places of worship would*
> *violate the Constitution. Prayers in our legislative halls;*
> *the appeals to the Almighty in the messages of the Chief*
> *Executive; the proclamations making Thanksgiving*

*Day a holiday; 'So Help Me God' in our courtroom
oaths—these and all other references to the Almighty
that run through our laws, our public rituals, our cere-
monies would be flouting the First Amendment.*

*A fastidious atheist or agnostic could even object to
the supplication with which the Court opens each
session: "God save the United States and this Honorable Court."*

*We are a religious people whose institutions presup-
pose a Supreme Being... When the state encourages
religious instruction... it follows the best of our
traditions. For it then respects the religious nature of
our people and accommodates the public service to
their spiritual needs. To hold that it may not would
be to find in the Constitution a requirement that the
government show a callous indifference to religious
groups. That would be preferring those who believe in
no religion over those who do believe...*

*We find no constitutional requirement which makes it
necessary for government to be hostile to religion and
to throw its weight against efforts to widen the effective
scope of religious influence... We cannot read into the
Bill of Rights such a philosophy of hostility to religion.*

When does it stop? Will we rename the cities of San Francisco (St. Francis) and Los Angeles (City of Angels)? Such political correctness doesn't seem far off. Overt hostility to religion is on the rise. At the very least, religion isn't viewed as "cool" by many today. Over time, the number of Americans who have become less interested or even dismissive of religion, and certain religions, has grown.

We can see this in polls that show fewer Americans attend church on a regular basis. While Gallup polls show about 40% of Americans say they attend church at least once a week, down from a high of 49% in the mid-1950s, other polls from various congregations have that figure at or below 20%.

Practicing religion, especially among Christians, is on the decline, as noted in polls. Buddhists believe in order to grow, three things are essential—the practice of the faith, the teaching and community. Without all three, Buddhism does not exist. Rohr argues religion, and specifically Christianity, "has probably never had such a bad name…and is now seen as 'irrelevant' by many," and often part of the problem, not a solution.

Says Rohr: "Some of us are almost embarrassed to say we are Christian because of the negative images that word conjures in others' minds. Young people especially are turned off by how judgmental, exclusionary, impractical, and ineffective Christian culture seems to be. The church seems hostile toward most science (the objective outer world) and thus unable to talk about its inner dimensions with any authority. As we saw in the [2016] U.S. election, Christians overall showed little prophetic or compassionate presence."

Truth, Father. Remember those texts I received after Election Day?

Because Christians rely more on teaching and community—and even that is arguable—and less on practicing what we know and believe, we're reaping what we sow, says the Franciscan.

"Most Christians have not been taught how to plug into the 'mind of Christ;' thus they often reflect the common mind of power, greed, and war instead. The dualistic mind reads reality in simple binaries— good and bad, right and wrong—and thinks itself smart because it chooses one side. This is getting us nowhere."

Our friend Meacham would agree that our compassionate presence is on the decline in this era of polarization. He would side with Justice Douglas on issuing opinions that are less hostile to religion while finding balance and more room for more people. He would agree with Justice O'Connor's necessary cautionary blueprint that keeps us out of trouble elsewhere. Says Meacham, "Our finest hours—the Revolutionary War, abolition, the expansion of the rights of women, fights against terror and tyranny, the battle against Jim Crow—can be traced to religious ideas about liberty, justice and charity. Yet theology and scripture have also been used to justify our worst hours—from enslaving black people to persecuting Native Americans to treating women as second-class citizens."

We can find a way out of this. The ruminations of Meacham, Rohr, Douglas, O'Connor and many others center on the subject. Their research and words provide the foundation for a strategic plan to ensure our guaranteed individual right to religious freedom shall be preserved on this earth. Those of us who have faith in a Supreme Being believe those rights have already been bestowed by the God we call our God, which is a victory unto itself. You can have your coffee bold or mild in our country, and that must continue.

Noise from fringe elements will always be here. But we must not give in to fear of religion or projected fear from religious zealots. We can always have Light.

We can welcome the view of our Creator, a public god as the Founders said, but be mindful that my god and yours may not be the same. Both gods, and others, are protected under our Constitution.

CRITICAL POINT:

The First Amendment is first for a reason. The practice of religion, which is in disfavor with an increasing number of Americans, must be preserved. "Separation of church and state" has become a distorted phrase that fewer Americans understand.

ACTION STEP:

Judicial activism prohibiting religious freedom and fundamental First Amendment rights must end. The great religions must look inwardly and seek more common ground with other religions, as Pope Francis is attempting to do. We have a role in our daily lives to support tolerant, open-minded judges and elected officials who always will support our constitutional rights and find common ground in situations where extremists want a different result.

HELPFUL LINKS AND RESOURCES:

Falling Upward and *The Divine Dance*, Richard Rohr
American Gospel: God, The Founding Fathers and the Making of a Nation, Jon Meacham
www.EndingOurUncivilWar.com

CONTEMPLATION:

"Without the contemplative and converted mind—
honest and humble perception—much religion is
frankly dangerous."

—RICHARD ROHR, "THE DUALISTIC MIND," 2017

CHAPTER 2: SPIRITUAL RENEWAL

COGNITIVE & POSITIVE— REWIRING OUR MINDS

Our minds are a center for our spiritual growth, so let's look at a little science and how the mind can react.

If you've dabbled in psychology, counseling or coaching, you're aware how easy it is for your mind to "go negative." With the bombardment of hopeless, distorted and incomplete stories and opinions from the media, one-sided websites and news aggregators, the growing polarization and intolerance aren't surprising.

In addition to these environmental factors, many of us recognize that our genetic makeup and childhood experiences influence how we process information. Some of these experiences have a lasting imprint. Maybe a parent yelled at you often, or even physically abused you. Perhaps a fellow student bullied you constantly. Or did someone lift you up and support your growth, like a family member, or a teacher, mentor, coach or best friend?

Regardless of whether your experiences were overly negative or positive, psychologists like Rick Hanson at the Greater Good Science Center at the University of California-Berkeley assert that people are "built to overlearn from negative experiences, but under learn from positive ones."

We all have negative thoughts. It's normal. The challenge is how to deal with them. Some folks completely ignore them, while others embrace the negativity because the energy has to go somewhere. It becomes who they are. We're seeing it on full display in social media.

So what is one to do, given the tsunami of angry tweets, posts and other rants from leaders like Tweeter-in-Chief Donald Trump or divisive ranting by entertainers like Samantha Bee or talk radio hosts like Mark Levin? It's difficult to hear their good points because of how negatively most are presented. How can one deal with this unending drumbeat of negativity—the blaming, shaming, castigation and anger? Why are more people in our culture so smug?

If you're in lockstep with Trump, Levin, Bee, or maybe Rachel Maddow, Rush Limbaugh or Sean Hannity, I'll ask you to ponder what Bee said in response to a question from CNN's Jake Tapper, who asked her if there is a "smug liberal problem." After dodging the question, Bee acknowledged what most of us already know.

"I do the show for me and people like me and I don't really care how the rest of the world sees it, quite frankly," she said. "We make a show for ourselves."

She's not alone. Many right-wing talk shows have contributed to a "smug conservative problem." Many talk-radio conservatives have a huge holier-than-thou problem, as well.

For example, Levin's shrill attacks on anyone who disagrees with him are just as unsettling as what occurs on much of late night TV. Levin has called Joe Scarborough, host of "Morning Joe" on MSNBC, a "pathetic troll" for speaking his mind on political miscalculations by the Republican Party. He's called MSNBC's Chris Matthews a "drunken lush."

MSNBC's Rachel Maddow and Keith Olbermann? MSLSD's Rachel Madcow and Keith Overbite.

Dana Milbank with *The Washington Post*? Dana Bankrupt with The Washington Compost.

Levin's endless ad hominem attacks can hard-wire the brain, if one continues to listen and accept.

Rush Limbaugh has called President Obama a "halfrican American" and "an affirmative action candidate," and played a song called "Barack the Magic Negro." He's one of several on the airwaves and cable TV whose racist, misogynist dribble is the other end of the pendulum that conservatives like to ignore or dismiss. More on that later.

Both sides come off as self-righteous. In their quest for attention and ratings, Levin, Limbaugh, Bee, Oliver and others are fueling the growing divide in our country. Many who listen rationalize that since their side is correct, they dismiss how dehumanizing the presentations have become. One can argue which brand of smugness arrived first, but both sides are in a tête-à-tête for ground in a low-lying swamp.

These media outlets and their shows' hosts and staffs bear much responsibility for the decline in civil discourse, along with Donald Trump. The president has had a significant role in creating an unhealthy response from many conservatives and greater incivility in a country seeking solutions to real, systemic problems.

In the May 2017 edition of *The Atlantic*, Caitlin Flanagan postulates "How Late Night Comedy Fueled the Rise of Trump: Sneering hosts have alienated conservatives and made liberals smug." First, she acknowledges how Trump's antics and pompous statements don't deserve respect:

> *The late-night political-comedy shows—principally Noah's "Daily Show," Samantha Bee's "Full Frontal," and John Oliver's "Last Week Tonight"—staked their territory during the heat of the general election: unwavering, bombastic, belittling, humiliating screeds against Donald Trump. Fair enough. Trump is a man who on any casual summer day during the campaign could be found inciting a crowd to violence. This isn't the slippery slope; this is the ditch at the bottom of the hill. Once a man stands before a mob and exhorts the powerful to beat the outlier, it's all over except for the cannibalism and the cave painting. "Government of the people, by the people, for the people, shall not perish from the earth," said Abraham Lincoln. "Knock the crap out of them," said Donald Trump.*

*... Trump and Bee are on different sides politically,
but culturally they are drinking from the same cup,
one filled with the poisonous nectar of reality TV and
its baseless values, which have now moved to the very
center of our national discourse. Trump and Bee share
a penchant for verbal cruelty and a willingness to
mock the defenseless. Both consider self-restraint, once
the hallmark of the admirable, to be for chumps.*

*During the campaign, Trump's mockery of a war
hero, grieving parents, and a disabled man showed us
much about his character. We know what he said about
Mexicans and in years past what he said about women.
There is no defense for this rhetoric. Nor is there defense
for the obsessive-compulsive, dawn-to-dusk media
coverage of Trump and the late-night responses to his
tweets and other cancerous after-hours presentations.*

*When John Oliver told viewers that if they opposed
abortion they had to change the channel until the last
minute of the program, when they would be shown
"an adorable bucket of sloths," he precisely encapsu-
lated the tone of these shows: one imbued with the
conviction that they and their fans are intellectually
and morally superior to those who espouse any of the
beliefs of the political right.*

Bee's shoot-from-the-hip statements and antics aren't pretty, either.
Noted Flanagan: "In March ... Bee's show issued a formal apology
to a young man who had attended the Conservative Political Action
Conference and whom the show had blasted for having "Nazi hair." As
it turned out, the young man was suffering from Stage 4 brain cancer—
which a moment's research on the producers' part would have revealed: He
had tweeted about his frightening diagnosis days before the conference."

"During the campaign, Bee dispatched a correspondent to go
shoot fish in a barrel at something called the Western Conservative
Summit, which the reporter described as "an annual Denver gathering
popular with hard-right Christian conservatives." He interviewed an

earnest young boy who talked about going to church on Sundays and Bible study on Wednesdays, and about his hope to start a group called Children for Trump. For this, the boy—who spoke with the unguarded openness of a child who has assumed goodwill on the part of an adult—was described as "Jerry Falwell in blond, larval form."

This isn't after-hours entertainment. It's a late-night assault on our humanity.

Hopefully, you've picked up on some helpful tips in previous chapters to keep your sanity and celebrate our humanity. It's worth looking, too, at what some experts of the mind say.

REWIRING TO POSITIVE

We all have negative thoughts. We're human, and we're going to have them. One mistake we make is trying to stop these thoughts. Maybe you were one who couldn't, or hasn't, let go of the election results. Fear of the unknown or your expectations of things to come invaded your psyche. Some thought, "I have to stop thinking like this," or "Why won't these thoughts stop?"

"Worry and obsession get worse when you try to control your thoughts," says Judith Beck, president of the Beck Institute for Cognitive Behavior Therapy in Bala Cynwyd, Pennsylvania. Beck encourages people in a negative cycle of thinking to own your thinking as soon as possible.

> *"I'm thinking negatively."*
> *"My thoughts are negative."*
> *"My brain isn't in a good place."*

Once this first step is achieved, the process of rewiring can begin, experts say. The goal is not to eliminate the negative thoughts but to recognize them quickly. Then, in this non-judgmental way of owning the behavior, one is encouraged to enter into "mindfulness meditation" over the course of a day. This can be highly complementary to full meditation at daybreak or at the close of a busy day.

Mindfulness meditation is an awareness and recognition of behavior. One doesn't need to change the behavior immediately or shortly thereafter. It offers an opportunity for owning and reflection. This calms the brain. It helps apply the brake to thinking that may be triggering negative rapid, strong responses to stimuli, like a ridiculous tweet.

If you're not convinced of the immediate benefits of meditation, consider the long-term benefits psychologists believe occur in a better state of being and daily thinking. Mindfulness meditation and meditation of your choosing (emptying thoughts, repetitive prayer, deep and slow breathing) are believed to help reduce stress and decrease the chances of illness or disease. They also increase productivity and outlook. This mental regimen also can keep us from going into darker places. Sounds pretty cool, right?

Dr. Rick Hanson, author of *Hardwiring Happiness: The New Brain Science of Contentment, Calm and Confidence*, argues our brains have a negativity bias that can serve us well, like animals use for survival. That bias, however, can be like Velcro for negative experiences and Teflon for positive ones. Unaddressed, we can become "frazzled, worried, irritated, lonely, inadequate, and blue."

In too many cases, we can become depressed or obsessed, which can lead to destructive personal behavior that can impact not only our lives but also our livelihoods and those we love. If depression or other mental disorders manifest, meditation likely won't help too much. The brain simply is wired too hard.

Cognitive behavior therapy, or the development of personal coping strategies to harmful thoughts, beliefs and attitudes, often is recommended to rewire the brain and promote emotional regulation. Psychologists are flourishing today, as their services are in great need with the rise in post-traumatic stress disorders, anxiety and substance abuse. Many are reporting they're spending more time with their clientele discussing politics, the culture and fear of authoritarianism imposed by the left and the right!

Before getting into those unfortunate states, we can take a lot of preventive actions. Certainly, getting enough sleep, eating healthily, staying hydrated and exercising regularly are highly important activities that keep the brain running properly, interfacing with our body. Garbage in, garbage out is true. So simple, yet we can stray. Goodness in, goodness out is also true. It's a matter of choice and habit.

One study shows that a 30-minute walk in a forest or park decreases negative feelings like stress, depression, anger, fatigue, anger, anxiety, and confusion, while improving cognitive skills. Have you noticed generally good patterns of thought and behavior in people who exercise and eat well? Have you noticed the opposite generally in people who eat too many fatty, sugary foods and watch TV all day?

Another preemptive action is to complement daily and mindful meditation by engaging with a coach. Some of us do this naturally with a mentor or role model. I have several—my friends Maureen and Mark, Dexter the priest at my church and others. Others may want or need an actual coach.

Most of us had coaches growing up, playing sports. The really good ones valued you as a person, promoted harmony on the team, offered good instruction and listened especially well. They empowered the players who reinforced the positive values that they wanted their teams to embody. Good coaches also cared greatly for each individual soul.

Other coaches promote empowering behavior. Business coaches work to adapt these positive practices into the lives of executives, who in turn seek to promote them in their businesses. Wellness coaches help their clients identify the tools and motivations to achieve physical and emotional health goals, like eating better and improving physical fitness. Life coaches can help provide avenues for their clients to improve the drive and focus necessary to improve their careers, relationships and work-life balance.

Life coaching is a $1 billion industry in America, and growing. These coaches help people deal with negativity by keeping clients focused on skills development, achieving dreams, adjusting life goals, and moving past specific challenges. A good life coach helps one acknowledge negativity and deal with it as soon as possible, before it can get out of hand and before a therapist is required. Practice may not actually make perfect, but its gets you closer.

Life coaches often cite the Law of Attraction, a concept rooted in Buddhist teachings and religious Taoism. Dr. Wayne Dyer's calls the concept behind the Law of Attraction the "Power of Intention."

"The law of attraction is this: You don't attract what you want. You attract what you are," said Dyer, author of *The Power of Intention*, *I Can See Clearly Now*, and other related works. "Most people's mistake in trying to apply the law of attraction is they want things; they demand things. But God doesn't work that way. It's all about allowing."

It's about removing the blockage each of us has.

Dyer, who passed away in 2015, gives credit to Lao Tzu, author of the *Tao Te Ching,* for this ancient but powerful philosophy that emerged 2,500 years ago. Tzu said virtue is a critical concept in the Law of Attraction, citing teaching Number 51 in the *Hua Hu Ching*:

> *"Those who want to know the truth of the universe should practice the four cardinal virtues. The first is reverence for all of life. This manifests as unconditional love and respect for oneself and all other beings. The second is natural sincerity. This manifests as honesty, simplicity and faithfulness. The third is gentleness, which manifests as kindness, consideration for others and sensitivity to spiritual truth. The fourth is supportiveness. This manifests as service to others without expectation of reward."*

Forgiveness, kindness, love and unselfishness are virtues that take oxygen away from retribution, hate and greed. That's how you win.

CRITICAL POINT:

What you think and accept, you become. Through modern media, hardliners are seeking to enter our minds and create a darkness that sells, resonates and proliferates. Our humanity is under attack by people who disagree, but tactically they are no different.

ACTION STEP:

Turn off the TV, and limit the ability of blowhards to corrupt the mind. Practice meditation early in the day and during those times when the attacks on humanity begin. Find mentors and coaches who help create positive thinking, which leads to better results, experiences and opportunities to find common ground.

RESOURCES:

Any business, wellness or life coach in your community. Books mentioned in this chapter or that your friends or coach would recommend that create balance and wellness in your life.

www.EndingOurUncivilWar.com

CONTEMPLATION:

"Spiritually speaking, no one else is your problem. You are first and foremost your own problem."
—RICHARD ROHR, **JESUS REVEALS THE LIE OF SCAPEGOATING**, 2016

CHAPTER 2: SPIRITUAL RENEWAL

MIND OVER MEDIA

"Kick 'em when they're up, kick 'em when they're down."
—DON HENLEY, "DIRTY LAUNDRY"

Two of my favorite years professionally were at *The City Paper*, an upstart local newspaper that started in 2000 in Nashville.

Reputable journalists will tell you getting every side of any story is a prerequisite to producing a fair, balanced account. As an editor and reporter, this was a primary function.

Many times, our team would hold a story if we didn't have another side's quotes or background, despite feeling pressure to run it because another outlet might break the news. Sometimes, we would call a person two or three times; if we didn't receive a response, we would note in the story that repeated calls weren't returned.

Our senior editors taught us well. Having an objective reputation was very important to being a trusted news source. People around town respected our team, and our list of sources grew. Folks called back often.

We made mistakes, but we learned from them. I recall one I made the day after 9/11, exhausted from producing a special afternoon edition after the morning's tragic terrorist attacks. The next day, we had information from what appeared to be a New York City website that a Vanderbilt graduate had survived the collapse of one of the towers, and we ran the story. It turned out to be incorrect. The story never should have run; I should have waited for several sources to call back. It was a hard lesson I will never forget.

The City Paper had a great run, but eventually folded after losing too much money. It was merged into a website version that exists to this day. It's an all-too-common event nowadays.

The consolidation of media over the last two decades has led to fewer sources and less competition. This trend is bad news for all. We've seen a rise in sensational, one-sided news aggregate sites, and cable TV and talk radio shows. Blaring commercials on these programs seem less loud than many of the hosts and guests who engage in exhausting free-for-alls.

Many national stations like Fox News, CNN and MSNBC run red banners the entire day with "Breaking News!" It's a high-energy push designed to keep you watching, afraid you'll miss something important. In fact, much of it isn't important or news. And very little is substantive.

Finding fair, balanced accounts on TV and radio and in print is getting more difficult. This is important, as noted previously, because of the certitude, fear and negativity that one-sided, or *incomplete*, media can have on our minds.

Let's look at a few examples at some of my favorite sources—NPR and *The Wall Street Journal*.

IS GOOD INFORMATION ENOUGH INFORMATION?

I listen to National Public Radio, which leans left, and a conservative morning talk radio show several days a week on my commute. I like NPR and a local talk radio show hosted by Ralph Bristol. I trust that the information I am receiving from both is correct; I've been disappointed rarely.

But I don't always get all sides of an issue from each source, hence my desire to move around the dial.

Some friends like NPR because there's no yelling. NPR's soft-spoken hosts offer a peaceful way to start a morning. NPR, to its credit, has credible sources, shares longer sound bites, and stays away from poisonous back-and-forths.

But it's not always offering a complete picture.

Take a recent energy and environmental issue, the fight over the Dakota Access Pipeline (DAP). Whether you are for or against this pipeline, this is a critique on information available versus information presented.

According to the main proponent's website, DAP is "a 1,172-mile underground state of the art pipeline...that will transport domestically-produced, light, sweet crude oil from North Dakota to major refining markets in a more direct, cost-effective, safer and more environmentally responsible manner than other modes of transportation, including rail or truck."

That's not how opponents see DAP. According to the *New York Times*, members "of the Standing Rock Sioux Tribe view the pipeline as a major environmental and cultural threat. They say its route traverses ancestral lands—which are not part of the reservation—where their forebears hunted, fished and were buried. They say historical and cultural reviews of the land where the pipeline will be buried were inadequate. They also worry about catastrophic environmental damage if the pipeline were to break near where it crosses under the Missouri River."

Other groups joined the Sioux. Some cited a 2012 *ProPublica* report that more than half of the country's pipelines are at least 50 years old, and that aging pipelines and lax federal oversight put public health and the environment at risk. Others simply said the flow of fossil fuels must stop.

Demonstrations began. Some of the protests were peaceful, but radicals then turned to more violent measures. In response, police on horseback in riot gear confronted and arrested many people, including 141 on October 28, 2016, to bring the total to more than 400 in three months, and many more since. The next month during another confrontation, protestors detonated an improvised explosive device on a public bridge in southern North Dakota.

These accounts were what most people saw or were hearing on the news. NPR and other sources either missed or ignored opportunities to report more about what proponents were saying or doing. According to its website, Energy Transfer, the main DAP proponent, is "a Texas-based company that [is]...one of the largest and most diversified investment grade master limited partnerships in the United States. Why not ask the company more about its motives, or report that repeated calls were not returned?

Many important questions remained, like which mode of transportation of the fuel (underground pipeline, above-ground pipeline, rail or truck) is safest and most economical? Would newer pipelines be safer than older pipelines, and could industry and government manage this area more effectively, and if so, how and at what cost (like repair and replacement of old pipelines)?

Those who wanted more information had to dig deeper. Those who did may have learned that Dakota Access Pipeline company leaders attempted to meet dozens of times in recent years with Standing Rock Sioux Tribe leaders, who refused. They knew also that the underground pipeline never touched Native American property, and that the economic benefits to thousands in the region and across the country would be profound, as cited in the main proponent's website, https://daplpipelinefacts.com. If you visit this site, it's worth clicking "Misconceptions" to see counter-arguments, since they're hard to find in most mainstream media accounts.

In short, both sides had their positions and facts. But most of us only had a few sound bites and video of activists clashing with law enforcement.

If you visit the NPR's *Morning Edition* website page, there is an obvious bent in DAP headlines, content and context; it looks like a pep rally against DAP. If you listened to "Dakota Pipeline Protesters, Nearby Residents Brace For 2017," on January 4, 2017, you primarily heard what protestors were saying. Nothing was inaccurate, but there is little information from proponents.

I like NPR because there is very good information. But it's not always complete. I like *The Wall Street Journal*, too. But it's not always complete, either.

In August 2017, several *Wall Street Journal* reporters said they were disturbed by their publication's soft coverage of Donald Trump's presidency. They began communicating their concerns by email up the chain to editor-in-chief Gerard Baker; eventually, several met with him.

Baker, who met with Trump right after his stunning election, had penned a somewhat celebratory column in *The Spectator*, a conservative British newspaper, in which he said Trump's "helmet of hair is even more golden than usual, having received a fresh post-triumphal, presidential burnishing." Baker later said he probably should not have written the column.

In an exchange with reporters, Baker said accusations of soft coverage were "a little irritating." Reporters specifically said they had been edited over a period of time to avoid certain euphemisms and told to refrain from being "overly opinionated."

One draft of a story of Trump's raucous speech in Phoenix on August 22, 2017, said it was "an off-script return to campaign form," in which the president "pivoted away from remarks a day earlier in which he had solemnly called for unity." That draft language, true (he was on a teleprompter the day before and clearly not the day after) and actually somewhat benign, was removed from the article's final version.

In one interview of Trump, Baker took the lead, unusual for an editor-in-chief. He talked about the president's recent golf outings and travel, and told Trump's daughter Ivanka in the Oval Office, "It was nice to see you out in Southampton a couple weeks ago."

None of this damning on its own, but much of it is curious. Is Baker being a soldier, or a scout? Baker's continued closeness to the family simply will hurt the *Journal*'s ability to be viewed as an objective source on the Trump presidency.

Where does one go for good journalism these days? NPR and the *Journal* are still very good, despite the hiccups. I particularly like the National Public Television show *Frontline*, which has a growing audience because it takes on tough topics, like the Middle East conflict, and engages in challenging interviews with policy makers with differing views or accounts.

Wherever you get your news, it's worth investing time to review multiple sources, if you're really going to probe any issue. Multiple means a lot. This ongoing quest for information leads to a well-rounded, better-formed opinion. It is a booster shot, too, against certitude, fear and negativity.

From this place, one can have more productive conversations. It becomes easier to listen well and acknowledge alternative viewpoints, rather than project certainty. We're seeing more people on TV and radio simply repeat—or shout—their positions with dangerously absolute conviction. If you're in or near that place, I encourage unlearning what's been learned.

THE LIMITATIONS AND DISTORTIONS OF TV JOURNALISM

Do you remember when we boarded our flight that the environmentalist and unemployed coal miner were seated together? The two couldn't be more in conflict. One wants to eliminate fossil fuels and reduce carbon emissions—a noble goal—while the other wants to keep their communities, homes and families together, which is also noble.

In January 2017, I saw a story about coal mining on CNN's show "Anderson Cooper 360" by reporter and commentator Van Jones, who leans left on many matters. Jones travelled to West Virginia to interview people who had voted for Trump and produced an old-school journalistic report, "Big Promises: What Coal Country Expects from Trump." These mountaineers had seen their livelihoods dramatically change under the Obama administration's tight regulating of their industry. He asked questions in a roundtable format and let everyone speak, with minimal editing in a bright room (remember that for later).

Not all of Jones' interviewees who voted for Trump liked the president; some said they didn't. These very independent people simply stated they were very afraid their existence was ending—uprooted families, growing poverty and dependence on government subsidies, homes they couldn't sell and more. They hadn't been paid much attention in recent elections, but Trump paid attention to them. They resented the view that some big-city elites viewed them as "uneducated."

Back in the studio, Cooper said, "It's just so great to hear from people, what's in their hearts and in their heads." Jones agreed, saying yes, "I was struck by the complexity of the political analysis.... [These people] were incredibly sophisticated."

Viewers who had determined anyone voting for Trump must be "an idiot" probably couldn't process the comments from the coal miners, or the fair-handed reporting from Cooper and Jones. That's not what they heard elsewhere.

I posted the CNN video on my Facebook page, and whoa did the reactions vary. Remembering everyone's contextual place is different, here's what folks posted, with their leanings and/or background noted:

"Van Jones is a communist." –REPUBLICAN PARTY OPERATIVE

"Great interview." –CENTER-LEFT FRIEND WHO DIDN'T VOTE FOR TRUMP

"I can't believe I'm going to say this, but Van Jones did a great interview here. Trump has to deliver or he will be fired as the gentleman in the NRA cap said." —RELIGIOUS CONSERVATIVE

"I'd like to see Wimpy Cooper go down in one of those mines and actually do that work for 15 minutes. All the years he has spent at the gym wouldn't mean a thing. God bless those people." —TRUMP SUPPORTER

"Very interesting... kind of shocking coming from CNN but I am glad to see that they were unbiased and told the real story."
—MODERATE INDEPENDENT

My Facebook page is tame, compared to many. But there was some name-calling, this time from the right. My hope is that, once off our plane, both the environmentalist and coal miner can acknowledge each other's strong views and find some common ground in the middle. The conversation just has to start differently. Questions are a great way to begin.

Maybe the environmental activist will ask, "What regulations are you OK with that will improve air quality?" Maybe the other will answer A, B and C, while D, E and F would wipe out half the state's economy. Maybe the West Virginian will ask, "What if we phased out coal production over a reasonable period of time so federal and state leaders can work to attract new industry to the region, perhaps even alternative energy, so families and communities can stay intact? Some of my kids don't want to mine, anyway. Would you help with that?" Maybe the activist will say, "That's a good idea, let's go talk to our politicians together."

While this may sound idealistic, it can be how conversations can start and how some common agreement can be achieved, instead of going negative, spreading fear and hoping for a better election in four years. Dualism is difficult; a third way often exists.

Even worse than dualism is complete distortion of an interview. That's what Katie Couric "achieved" in a 2016 documentary "Under the Gun."

In a dimly lit room, Couric assembled 10 members of the Virginia Citizens Defense League (VCDL) whose motto is "Defending Your Right to Defend Yourself." TV viewers heard her ask the gun right advocates: "If there are no background checks for gun purchasers, how do you prevent felons or terrorists from purchasing a gun?"

According to the Erik Wemple, a media critic with the *Washington Post*, what ensued in the film is "nearly 10 seconds of silence, as if no one has an answer to Couric's rather straightforward question." If you watched at home, you likely would have concluded the advocates were stumped, unprepared and maybe even moronic.

But that's not what happened at all.

VCDL President Philip Van Cleave audiotaped the session. First, Couric's question was very different from the one in the video: "If there are no background checks, how do you prevent—I know how you all are going to answer this, but I'm going to ask it anyway. If there are no background checks for gun purchasers, how do you prevent felons or terrorists from walking into, say, a licensed gun dealer and purchasing a gun?"

So were the responses.

One VCDL member said, "Well, one—if you're not in jail, you should still have your basic rights." Others chimed in quickly.

After he saw Couric's film, Van Cleave emailed his concerns to Producer Kristin Lazure with Atlas Films. "So a 'balanced' piece gives 15 minutes to the pro-gun side and 1-1/2 hours to the opposition?" He cuts to the chase, saying the "response" to the background checks question "shows our members just sitting there and then one looking down. The editors merged some 'b-roll' (video shot separately, usually for background) of our members sitting quietly between questions, followed by Katie asking the felon question. I have the audio of that entire interview and I know for an absolute fact that our members immediately jumped in to answer the question and did NOT just sit there quietly. To the person watching the video, it gave the intentionally false appearance of no one in our group having an answer."

Lazure responded, "I'm truly sorry to hear you were disappointed with the final product. We knew when we set out to make a film on such a divisive issue that we weren't going to make everybody happy. However, we have heard from many gun owners following our screenings and the television premiere who felt we gave the issue a balanced look and reflected their views accurately."

Their views? What about the views of VCDL members?

Couric later said she was "very proud of the film."

Van Cleave later told the media he came away from the interview with a largely favorable impression of Couric, saying her questions were tough but fair and she played devil's advocate but never attacked.

"Nothing in the interview made me think she would do what she did," Van Cleave told NPR. "We've got to be able to trust the press."

Yes, we do. Understandably, not as many do anymore. We've come a long way since Walter Cronkite and Tom Brokaw.

Importantly, the specific issue isn't what's most important, though it is significant; the misrepresentation of any issue, controversial or straightforward, is. If you're for gay marriage and a conservative news outlet rearranged the question and responses through editing, you would have a right to be disappointed and upset.

'AN EDUCATED CITIZENRY'

I've noticed friends who visit sources that challenge their views or make them uncomfortable are better at listening and debating. They can walk away from any argument without enmity for their opponent. They are scouts in a true sense.

I visit the news aggregate site *Drudge Report* and website *Huffington Post*. I like to read what others are reading. It's not easy some days. They're sometimes outrageous and their presentations oftentimes are sensational, unlike accounts on NPR, *Frontline*, the *Wall Street Journal*, *Washington Post* and *New York Times*.

But are we educated when we only visit conservative websites, or liberal ones? Are we going to become a nation with a soldier mentality, or will we be good scouts?

Staying educated and engaged, in a time when more media seemingly want to wear us down with "Breaking News," and shouting matches, isn't easy. But it's best for the mind that we think critically and process cautiously when reviewing media.

In April 2016, my friend Jim Bryson, a successful businessman and former state senator in Tennessee, scribed one of the best posts I've read on Facebook about the avalanche and negative drumbeat of people's opinions on social and mainstream media. Hundreds liked and commented on this post:

I am tired. I am tired of Christians being mean to other Christians because they disagree. I am tired of talking about gay, lesbian, transgender, whatever. I am tired of talking about whether God is for homosexuality or not. I am tired of talking about what bathroom someone can use (are we really even having this conversation?). I am tired of our society's obsession with sexuality. I am tired of people believing they are persecuted just because they are different. I am tired of mean people who think they can call other people names in the cause of politics or "culture wars" or, even worse, to defend Jesus. I am tired.

Through his exhaustion and raw honesty, Jim Bryson captured how many of us feel. Jim is wise, too. He isn't disengaging or over-engaging like some. He's in the game, where all need to be.

As Thomas Jefferson said, "An educated citizenry is a vital requisite for our survival as a free people."

CRITICAL POINT:

Information doesn't mean a story is balanced. Mainstream and social media can be an assault on our senses. Fear, certitude and negativity can result from whom, how and where we receive our information.

ACTION STEP:

Seek more information from alternative sources, especially those outside your comfort zone. Limit the amount of time you spend on social and mainstream media, but get information from all types—online, TV, radio and print. Stay educated and engaged.

RESOURCES:

www.cac.org (Center for Action and Contemplation website)
www.EndingOurUncivilWar.com

CONTEMPLATION:

"Don't waste any time dividing the world into the good guys and the bad guys. Hold them both together in your own soul—where they are anyway—and you will have held together the whole world. You will have overcome the great divide in one place of spacious compassion."
—RICHARD ROHR, "THERE IS NOTHING TO REGRET," 2017

After the 2016 election, an English bar owner, weary of the gloating and despair from tourists across the pond, chalked a conditional invitation.

Photo by Arsal Aleem via the *Evening Standard*

Father Charlie Strobel (left), founder of Room in the Inn, says, "The people you serve have no means to pay you, but they will repay you spiritually." Room in the Inn volunteers Amanda Livsey and Michael Bess, shown here with Charlie, are not just good friends but great role models of regular "service in love."

Photo by Jim Brown

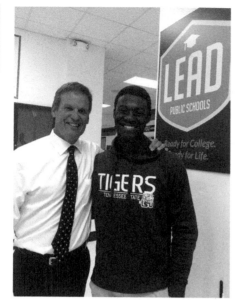

Knowing him gives me hope," says Adam Smith (right) of his mentor Bill Lee. "I hope one day I can get into a position to give back because I want to do the same thing." Service in love is simple, profound and reciprocal.

Photo courtesy of Bill Lee

I love uplifting social media. Here's a favorite from May 2017 about Bono, whose commitment to service has improved our world. @georgewbush: "Bono … has a huge heart and a selfless soul, not to mention a decent voice. … [We] are grateful he came to the ranch to talk about the work of @thebushcenter, @onecampaign, @PEPFAR, and our shared commitment to saving lives in Africa."

Photo courtesy of @georgewbush Instagram

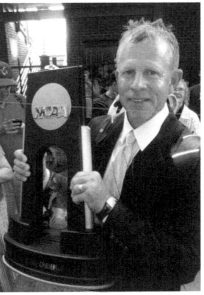

What a win! Vanderbilt Baseball Coach Tim Corbin didn't get much sleep after his team won the College World Series in 2014. He's a role model who showed my wife, Dori, and my family uncommon grace, love and compassion during her four-year journey with cancer.

Photos by Jim Brown

Digital Detox #1:

Staying connected to each other can be very challenging with so many "connections" elsewhere. One way I "unplug" is participating in a group we call En Masse Circle. No one interrupts. Everyone listens. No one judges. It happens.

Photo by Jim Brown

Digital Detox #2:

Alone or with family, being in nature is my favorite way to unplug. Two of our favorite Tennessee spots are the Savage Gulf State Natural Area in Grundy County and the Big South Fork National River & Recreation Area.

Photos by Jim Brown

Digital Detox #3:

Life is a journey, like climbing Ireland's Holy Mountain, Croagh Patrick. My friend Maureen found a beautiful prayer book in the visitor center that encourages reflections up and down the mountain. One prayer, "Breathe," is now part of my daily meditation routine that keeps the negative assault of media in check.

Photos by Jim Brown

Digital Detox #4:

Oregon, Montana and Ireland, oh my. No Internet "bars" out here.

Photos by Jim Brown

Silence is golden. Daily reflections and regular meditation help counteract incessant negativity in today's media. Stay positive with regular exercise, good food and rest. Be good to yourself.

Photo by Jim Brown

Lipscomb University in Nashville is being proactive on and off its campus promoting civil discourse. In 2017, several community leaders met to discuss Czechoslovakian President Václav Havel's famous essay.

Photo by Jim Brown

I love when friends see my favorite bumper sticker and share it. Photo by friend of Jim

CHAPTER 3: SCHOLASTIC INDEPENDENCE

THE ASSAULT ON FREE SPEECH

"Colleges owe students turbulence, because it's from
a contest of perspectives and an assault on pre-
sumptions that truth emerges— and, with it, true
confidence."
—FRANK BRUNI, **NEW YORK TIMES** OPINION EDITOR

"Congress shall make no law respecting an establishment of religion, or prohibiting the free exercise
thereof; or abridging the freedom of speech, or of
the press; or the right of the people peaceably to
assemble, and to petition the Government for a
redress of grievances."
—FIRST AMENDMENT TO THE U.S. CONSTITUTION

In early March 2017, at a small elite college in Vermont, free
speech suffered a glancing blow when students erupted into a raucous
protest intended to stop a speaker.

Not only did it work, but it also resulted in sending one of its own
professors to the hospital.

What sparked the screaming and excessive aggression? A few conservative students at Middlebury College asked school officials to invite political scientist Charles Murray to speak in an open forum. In the interest of offering varying views on social and racial issues, the administration agreed. What transpired became a national story.

In 1994, Murray co-wrote *The Bell Curve*, a highly controversial account that in part sought to link IQ to race. Murray argued that inherited and environmental factors are better predictors of financial income, job performance, crime involvement and out-of-marriage births more than parents' socioeconomic status. Further, he asserted America's "cognitive elite" has become separated from those of average and below-average intelligence.

Some in academia accept Murray's postulates, but the vast majority of scientists remain critical and hammer him over his assumptions, statistical methods, use of IQ testing and cognitive sorting. They said Murray's conclusions—that there aren't really any means to boost intelligence, that affirmative action is counterproductive because it stresses equal outcomes rather than equality of opportunity, and that immigration and welfare should be curtailed to stem an increase in people with lower IQs—are racist and rooted in hate.

Obviously, this is highly controversial stuff. It's subject matter that people contemplate often but less frequently discuss openly or freely in this time of polarization, racial tension and class warfare. President Trump's rhetoric, for instance, has fueled fire to some of Murray's conclusions, for proponents and opponents.

When Murray showed up on the Vermont campus, students went bonkers. Rather than hearing him out and challenging his methodology and countering his arguments with their own facts and figures, hundreds stood up in unison as he began to speak, then denounced Murray for 20 minutes before he left for a private room to record his remarks.

Protestors weren't through, however. They pulled fire alarms, banged windows, and then muscled Murray and an escorting professor, Allison Stanger, whose neck was injured in the melee, which led to a hospital visit. In an ironic twist, Stanger was supposed to provide counter-arguments after Murray's speech and lead the Q&A session. Stanger later wrote this in the *New York Times*:

> *Intelligent members of the Middlebury community—*
> *including some of my own students and advisees—*
> *concluded that Charles Murray was an anti-gay white*
> *nationalist from what they were hearing from one*
> *another, and what they read on the Southern Poverty*
> *Law Center website. Never mind that Dr. Murray*
> *supports same-sex marriage and is a member of the*
> *courageous 'never Trump' wing of the Republican*
> *Party. Students are in college in part to learn how to*
> *evaluate sources and follow up on ideas with their*
> *own research. The Southern Poverty Law Center in-*
> *correctly labels Dr. Murray a 'white nationalist,' but if*
> *we have learned nothing in this election, it is that such*
> *claims must be fact-checked, analyzed and assessed.*
> *Faulty information became the catalyst for shutting*
> *off the free exchange of ideas at Middlebury. We must*
> *all be more rigorous in evaluating and investigating*
> *anger, or this pattern of miscommunication will con-*
> *tinue on other college campuses.*

Bravo, Ms. Stanger, and lead on.

While the vast majority of students were not involved, *New York Times* editor Frank Bruni sagely noted in a column titled "The Dangerous Safety of College" that the Middlebury Melee, as it came to be called, amounted to "intellectual impoverishment" that serves as a wake-up call for what is occurring on campuses across our country. He lamented the "extraordinary demands... that students at other campuses have made, and it's the fruit of a dangerous ideological conformity in too much of higher education."

Bruni's conclusion is spot-on. Teaching liberal arts is no longer liberal if it's no longer tolerant of alternative thought. Thankfully, some on the left are calling out the disturbing behavior, and hopefully more will. Six days before the mess at Middlebury, CNN commentator and prominent Democrat Van Jones confronted students at the University of Chicago for demanding to be in safe spaces and cowering inside of protective bubbles.

*"I don't want you to be safe, ideologically. I don't
want you to be safe, emotionally. I want you to be
strong. . . . Put on some boots, and learn how to deal
with adversity.*

*You are creating a kind of liberalism that the minute
it crosses the street into the real world is not just use-
less, but obnoxious and dangerous. I want you to be
offended every single day on this campus. I want you
to be deeply aggrieved and offended and upset, and
then to learn how to speak back. Because that is what
we need from you."*

Before we can speak back, students—and you and I—must listen to
anyone and everyone with a viewpoint. I mean *really listen*, in stillness.
This predilection, unfortunately, is missing in our schools and homes
today. Many parents and educators—and thus their children and
students—dismiss this critical tenet of learning. The unfortunate and
often dangerous response is either to flee to a "safe space" or to scream
at the speaker. These undignified tactics are fueling our uncivil war.

After the Middlebury melee, *The Boston Globe* reported more
than 30 students accepted disciplinary sanctions for their actions, but
the college declined to offer details.

At Claremont McKenna College in early April 2017, officials announced likely repercussions for student protestors who successfully
blocked other students and professors from entering an on-campus
building to hear a pro-police speech by Heather MacDonald with the
conservative Manhattan Institute.

President Hiram Chodosh almost immediately issued a statement:
"Blocking access to buildings violates college policy. CMC students
who are found to have violated policies will be held accountable."
The school conducted a thorough review and indeed held students
accountable, issuing another statement in July.

"The blockade breached institutional values of freedom of
expression and assembly. Furthermore, this action violated [school]
policies . . . that prohibit material disruption of college programs and
created unsafe conditions in disregard of state law. Through a review

of available video and photographic evidence, the College...charged 10 students with violations of College policy."

In the end, three students received one-year suspensions, two received one-semester suspensions, and two were put on conduct probation. More schools that experience such incidents must follow the lead of administrators at Claremont McKenna.

Healthy liberalism has evolved into an unhealthy illiberalism. This growing illiberalism has enabled a culture of narrow-mindedness and unscholarly pursuit, which is being countered by an intolerant conservatism that doesn't look anything like what Ronald Reagan espoused.

No longer can one side of an argument hold some measure of truth. It's all or nothing, to many on the left and right.

Before we proceed, let's look again at the First Amendment and read the end, which endorses "the right of the people peaceably to assemble, and to petition the Government for a redress of grievances."

Protesting is an essential First Amendment right, as it should be. Without it, Martin Luther King Jr. and many others would not have been able to move the needle on civil rights. Middlebury students had every right to protest Murray's controversial views, but what they were doing wasn't protesting and it certainly wasn't non-violent. They were ignoring the First Amendment by not "peaceably" assembling and by "abridging" Murray's right to speak.

Will we end racism, sexism, homophobia, misogyny, and other bigotry, as some seem to think is possible by retreating or screaming? Or do such tactics make it much worse, by enabling fear and greater weakness, as Jones posed in Chicago? Bruni argues "the policing of imperfect language, silencing of dissent and shaming of dissenters runs counter to that goal, alienating the very onlookers who need illumination."

The same can be said for many on the right, who have staked camps in places like rowdy talk radio and alternative websites that play loose with facts or provide no balance to their stories. Before taking a deeper look at speech problems on many college campuses, it's important to note conservatives have a significant problem with speech and civility, as well. Much of their speech is beyond shrill.

Case in point: Stephen Bannon, who headed the website Breitbart before working on the Trump campaign. After the campaign, he became the White House's chief strategist before he was shown the revolving door like many in the first year of the Trump presidency. He didn't hold back, of course, when interviewed by *The Weekly Standard*.

"Now I'm free. I've got my hands back on my weapons," he said. "Someone said, it's 'Bannon the Barbarian.' I am definitely going to crush the opposition. There's no doubt. I built a f**** machine at Breitbart. And now I'm about to go back, knowing what I know, and we're about to rev that machine up. And rev it up we will do."

This kind of caustic rhetoric is infecting the ears and minds of too many Americans. Listening to people like Mark Levin, Rush Limbaugh, and maybe your hometown shouter doesn't help our political road rage. Desensitized, some loyal listeners are no longer able to have conversations. You see, they heard it on Rush, so it must be true. Rush regularly says he's right, 99.7% of the time. This type of speech feeds our certitude and fear problem.

Shouting and shaming isn't exclusive to talk radio and liberal campuses. It's penetrated hallowed spaces, as we saw during President Obama's State of the Union address before Congress in 2009. Arguing his healthcare plan didn't cover illegal immigrants, South Carolina Congressman Joe Wilson didn't hold back.

"You lie!" Wilson bellowed, to the amazement of all in the House chamber and a national audience watching at home. Wilson quickly apologized, but other Republicans grumbled throughout the speech. Texas Congressman Louie Gohmert wore a sign around his neck that said, "What bill?"

Such rejoinders diminish credibility and solve nothing.

CAMPUS SPEECH POLICE

Speech that is deemed "hateful" is often in the ear of the beholder. What's offensive to one person may not be offensive to another. I believe most of us can agree fringe rhetoric is on the rise, but I want to pause here and say something very important.

"Hate speech" and fringe rhetoric are protected by the First Amendment, as is anything someone says that is disagreeable or contrary to your beliefs or mine. Unfortunately, too many schools have an unhealthy penchant for "policing" speech.

First, some encouraging news: According to the Foundation for Individual Rights in Education (FIRE), there has been a decline in unconstitutional speech codes on college campuses since 2008. But according to Adam Goldstein with FIRE, we have a long road ahead to protect speech. "It is astonishing to see how few schools are willing to stand up and actually say, 'I'm going to follow…constitutional law,'" he says.

Goldstein says schools are missing the mark when they settle on the false conclusion that "if protest is speech, than disruptive protest is also speech. [But] that just isn't the way the Constitution works….If they don't or can't shout you down, they seek to shame you or state their well-being is in jeopardy if they hear something offensive."

According to FIRE's website, "too many universities—in policy and in practice—censor and punish students' and faculty members' speech and expressive activity. One way that universities do this is through the use of speech codes—policies prohibiting speech that, outside the bounds of campus, would be protected by the First Amendment."

In 2016, FIRE surveyed 440 schools and found 49.3% maintain severely restrictive "red light" speech codes—policies that clearly and substantially prohibit protected speech. In 2017, only 31 schools earned FIRE's highest "green light" rating, but that's up from 22 in 2015 and 18 in 2014. This decline in speech codes is good news that must continue, and can with ongoing healthy pressure.

Before we dive into what's unfolding on college campuses, I want to acknowledge this issue of protection of speech isn't polling as bipartisan as some issues we'll cover later. Republican and Republican leaners "who say colleges and universities have a positive effect on the way things are going in the country" had dropped significantly since 2015, from 54% then to 36% today. However, 72% of Democrats and Democrat leaners continue to say colleges have a positive effect. That's a wide gap—36 percentage points. The good news is many liberals are starting to speak out about the issue.

I also want to acknowledge that many schools continue to invite speakers who are considered controversial by some. My alma mater Vanderbilt University continues to host conservative speakers through the Chancellor's Lecture Series like former Florida Governor Jeb Bush, *Wall Street Journal* columnist Peggy Noonan, former Attorney General Alberto Gonzalez, Fox News contributor Charles Krauthammer and others.

The University of California at Berkeley, which has been criticized in recent years for not protecting conservative speakers, also is making efforts to protect free speech, much like it did in the 1960s. In August 2017, Carol Christ, the first woman to lead the nation's top public research university, said 2017-2018 would be a "Free Speech Year." Right-wing speakers would be invited, and "point-counterpoint" panels would be held to demonstrate how to debate views respectfully.

"Now what public speech is about is shouting, screaming your point of view in a public space rather than really thoughtfully engaging someone with a different point of view," Christ said. "We have to build a deeper and richer shared public understanding."

Cal-Berkley announced the initiative after dealing with the fallout from violent skirmishes between alt-right vs. alt-left over cancelled appearances by agitator Milo Yiannopoulos and ultra-conservative commentator Ann Coulter.

The university's security costs to host these speakers can be tens of thousands of dollars. It's worth every penny.

Another Nashville school, Lipscomb University, not only is placing emphasis on civil discourse on campus but also taking that message off campus into the community on a regular basis. The school, which has established a College of Leadership & Public Service, hosts forums through its Spark Idea Center.

I participated in one, "Politics, Morality and Civility" with a diverse group of business and community leaders. The school structured the program on an essay by the dissident Václav Havel who eventually became Czechoslovakia's president. Not unlike Dr. King, Havel spoke out against social injustice and spent time in jail on his iconic rise. Havel eventually spoke to Congress in the early 1990s, recognized as one of the world's greatest proponents of civil discourse, living a moral life and active political engagement. He proved the three could co-exist, even amidst Communist oppression. Many universities in turmoil would be wise to consider such programs beneficial to them and their communities.

Washington & Lee University in Lexington, Virginia, is another institution having few problems in today's hypersensitive political environment. They advertise a "Speaking Tradition" that "members of the W&L community regularly say 'hello' to one another, whether passing on the Colonnade or meeting in the Commons. This simple courtesy, which affects and reflects the warmth and civility of life on campus, is also extended to visitors, who instantly feel a part of the community." On two separate college visits with my children, students and faculty indeed said hello, instead of passing by checking out their smartphones.

From our high altitude plane ride, the scenes on other college campuses aren't as pretty. Young adults are walking on eggshells of our own making.

One example is a recently released seven-page guide by James Madison University, which encouraged orientation leaders to use with freshmen students. The newly arrived were told they should avoid saying 35 particular phrases, including "you have such a pretty face," "love the sinner, hate the sin," "we're all part of the human race," "I treat all people the same," and "it was only a joke." Other phrases include "I never owned slaves," and "people just need to pick themselves up by their bootstraps."

School officials believe such phrases "widen the diversity gap" and do not "create a safe and inclusive environment." Having reviewed the 35 phrases, I would agree several phrases could land hard on someone sensitive to slavery or sexual orientation. But why not have a conversation about that with someone who receives any of these 35 saying as offensive, rather than start a list of phrases that could have very different meanings to those saying it ("we're all part of the human race") or in different contexts of conversations? Soon, 35 will become 350, and 3,500, and so on, and the ability to speak freely, without worrying over various intended or unintended consequences, will be a thing of the past.

When put on notice, the speaker might take it as his or her view is wrong or inappropriate; there's also a missed opportunity to discuss possible unintended consequences. Opportunities to understand one another, as Martin Luther King said so well, are replaced by an adversarial admonishment, which can lead to greater division and less diversity in thought, the opposite of what JMU seems to be intending. The irony this effort is occurring at a school named after a Founder is not lost.

In 2012, according to the University of Maryland's website, the "Department of Resident Life and the Multicultural Involvement and Community Advocacy office [partnered] to create a comprehensive, multi-layered, inclusive *language campaign* that engages all students. Our students frequently express feeling unwelcomed and uncomfortable on campus, and in the residence halls, because of the derogatory language used by their peers. This type of language impacts many students based on their class, race, ethnicity, religion, sexual orientation, ability status, sex, and gender identity."

"Language campaign" is clearly code for something else. Who gets to define "inclusive," "unwelcomed," "uncomfortable," and "derogatory"? Once we're on this slope, anyone can claim anything to be these terms, and the aggrieved will demand action or retribution for something that's not illegal.

Jones and King have the better answer, rather than having speech policies and signed diversity statements. Follow the law, or change the law if you believe it needs to be changed. Many laws protecting civil rights, like the Equal Pay Act of 1963 and Civil Rights Act of 1964, have been enacted and expanded. The Fourteenth Amendment has expanded individual rights, whether you agree or disagree with some of the court decisions and agency rules. Are we going to eliminate or alter the First Amendment, so certain people feel safer? Is that the goal, or is conformity to the other's viewpoint really the goal? The latter leads to totalitarianism and authoritarianism, for those familiar with history. The First Amendment is first for a reason.

The University of Maryland further states its "goals for this campaign are to help students understand that their words have power and impact others sense of belonging on campus; provide students with helpful strategies and teach them to engage others about language in a way that creates 'aha moments'; help our students understand the impact, origin, and context of words; and create a student-driven process via focus groups and surveys, so that students can express the power of language in their own words."

I would recommend any Maryland or James Madison University alumnus or alumna acknowledge the university's desire to improve understanding of the meaning of words but encourage a different approach. Rather than setting up a new speech bureaucracy, why not require every student to enroll in a classic debate course, with any topic fair game? Instead of having focus groups and surveys on "class, race, ethnicity, religion, sexual orientation, ability status, sex, and gender identity," why not feature debates on these and other topics? Let them "express the power of language in their own words" in a classroom setting.

Students would be encouraged to learn the laws and existing protections that have occurred, and argue for further protections, modifications or repeals, based on their own research and beliefs. That would be a great introduction to a classic liberal arts education, rather than be told what to say and not say. Both the insensitive student and overly sensitive student would learn how to stand their ground, and hopefully learn from each other, by engaging.

Too many schools, as FIRE's research has found, have "inclusive language campaigns" such as one adopted in 2015 by the University of Michigan. Posters across campus espoused: "Stop. Think. YOUR WORDS MATTER," with questions like, "If you knew that I grew up in poverty, would you still call things 'ghetto' and 'ratchet'?"

Hmmm. When those students return to their dorms, they can turn on their Spotify, select their favorite rapper, and hear those terms and much more. The term ratchet, for instance, is in recent songs by Beyonce, LL Cool J, Juicy J, and Nicki Minaj, who laments "all them b***** is ratchet" in "Right by My Side."

So is it OK to have it both ways, for them to listen to African-American rap stars or comedians who use the words "n****r" or "cracker"? Will the university step in and remove such materials from dorms? Will the Michigan football star playing such music be held to the same standard as the white fraternity member who plays it at a party? Will the Michigan football star be justifiably angry and offended when he hears it at an all-white party? Where is this going, and where does it end?

This reconstruction of racial views seems to be an impossible and implausible task that is advancing tension, not ameliorating it. Northwestern University offered a class called "Deconstructing Whiteness," a six-session seminar that is part of its "Social Justice Education" office, which "creates co-curricular educational opportunities in partnership with our student community that foster self-exploration, facilitate conversations across difference and support actions that create social change on campus. Posters for the class posed: "What is my role in doing anti-racist work?" or "why do I have to feel guilty about being white?" and "how can I talk about race as a white person?"

At Princeton University, the word "man" has by and large been eliminated. Ivy Leaguers in New Jersey are encouraged to say: "Instead of 'man and wife' use spouses or partners. Switch out 'man made' with artificial, handmade or manufactured. Don't use the verb "to man," as in to work something, instead use to operate or to staff. Throw out workmanlike and replace it with skillful."

In addition, use "business person instead of businessman, fire-fighter instead of fireman, ancestors instead of forefathers, and so on."

"Consistent with style guidelines issued by Princeton's Office of Human Resources and Office of Communications, and as endorsed by the Institutional Equity Planning Group as a preferred University practice, HR has developed these gender inclusive style guidelines, to be utilized by all HR staff members in HR communications, policies, job descriptions, and job postings," the memo states.

Princeton's LGBT Center also offers a guide on gender pronouns for those who identify as "transgender, genderqueer, and other gender-variant," suggesting "ze, zie and hir," "they and theirs," and "Ey, em, eir and emself." This didn't seem to set off much controversy at the private institution in New Jersey, but when it happened in my home state of Tennessee at a public university, the you-know-what hit the fan.

In 2015, the University of Tennessee's Office for Diversity and Inclu-sion encouraged students begin using the pronouns ze, xe, hir, hirs and zirs, and others, for those who don't identify with a particular biological sex. Lawmakers in Nashville were flooded with calls and emails, demanding action against the school for issuing guidance contrary to their beliefs. Was the university promoting, or stifling, diversity? Read on.

Later that year, the office issued holiday party guidance that reignited fire across the state (italics mine): "Holiday parties and celebrations should celebrate and build upon workplace relationships and team morale with no emphasis on religion or culture. *Ensure your holiday party is not a Christmas party in disguise.*"

Tennessee's General Assembly contemplated pulling funding of the office, which some students counter-protested. Federal and state lawmakers went on the attack, issuing pointed press releases.

> "The Office of Diversity is not welcoming to all
> and hostile to none as they claim," State Senator

Dolores Gresham said. "They are very hostile to students and other Tennesseans with Christian and conservative values. By placing a virtual religious test regarding holiday events at this campus, every student who is a Christian is penalized."

"This is a public university, supported by taxpayer dollars, where the precious resources provided to them should be directed at what we are doing to give our students a world class education," State Senator Mike Bell said. "The people want us to ensure that their money is being spent wisely and we have lost confidence that this is being done."

East Tennessee Congressman Jimmy Duncan, who serves the district where UT Knoxville resides, didn't mince words: "People all over the country are sick and tired of this extreme, radical political correctness."

Neither did Congressman Diane Black from Middle Tennessee: "The University of Tennessee's 'holiday party' guidelines would be laughable if only the implications for students were not so serious. With these rules, the UT Office of Diversity and Inclusion is not promoting diversity—it is stifling it.... Between these offensive, Scrooge-like guidelines, and the school's much-maligned attempt at regulating gender-neutral pronouns, it is past time for Chancellor Cheek to get a handle on the University's affairs or make way for someone who can."

The Office responded by saying its words were misconstrued, in both instances: "We recognize that most people prefer to use the pronouns he and she; we do not dictate speech. We do strive to be a diverse and inclusive campus and to ensure that everyone feels welcome, accepted and respected."

Later, the Office said the lines about holiday celebrations are "not a policy [but] a list of suggestions for inclusive celebrations."

After fumbling over itself, the university shut down the office for a period, prompting Chancellor Jimmy Cheek to say: "This in no way diminishes our commitment to diversity and inclusion. We will use the coming year to determine how to more effectively advance diversity and inclusion on our campus."

The University of North Carolina at Chapel Hill, Marquette University and many others now have an exhaustive list of words that contain potentially biased or offensive implications, such as businessman, policeman, and even freshman, so that students can avoid using them in their writing. Some schools have started calling freshmen "first-years," for instance.

"When you are writing about people in general, many of your professors will expect you to use 'inclusive' or 'nonsexist' language, that is, gender neutral language," Marquette's website states, adding that many people find non-neutered language "not only inaccurate but offensive."

Knowingly or unknowingly, Marquette is dangerously accommodating one view, and only one view, that is disagreeable to many if not the majority of Americans. It is sending an explicit message it wants to admit students with certain views on sexuality, and likely implicitly on other topics. Some who are being prepared in such a way will have difficulty entering the workforce and tackling the many complexities in our world.

There are many who view these workshops, seminars, posters, HR policy issuances, emails from professors, and guidance memos as attacks on free speech and religion. Count this author as one of them. Free speech advocates are concerned, not solely because of the political correctness of such attempts to redefine traditional terms that have no inherent bias in them. We see what's happening outside university borders to enforce new sexual orientation terminology, like in New York City.

In 2015, the city's Commission on Human Rights announced new protections for the city's 25,000 transgender and gender-nonconforming individuals under its Human Rights Law. The "guidelines" require employers and covered entities to use an individual's preferred name, pronoun and title regardless of the individual's sex assigned at birth, anatomy, gender, medical history, appearance, or the sex indicated on the individual's identification.

Pronouns such as "they/them/theirs or ze/hir," instead of the conventional binary pronouns of "he/him/his" or "she/her/hers" are to be used. In May 2016, the commission confirmed individuals could use 31 accepted pronouns protecting their gender identities, including "gender bender," "two spirit," "third sex," "androgynous," "gender gifted" and "pangender." The city's website listed the identities without defi-

nitions. Those definitions, however, could be found at certain universities' websites—like the University of Wisconsin and the University
of California-Berkley. The number of definitions most certainly will
grow, something the city and employers in their spare time (tongue-
in-cheek planted) will be monitoring closely.

Now for the kicker: *Any employer committing violations deemed
"willful, wanton, or malicious conduct" is subject to fines of $250,000
per incident.* A lawsuit against Whole Foods has already been filed.

Other standard violations of the law, such as refusing to allow
individuals to use single-sex facilities like bathrooms "consistent
with their gender identity," failing to provide employee health benefits for "gender-affirming care" and "imposing different uniforms or
grooming standards based on sex or gender," can be fined $125,000.
Examples include "requiring female bartenders to wear makeup," or
"requiring only individuals who identify as male to have short hair."

Advocates of the extremely heavy-handed law and rule, like
Commission Chairman Carmelyn P. Malalis, dismiss how extreme it
is. "Accidentally misusing a transgender person's preferred pronoun
is not a violation of the law and will not result in a fine," Malalis
said. "In fact, our guidance encourages people to ask transgender
and gender non-conforming individuals how they would like to be
addressed.... We issued this guidance [in 2015] so employers and
individuals understand what the law says and to ensure that every
transgender individual in New York City is treated with the respect
and dignity they deserve."

It's hard to put wrapping paper and a bow around such extremism, but give Chairman Malalis credit for trying. Besides creating
opportunities for a more contentious work environment and telling a
business owner how it will conduct business, with everyone watching
every word that's being said and wondering who should wear what,
employers are now faced with penalties that don't feel encouraging in
the least. Any claim filed, real or bogus, will be a nightmare. Besides
being at the mercy of unelected government bureaucrats, a defendant
most certainly will incur exorbitant legal fees, not to mention deal
with the tremendous stress wondering if fines alone will shut down the
business owner's dream.

In Canada, incorrect use of gender pronouns could mean jail

time. In June 2017, our northern neighbor overwhelmingly passed legislation that says improper use of gender pronouns will result in jail time, fines and mandatory anti-bias training.

In testimony to the Canadian Senate, Jordan Peterson, a professor at the University of Toronto, argued the legislation infringes upon citizens' free speech rights.

"Compelled speech has come to Canada," Peterson said. "We will seriously regret this....[Ideologues are] using unsuspecting and some-times complicit members of the so-called transgender community to push their ideological vanguard forward. The very idea that calling someone a term that they didn't choose causes them such irreparable harm that legal remedies should be sought [is] an indication of just how deeply the culture of victimization has sunk into our society."

Speech policing, victimization and thought control are on the rise, in our schools and in government. Shaming, blaming and screaming have taken root. For too long, administrators have accommodated many demonstrators because they are afraid of being called insensitive or lacking understanding. Other school leaders are afraid their boards, fearing negative publicity, might fire them.

Some clear-headed administrators like at Claremont McKenna have begun to take on the demonstrators and are holding them accountable for the disturbing, illegal behavior with suspensions and other actions. It is critical many more join them, especially chancellors, board mem-bers, and alumni and alumnae who support these elite institutions charging up to $65,000 a year. You may be one of them. Money talks, emails and calls matter, and spreading the word won't hurt a bit.

When young people arrive at college or enter the workforce, each one arrives very differently than we did. They have been bombarded with edgy, one-sided opinions, without receiving much information in short news accounts in our attention-deficit disorderly world. Mom and Dad listen to it, or don't warn against the risks, so why shouldn't I listen to and believe it?

There are so many things to click and review that any story or video that requires more than a minute of our time often doesn't make the cut. It's easier to rely on an email from a one-sided political party, or post from a passionate blogger or Facebook friend, for our daily affirmations.

Thus, in this information age without much information, more of us have become susceptible to a herd mentality of thinking. Fewer stand alone in their well-researched convictions. As Bruni notes, healthy turbulence *and* true confidence are lacking.

When challenged with information from the other side of an argument, young adults often don't know what to do. Some reactions are innocent, like "No way, I didn't know that." Other reactions are dismissive. The listener tunes out what is contrary to the firmly held belief. Worse, he digs in and ramps up the volume, or even worse, he attacks the messenger.

And then there is what's unfolding on college campuses—shaming and screaming.

If this is your child, invite him, right now, onto our plane. The Middlebury or Claremont McKenna student who went apoplectic should sit next to Charles Murray or Heather MacDonald. And if you've been watching what they've been watching, turn it off and tell your child you're seeking more balanced ways to receive your information and they should, too. Be the change you wish to happen. I promise you'll feel better about yourself as your blood pressure lowers.

As we prepare to move on, FIRE's website can make you and your children aware of restrictive policies at your alma mater or child's school. FIRE says your voice matters and they're right: "Public pressure is still perhaps the most powerful weapon against campus censorship, so it is critical that students and faculty understand their rights—and are willing to stand up for them when they are threatened.... To paraphrase Justice Louis Brandeis, sunlight really is the best of disinfectants.

Your voice in state legislatures also carries weight. States are passing specific legislation to protect free speech on college campuses and to defend college professors.

In 2015, Missouri enacted the Campus Free Expression Act (CAFE Act), "which prohibits Missouri's public colleges and universities from limiting students' expressive activities to small or out-of-the-way 'free speech zones.'" Virginia also enacted a similar law in 2014. Others have joined in, including Tennessee, which passed its own bill in 2017. FIRE called the Tennessee bill "the most comprehensive state legislation protecting free speech on college campuses that we've seen passed anywhere in the country."

Specifically, Tennessee's new law says: "Although faculty are free in the classroom to discuss subjects within areas of their competence, faculty shall be cautious in expressing personal views in the classroom and shall be careful not to introduce controversial matters that have no relationship to the subject taught, and especially matters in which they have no special competence or training and in which, therefore, faculty's views cannot claim the authority accorded statements they make about subjects within areas of their competence; provided, that no faculty will face adverse employment action for classroom speech, unless it is not reasonably germane to the subject matter of the class as broadly construed, and comprises a substantial portion of classroom instruction."

The American Association of University Professors (AAUP) didn't like the bill. It opposed the legislation because they said it "interferes with the institutional autonomy of colleges and universities by undermining the role of faculty, administration, and governing board in institutional decision-making and the role of students in the formulation and application of institutional policies affecting student affairs."

But that's not what AAUP said 77 years ago. In fact, the language in Tennessee's statute closely mirrors the text of the American Association of University Professors' 1940 Statement of Principles on Academic Freedom and Tenure, which reads in relevant part: "Teachers are entitled to freedom in the classroom in discussing their subject, but they should be careful not to introduce into their teaching controversial matter which has no relation to their subject."

How things have changed. Today, AAUP is saying butt out, which government should usually do. But when their own professors' civil liberties are not protected, something is necessary legislatively.

According to FIRE: "Had this law been in effect in Colorado, sociology professor Patti Adler would not have been subjected to a lengthy harassment investigation and forced into retirement for including a skit involving volunteer teaching assistants dressed as and portraying prostitutes as part of her 'Deviance in U.S. Society' course at the University of Colorado. If…New Jersey had this law, sociology professor Dawn Tawwater would not have been terminated from her tenure-track position for her occasional use of profanity in the classroom and her screening of a racy feminist parody of the music video for the Robin Thicke song 'Blurred Lines.'" Professors Hyung-il Jung, James Tuttle, Elizabeth Ito, and Andrea Quenette are other examples of instructors who would not have faced adverse employment actions for their classroom speech if their states had similar laws.

Most people taking a geology class want to keep it to geology and not drift into political science for substantial periods. Wherever you stand on Tennessee's law, we can probably agree it's unfortunate that government is stepping in to settle something that was accepted by the professors themselves years ago.

Let's piggyback off this onto our next subject: teaching both sides of issues.

CRITICAL POINT:

Free speech is under dangerous attack at our colleges and universities. One comprehensive survey shows almost half of our universities have unconstitutional speech codes.

ACTION STEP:

Support administrations that protect free speech and call out those with speech codes. Learn where your alma mater stands and engage, discontinue donating and educate your friends until your school promotes and protects free speech.

RESOURCES:

Is your alma mater a green, yellow or red light school for free speech?
https://www.thefire.org
www.EndingOurUncivilWar.com

CHAPTER 3: SCHOLASTIC INDEPENDENCE

'SETTLED' OR NOT, HERE IT COMES

Parents, by and large, want their kids to get a great education so they can be prepared for whatever career they choose. It may be graduating from high school or receiving appropriate vocational training, or it may be getting a bachelor's degree or graduate degree from a university or college.

There is some controversy about what's being taught in elementary and high school textbooks, but it pales in comparison to what's going on in higher education. More and more, university leaders and professors are emphasizing a certain point of view, eliminating instruction of other viewpoints. This defames the integrity of liberal arts instruction, and threatens to further corrode our discourse, undermine commonsense civility and destabilize our society.

At dinner parties with friends and business and political contacts with very diverse viewpoints, I continue to be amazed at the conversations. Maybe you hear what I'm hearing.

"What's happening at our universities? My child now believes most rich people are greedy, many companies are bad, pretty much everyone is racist, and people with a different view aren't to be believed or trusted. I feel like my son has been brainwashed."

One friend who sent his son to an elite Ivy League school re-marked how the young man came home and said no one he knows on campus—students and professors—understands why anyone could vote for Trump. When he came home and volunteered at a hospital, the student attended to patients and had many conversations with Trump supporters. In that setting outside the classroom, he listened to people who had lost their manufacturing job and were working for lower wages or two jobs to pay the bills. Some had lost their health insurance or seen their rates triple in five years. Others wondered why any city would harbor someone who is here illegally that had committed violent crimes.

They were afraid, the student told his dad, for different reasons. The undergraduate may not have agreed with Trump's solutions, but he could see why they were willing to go in a different direction at the ballot box. Back on campus, he returned to a different world, where the bewilderment continued.

Before you read further, know this: I believe good has been accomplished through some liberal policies. I also believe harm has been done. I believe good, too, has been accomplished through some conservative policies. I also believe harm has been done. Now let's look at an area where most liberals say there is no room for disagree-ment: climate change.

NO ROOM FOR DEBATE

In April 2017, *New York Times* columnist Bret Stephens, previ-ously with the *Wall Street Journal*, authored an opinion piece titled "Climate of Complete Certainty." Some of his cautionary and balanced words were directed at climate change advocates who maintain tight adherence to various scientific conclusions. Said Stephens:

> *Claiming total certainty about the science traduces the spirit of science and creates openings for doubt when-ever a climate claim proves wrong. Demanding abrupt and expensive changes in public policy raises fair*

questions about ideological intentions. Censoriously
asserting one's moral superiority and treating skeptics
as imbeciles "and deplorables" wins few converts. None
of this is to deny climate change or the possible severity
of its consequences. But ordinary citizens also have a
right to be skeptical of an overweening scientism. They
know—as all environmentalists should—that history
is littered with the human wreckage of scientific errors
married to political power.

Already struggling to maintain its readership, like so many news outlets, the *Times* response page and social media was peppered with outrage from subscribers and others.

"Go eat dog d******," fumed one Twitter user.

"When is the Times going to get rid of you?" said another.

Fellow journalists chimed in.

"You're a s******, a crybaby lil f**** weenie. a massive t*** too," tweeted Gizmodo staff writer Libby Watson.

"I'm gonna lose my mind," said Eve Peyser, politics writer at Vice. "The ideas ppl like @BretStephensNYT espouse are violently hateful & should not be given a platform by @NYTimes."

Said another on Twitter: "Each and every one of us should fully boycott the NY Times—don't link to them, don't click on their links. Their actions are inexcusable...You cannot be an ostensible paper-of-record and allow a science denier to spread propaganda."

NYU professor Adriana Heguy tweeted: "Composing my letter to the editor today and canceling @nytimes. Balance' means a VALID alternative opinion, not pseudoscience. I'm so sad."

Tens of thousands signed a petition on Change.org: "The issue is not that climate denial makes *New York Times* readers uncomfortable. The issue is that climate denial relies on a foundation of lies. To present lies as if they were reasoned opinion compromises the impartiality, accuracy, and integrity of *The New York Times*."

Times Publisher Arthur Sulzberger Jr. attempted damage control as many in his readership ran to one side of a listing ship.

"Our customer care team shared with me that your reason for unsubscribing from *The New York Times* included our decision to hire

Bret Stephens as an Opinion columnist. I wanted to provide a bit more context," his email begins. Sulzberger then had to explain that the newsroom functions separately from the opinion department and that much of its coverage had shown the impact of climate change.

"No subject is more vital," Sulzberger said. "Meanwhile, *The Times*'s Opinion pages remain an independent and unblinking forum for debate from a wide range of viewpoints among open-minded, informed writers and readers. I don't think, in these polarizing and partisan times, there's anything quite like it in American journalism."

Sulzberger noted so many people are "talking past each other about how best to address climate change," and how "putting different points of view on the same page will hopefully help" advance real solutions.

"Challenging our assumptions and forcing us to think harder about our positions," he wrote, "sharpens all our work and benefits our readers.... In the coming years, we aim to further enrich the quality of our debate with other honest and intelligent voices, including some currently underrepresented in our pages. If you continue to read *The Times*, you will encounter such voices—not just as contributors, but as new staff columnists."

Sulzberger spoke like a true journalism professor, brilliantly defending his new hire as readership declined.

Stephens, who had spent nearly two years being bashed by *Journal* readers for taking on many comments by Donald Trump, left one hot seat for another. As he learned, the debate over climate change has ended for many, including President Obama. It's also the way it's being taught at hundreds of our universities.

"The debate is settled. Climate change is a fact."

With those words in the 2014 State of the Union, Obama closed the book on being open to alternative viewpoints, negotiation, levels of truth and uncertainty, conflicting data, or new science and information. Shortly thereafter, he began to go well outside his constitutional authority by signing an international climate change treaty, artfully called the Paris Agreement in late 2015. The president called it a "turning point" that "would save our planet," a noble notion.

Set aside your view of the Paris Agreement for a moment, and let's look at how our country "agreed" to it.

Pesky constitutionalists like Steven Groves at *The Freedom Project* noted several causes for alarm, chiefly, "The [administration's] uni-lateral treatment of the Paris Agreement...has all the hallmarks of a treaty that should be submitted to the Senate for its advice and consent under Article II, Section 2, of the U.S. Constitution, and...contains 'targets and timetables' for emissions reductions and, as such, the administration's failure to submit the agreement to the Senate breaches a commitment made by the executive branch to the Senate in 1992 during the ratification process of the United Nations Framework Con-vention on Climate Change."

Basically, been there done that, so you must do it again.

The administration knew this and began to throw up flak. Several months prior to Paris, White House press secretary Josh Earnest was asked if "Congress should have the ability to sign off" on any deal, to which he retorted: "...It's hard to take seriously from some members of Congress who deny the fact that climate change exists, that they should have some opportunity to render judgment about a climate change agreement."

Basically, we're right, they're wrong so our nation's rules don't apply. This is a very, very slippery slope we're on, as some Obama sup-porters are now seeing with some of his successor's actions.

Unabashed, Obama then used the regulatory system to strangle the fossil fuel industry, something many of his supporters wanted him to do. Business groups and state leaders said executive actions like the Clean Power Plan and others killed thousands of jobs. I believe, in part, unbri-dled rulemaking contributed to Democrats losing the 2016 election.

If you agreed with Obama's means to his ends, consider that many were aghast by such means, even those who largely or to some extent agreed with him on climate change. They saw a republic charting new territory, with a determined president outside the legal bounds to which he took an oath. They viewed his actions as illegal, autocratic decrees and feared electoral responses that would embrace an equally if not greater autocratic approach to solving problems. They knew seemingly permanent gridlock, though frustrating at times, was and is necessary to temper extreme or illegal actions by any president of any party.

True, Mr. Obama was unable to sway his opponents, who were in the hip pockets of the oil industry and disinterested in disrupting the status quo. Frankly, climate change opponents bear some blame, since the status quo needed an update. They missed an opportunity to achieve some of their own energy goals as well. The lost art of compromise, so hard to achieve in this hardline era, was there for the taking. Go with me for a second...

What if Republicans and Democrats agreed to incentivize alternative energies with reputable companies using measurable accountability standards (gradual funding, oversight and no blank checks to political friends)? What if these investments would be made in states that rely more heavily on fossil fuels, while training their workers in the new technologies? What if politicians agreed to lower carbon emissions further in exchange for development of safely transported domestic fossil fuels via new pipelines, while repairing older ones and getting away from less safe means, like rail and truck? What if Congress and the president agreed to stop buying oil from countries with a history of human rights' violations and support of terror? What if we turned up, gradually, economic pressure on countries that have far worse emission standards than us?

Those things could happen more easily, under a better system of government, which will be where we'll end our plane ride.

Instead, Obama felt he had no choice but to use his pen and phone to right what he and others saw as wrongs. Problem is, the next guy has a pen and a phone too. President Trump, for example, issued an executive order on immigration that triggered court action.

Climate change and global warming have been emphasized at many learning institutions for a long time. This is a good thing, since energy consumption is a big part of our economy and few would deny having a clean environment is important. Even so, instructional mantra denies scrutiny of available information. Armed with degrees and their side of the story, these graduates continue to enter positions of influence—like the media, where we've seen less fondness for deliberation. Instead the tone and volume over "settled" science at our schools has made its way into our culture, and not just on this issue.

Before we look at how one-sided teaching has become in various schools, here are a few statements about global warming and climate change some may recall, starting around 1970 when Earth Day was conceived:

"Civilization will end within 15 or 30 years unless immediate action is taken against problems facing mankind."
—GEORGE WALD, NOBEL LAUREATE BIOLOGY PROFESSOR AT HARVARD UNIVERSITY, 1970

"The battle to feed all of humanity is over. In the 1970s hundreds of millions of people will starve to death in spite of any crash programs embarked upon now. At this late date nothing can prevent a substantial increase in the world death rate." —PAUL EHRLICH, STANFORD UNIVERSITY BIOLOGIST AND AUTHOR OF **THE POPULATION BOMB**, 1970

"In 10 years, all important animal life in the sea will be extinct."
—EHRLICH, WHO WON 16 AWARDS, INCLUDING THE 1990 CRAFOORD PRIZE, THE ROYAL SWEDISH ACADEMY OF SCIENCES' HIGHEST AWARD

"If I were a gambler, I would take even money that England will not exist in the year 2000." —EHRLICH, 1969

"The threat of a new ice age must now stand alongside nuclear war as a likely source of wholesale death and misery for mankind." —NIGEL CALDER IN **INTERNATIONAL WILDLIFE**, 1975

"The world has been chilling sharply for about 20 years. If present trends continue, the world will be about 4 degrees colder for the global mean temperature in 1990 but 11 degrees colder in the year 2000. This is about twice what it would take to put us into an ice age." —KENNETH WATT SPEAKING AT SWARTHMORE COLLEGE, 1970

"We have to offer up scary scenarios, make simplified, dramatic statements, and make little mention of any doubts we might have.... Each of us has to decide what the right balance is between being effective and being honest."
—ACTIVIST STEPHEN SCHNEIDER IN **DISCOVER MAGAZINE**, 1989

"We've got to...try to ride the global warming issue. Even if the theory of global warming is wrong...we will be doing the right thing anyway in terms of economic policy and environmental policy." —SENATOR TIMOTHY WIRTH (D-COLO.), 1988

Those statements and many others have hurt valid arguments by environmentalists, as have these prognostications:

- In his 2006 movie *An Inconvenient Truth*, Al Gore predicted shores would flood and sea-bordering cities would sink below water, leaving millions homeless amid catastrophic property damage we couldn't afford. Due to global warming, melting ice could release enough water to cause at 20-foot rise in sea level "in the near future." In 2008, Gore told a German audience "the entire North 'polarized' cap will disappear in five years." That same year, *ABC News* (Bob Woodruff on *Good Morning America*) predicted New York City would be under water by 2015.
- In 1970, in *Look* magazine, Sen. Gaylord Nelson (D-Wis.) said: "Dr. S. Dillon Ripley, secretary of the Smithsonian (Institution), believes that in 25 years, somewhere between 75 and 80% of all the species of living animals will be extinct."
- Scientist Harrison Brown in Scientific American said mankind would run out of copper shortly after 2000, while lead, zinc, tin, gold and silver would disappear before 1990.
- Government has a history of wild predictions, too: In 1939, the U.S. Department of the Interior said American oil supplies would last another 13 years. In 1949, the Secretary of the Interior said the end of U.S. oil supplies was in sight. In 1974, the U.S. Geological Survey said the U.S. only had a 10-year supply of natural gas. In fact, in 2014 our nation had 2.47 quadrillion cubic feet of natural gas, which should last about a century.

It should come as no surprise, then, how such matters are handled today at some universities. Recently, three professors at the University of Colorado-Colorado Springs co-teaching the course "Medical Humanities in the Digital Age," issued the following email to students:

"The point of departure for this course is based on the scientific premise that human induced climate change is valid and occurring. We will not, at any time, debate the science of climate change, nor will the 'other side' of the climate change debate be taught or discussed in this course."

The professors issued the email after a student had inquired if alternative science or views could be researched, incorporated or presented.

"Opening up a debate that 98% of climate scientists unequivocally agree to be a non-debate would detract from the central concerns of environment and health addressed in this course the professors stated.

"If you believe this premise to be an issue for you, we respectfully ask that you do not take this course, as there are options within the Humanities program for face-to-face [teaching] this semester and online next."

This ban on debate extended to discussion among students in online forums. Students also were required to use only those resources that had been peer-reviewed by the United Nations' Intergovernmental Panel on Climate Change (IPCC). Stray, and your grade will be low.

The professors incorporated fracking, the controversial process of using water to extract oil and natural gas from shale plays, into the course. Several studies have shown fracking is safe, while other studies have come to different conclusions. It shouldn't come as a surprise that only anti-fracking studies made it into the course materials. Wouldn't it have been thought provoking to have two of each, or more of each?

Lastly, one course activity was for students to estimate their carbon footprint, a reasonable exercise. The syllabus, however, states the purpose of the activity "is not to create guilt or shame, though those emotions are entirely common." Just in case you don't get the point, right?

Classes like these are nothing less than programming or indoctrination, much different than even-handed instruction. They stray far from classic liberal arts teaching and detract from questions about climate change and the estimated impact of our consumption of fossil fuels. (More to follow, I promise to share both sides.) And it's a trend: debate isn't allowed at more schools since the case for man-made climate change has been "settled," a word frequently used by university communication departments and politicians. Here's more proof:

- In May 2016, the Portland, Oregon Public Schools Board unanimously voted to ban classroom materials that express doubt on climate change.
- In March 2016, a group at the University of Michigan called Young Americans for Liberty organized an event, "The Moral Case for Fossil Fuels" by Professor Pierre Desrochers. Flyers across campus were vandalized, not uncommon in Ann Arbor. Remember, flyers promoting a panel of Jewish conservatives also were torn away from a public wall, while a banner advertising an appearance by conservative Ben Shapiro was defaced.
- Schools like Michigan and the University of California-River-

side are offering degrees in "environmental justice." In California, students explore how climate change allegedly impacts
unhealthy eating habits and academic progress of school
children, and study how big business and "racist" policies have
combined to create unhealthy living environments for minorities and the poor, which is called "environmental racism."

In addition to agreeing that the debate has been settled, President
Obamas also said in his 2014 State of the Union, "the shift to a cleaner
energy economy won't happen overnight, and it will require tough
choices along the way."

The first part is reasonable. Change of this nature, and on this
scale, will take time. Also, requiring "tough choices along the way"
makes some sense, until you saw what that really meant: Shortly after
this speech, the administration announced its very aggressive Clean
Power Plan rule. As you may recall, before the courts blocked the rule,
its estimated annual cost was $1,700 a year for a family of four, includ-
ing already-struggling poor families. The government's own estimated
job losses were half a million a year by the late 2020s. I wonder how
many universities teaching environmental justice classes used these
estimates, just to show another facet of the issue.

What about that 98% number that pervades our politics? You can
find it in several places. A 2010 study published by the United States
National Academy of Sciences found approximately 97 to 98% of 1,372
climate researchers surveyed believe climate change is anthropogenic,
or man-made. A 2009 survey published by the American Geophysical
Union surveyed 3,146 scientists and asked: "Do you think human
activity is a significant contributing factor in changing mean global
temperatures?" Approximately 82% of the surveyed scientists answered
yes to this question. Of those climate change specialists surveyed, 97.4%
answered yes to this question.

There are other polls on the subject, however, with less than 98%
consensus. In 2012, the American Meteorological Society polled 1,862
members. Interestingly, only 59% said human activity was the primary cause of global warming, while 11% attributed "the phenomenon
to human activity and natural causes in about equal measure," and
23% said not enough is known yet to make a determination. 76%

said warming over the next century would be "very" or "somewhat" harmful, but of those, only 22% thought that "all" or a "large" amount of the harm could be prevented "through mitigation and adaptation measures."

In a 2015 study conducted by the PBL Netherlands Environment Assessment Agency, three in 10 of 1,868 climate scientists responding said that less than half of global warming since 1951 could be attributed to human activity, or that they did not know.

That isn't 98%, but it is strong evidence that there is some uncertainty of the impact of fossil fuels and human activity. But is it "settled" or a "fact"? The 98% number underscores what many of us are thinking—that our energy consumption has had an impact on the environment. But have you ever heard a politician or Colorado professor ponder to what measurable extent has anthropogenic activity had on water quality, or air quality, or soil quality, or anything else? Is it improving or getting worse? What are the differing opinions and data on ice cap measurements, and why? And just for shivers and giggles, why not allow the arguments from the 2% of scientists with dissenting views?

Of course, these things have been and are being measured, but they don't make it into our public discourse or course curriculums in a balanced way.

It's easier to push an anti-fossil fuels agenda, using fear as a tactic, like Schneider and Wirth said in the late 1980s. It's also easy to deny there is some concerning scientific data and instead blast environmentalists and group them as "environmental wackos," like Rush Limbaugh likes to do. This rough rhetoric hurts valid arguments from those who oppose many environmentalist proposals.

Let's look at some of the science that's in the mainstream. An IPCC study from 1995 – 2006 said during that period the planet registered 11 of the 12 warmest years on record since instrumental measurement began in 1850. It said global surface temperature rose 0.76 degrees Celsius from the end of the 19th century (1850 – 1899) to the beginning of the 21st (2001 – 2005). The U.S. Global Change Research Program (GCRP) reported similarly in 2009, finding the average global temperature increased 1.5 degrees Fahrenheit since 1900.

According to the GCRP report, "Observations show that warming of the climate is unequivocal. The global warming observed over the past 50 years is due primarily to human-induced emissions of heat-trapping gases. These emissions come mainly from the burning of fossil fuels (coal, oil and gas), with important contributions from the clearing of forests, agricultural practices, and other activities."

From 2002 – 2006, another study asserted Greenland lost 36 to 60 cubic miles of ice, while Antarctica lost 36 cubic miles of ice during the same time period. In 2007, the BBC reported the Arctic could be ice free by 2013, an alarming statement.

Is there another side to all this? Of course, but one has to hunt for it. In 2012, according to the *Daily Mail*, the Artic ice surface began to expand dramatically, by 533,000 square miles, a 29% increase. That was as alarming as the BBC's 2007 prediction.

In the IPCC's 2013 draft report, the UN said it was 95% confident that human behavior was the cause for global warming—up from 90% in 2007. But contrary data rolled in, and some scientists challenged the IPCC findings.

U.S. climate expert Professor Judith Curry said, "In fact, the uncertainty is getting bigger. It's now clear the models are way too sensitive to carbon dioxide. I cannot see any basis for the IPCC increasing its confidence level." Curry said other factors were in play, including long-term cycles in ocean temperature, which have a significant influence and suggest the oceans were approaching a cooling trend similar to one from 1965 to 1975.

Professor Anastasios Tsonis from the University of Wisconsin, an expert on ocean cycles, was bolder: "We are already in a cooling trend, which I think will continue for the next 15 years at least. There is no doubt the warming of the 1980s and 1990s has stopped."

Later, as more information emerged from government sources, one might have expected a more robust dissection of the information. In 2015, NASA issued a study saying that an increase in Antarctic snow accumulation that began 10,000 years ago is currently adding enough ice to the continent to outweigh the increased losses from its thinning glaciers. NASA's research challenged the conclusions of other studies, including the IPCC's 2013 report that said Antarctica is losing land ice. Using satellite data, NASA said the Antarctic ice sheet showed a net gain of 112 billion tons of ice per year from 1992 to 2001. That net gain slowed to 82 billion tons of ice per year between 2003 and 2008.

"The good news is that Antarctica is not currently contributing to sea level rise, but is taking 0.23 millimeters per year away," said Jay Zwally, a NASA glaciologist and lead author of the study published in the *Journal of Glaciology*. "But this is also bad news. If the 0.27 milli-meters per year of sea level rise attributed to Antarctica in the IPCC report is not really coming from Antarctica, there must be some other contribution to sea level rise that is not accounted for."

"The new study highlights the difficulties of measuring the small changes in ice height happening in East Antarctica," chimed in Ben Smith, a glaciologist with the University of Washington in Seattle who was not involved in NASA's study.

So whom should one believe? IPCC? NASA? Somebody else? No one? At the University of Colorado-Colorado Springs, there is only one correct answer and no opportunity for debate: IPCC.

You may be thinking about where you are on climate change. Maybe you're wondering where this author stands on environmental issues. I'm glad you asked…

I believe, like many, that the issue isn't as simple as hardcore environmentalists and ardent opponents say. It's complex. Both sides have good arguments, to varying degrees, depending on the specific topic. Both are well funded enough to conduct ongoing research that backs their suppositions.

I believe some of our consumption over a long period of time has had a negative impact on the environment, significant in some areas of science, and more recently and especially in areas of the world like India and China. Remember when China shut down factories weeks in advance of the 2008 Olympics in Beijing in an attempt to clear the air? After the medals were awarded, the factories with little regulatory oversight started up again.

I believe the ocean's acidity has increased—30% by one study since the 1800's—which has stunted growth of coral reefs off the coast of Australia. I'm concerned when I hear about significant declines in the honeybee population, and the potential impact on pollination. I believe the ozone has deteriorated over the last 60 to 70 years and am glad aerosol cans have been outlawed.

I also believe we're doing great things that are being lost during this highly uncivil struggle. Significant improvements in air and water quality are being made through private and public investment in technologies via coal scrubbers and better storm water and wastewater management. Private industry, including Big Oil, is investing billions in cleaner energy technologies.

Evidence is around me, and I hope for you, too. Air quality, which has been a problem over the years in East Tennessee near the Smoky Mountains, has been improving. In fact, in summer 2017 the EPA concluded the entire state achieved compliance with federal air quality health standards for particle pollution, when the last five of 95 counties came into compliance. According to Tennessee's Department of Environment & Conservation the state has seen almost a 25% reduction in ozone pollution (smog) from 2000 to 2016 and a 50% reduction for particle pollution (soot) over the same period. This is great news that hardly made news.

Water quality is better, too. I recall seeing polluted rivers in the 1970s, like at my boyhood summer camp in Monterey, Tennessee, where no one would swim in or fish. I am glad those days are behind us and appreciate reasonable local, state and federal oversight that protects us.

Watching people attack, blame and shame, and not acknowledge progress, is frustrating. Wouldn't it be wiser to create urgency differently—get all the information, build consensus with stakeholders, then encourage, activate and incentivize better behavior and pursue reasonable, bipartisan and affordable energy policies? The all-out war on fossil fuels from the post-modern left is alienating and would damage our economy greatly. I share some urgency environmentalists have, but believe much harm will be done with some of the current proposed policies and tactics. Just ask the West Virginians that CNN's Van Jones interviewed.

Rewind to 25 years ago, when I read Al Gore's book *Earth in the Balance*. I recall his and others' assertions about global warming that grew in intensity in the years ahead. A rise in the number of major hurricanes, tsunamis, more powerful tornadoes, epic flooding events and more...

What does the UN's own IPCC say about hurricane activity over time?

Current data sets indicate no significant observed
trends in global tropical cyclone frequency over the

past century and it remains uncertain whether any
reported long-term increases in tropical cyclone fre-
quency are robust, after accounting for past changes
in observing capabilities...No robust trends in annu-
al numbers of tropical storms, hurricanes and major
hurricanes counts have been identified over the past
100 years in the North Atlantic basin.

What about tornado activity? According to the National Climatic Data Center (NCDC), part of the National Oceanic and Atmospheric Administration:

To better understand the variability and trend in
tornado frequency in the United States, the total num-
ber of EF-1 and stronger, as well as strong to violent
tornadoes (EF-3 to EF-5 category on the Enhanced
Fujita scale) can be analyzed. These tornadoes would
have likely been reported even during the decades
before Doppler radar use became widespread and
practices resulted in increasing tornado reports. The
bar charts below indicate there has been little trend in
the frequency of the stronger tornadoes over the past
55 years.

In fact, NCDC notes tornadoes at EF-3 and above have been less frequent, relative to the period from 1955-1975.

The IPCC previously reported droughts were on the rise, but later issued this statement after further study:

In summary, the current assessment concludes that
there is not enough evidence at present to suggest
more than low confidence in a global-scale observed
trend in drought or dryness (lack of rainfall) since the
middle of the 20th century, owing to lack of direct ob-
servations, geographical inconsistencies in the trends,
and dependencies of inferred trends on the index
choice. Based on updated studies, AR4 conclusions

regarding global increasing trends in drought since the
1970s were probably overstated.

So is all of this settled, as we have heard so confidently for many decades? Once again, is it "either-or," or is "both-and" possible? What about a scout mentality when new studies are released, such as over the last five years, that conflict with older studies?

If we insist on preaching instead of teaching young adults at our institutions of higher learning, we're inviting more coarseness and intransigence in the arena of public policy formation. We've cued up our media similarly, and we enable it too often around the dinner table and on social media.

We must unlearn "either-or," like any good Buddhist or Franciscan would advise. We need more "both-and" in our schools, as well as our homes, media and legislatures. That, and a whole lot more love of each other.

I came across this valuable approach with one of the aforementioned events—the campus event organized in favor of fossil fuels at the University of Michigan. UM President Mark Schlissel, who like many university administrators is dealing often with hard-lined camps, told event protesters he appreciated their "commitment and passion," and acknowledged their request to divest from fossil fuels.

"[Your concerns are not] linked to immoral and unethical actions and ideologies," he said. "Fossil fuels enable us to operate the university, to conduct research and to provide patient care. At this moment, there is no viable alternative to fossil fuels at the necessary scale. In addition, most of the same companies that extract or use fossil fuels are also investing heavily in a transition to natural gas or renewables, in response to market forces and regulatory activity. I do not believe that a persuasive argument has been made that divestment by the UM will speed up the necessary transition from coal to renewable or less polluting sources of energy."

Sounds like the kinda fella you could grab a beer with and talk through, reasonably, about most anything.

To be fair, we could pick a number of topics where conservatives say some matters are completely settled. But they're not being taught as gospel at our universities. Conservatives have a "my way or the highway" problem, too, but they haven't figured out (yet) how to include their views in college curriculums around the country. The make-ups of university administrations and faculties will have to change dramatically over the next generation or two before that would happen. Let's work to get the pendulum in the middle.

CRITICAL POINT:

Very few controversial or important issues are settled in life. Some universities are teaching that they are, which is infecting public discourse and our ability to come together to sort out and work on important issues, like protecting our environment.

ACTION STEP:

Engage your alma mater, children and circles of influence to avoid certainty. Seek and share illuminating or contrary information in a civil way. Debate, debate, debate! Support schools that foster this; withhold financial support from those that do not.

RESOURCES:

www.EndingOurUncivilWar.com

TRIGGERED: THE GROWING PROBLEM OF SAFE SPACES, CULTURAL APPROPRIATION, VICTIMIZATION AND DIVERSITY STATEMENTS

"Safe spaces, physical and intellectual, are for children. You are grown-ups now. If your diplomas mean anything, it's that it is time you leave those spaces behind forever."
—BRET STEPHENS, **NEW YORK TIMES** COLUMNIST AND FORMER **WALL STREET JOURNAL** COLUMNIST, IN HIS 2017 COMMENCEMENT SPEECH AT HAMPDEN-SYDNEY UNIVERSITY

"Playing the victim is another way to deal with pain indirectly. You blame someone else, and your pain becomes your personal ticket to power because it gives you a false sense of moral superiority and

outrage. You don't have to grow up, let go, forgive, or surrender—you just have to accuse someone else of being worse than you are. And sadly, that becomes your very fragile identity, which always needs more reinforcement."
                        —RICHARD ROHR, "AVOIDING TRANSFORMATION," 2017

"It's not happening to you. It's happening for you."
                        —MAUREEN DOYLE, AUTHOR AND LIFE COACH

In May 1991, Yale University President Benno Schmidt penned an editorial in *The Wall Street Journal* that expressed his growing concerns with the lockstep marching of thought control and conformity in our higher education system. The balance of the statement read:

> *The most serious problems of freedom of expression in the U.S. today exist on our campuses. Freedom of thought is in danger from well-intentioned but misguided efforts to give values of community and harmony a higher place than freedom. The assumption seems to be that the purpose of education is to induce 'correct' opinion rather than to search for wisdom and to liberate the mind.*
>
> *On many campuses, perhaps most, there is little resistance to growing pressure to suppress and to punish, rather than to answer, speech that offends notions of civility and community. These campuses are heedless of the oldest lesson in the history of freedom, which is that offensive, erroneous and obnoxious speech is the price of liberty. Values of civility, mutual respect and harmony are rightly prized within the university. But these values must be fostered by teaching and by example, and defended by expression. When the goals of harmony collide with freedom of expression, freedom must be the paramount obligation of an academic community.*

*Much expression that is free may deserve our contempt.
We may well be moved to exercise our own freedom
to counter it or to ignore it. But universities cannot
censor or suppress speech, no matter how obnoxious
in content, without violating their justification for existence. Liberal education presupposes that a liberated
mind will strive for the courage and composure to face
ideas that are fraught with evil, and to answer them.
To stifle expression because it is obnoxious, erroneous,
embarrassing, not instrumental to some political or
ideological end is—quite apart from the invasion of the
rights of others—a disastrous reflection on the idea of
the university. It is to elevate fear over the capacity for a
liberated and humane mind....*

*A more vexing question of freedom of expression con-
cerns the actual use of university authority to suppress
freedom. This is the most serious example of confusion
and failure of principle in university governance today.
It reminds us how frequently in history threats to free
expression have come not from tyranny but from
well-meaning persons of little understanding.*

Schmidt, who left Yale the next year and is now Chairman of the
Board at The City University of New York, can't be pleased with what's
happened since. In April 2017, The William F. Buckley Jr. Program at
Yale commissioned a survey by McLaughlin & Associates that polled
872 Yale undergraduates.

On the surface, the results would seem to lend reassurance to
Schmidt and others that free speech is alive and well on Yale's campus
and others. Only 5% of Yale students agreed that the school "should
forbid people from speaking on campus who have controversial views
and opinions on issues like politics, race, religion or gender." One
in six of Yale's students however, support "having speech codes to
regulate speech for students and faculty." While that's a minority, it's a
disturbing one, along with the 5% result. Other alarming results from
the survey reinforce Schmidt's warnings:

- More than 40% said they're "not comfortable" expressing their opinions in class on issues ranging from politics to race to gender; 75% of Republicans said they do not feel comfortable, while 74% of Democrats said they did.
- More than half the students said they feel "intimidated" about voicing their opinions in class; 83% were Republican, 51% Independent and 31% Democrat.
- Only 60% of students approve of the job Yale is doing promoting free speech; 76% of liberals approve, while 66% of conservatives disapproved.

Eye-popping numbers. But how has this manifested on the campuses of Yale and elsewhere? What are students experiencing? At Emerson College in downtown Boston, it's not easy if you're not in lockstep with the post-modern left students and faculty. Just ask the kids.

- "[Emerson] has been very not open to the idea of people who have different opinions and it's really come to a boiling point over the past few months." Sophomore Erik Picone said. "Anything I will say will be dismissed because I'm a straight white male. As if that has anything to do with the argument I'm saying."
- Freshman Lexie Kaufman said her first-year experience has been so "awful" that she's transferring after being called a white supremacist. "It's hostile and there's a lot of tension, just sitting in a classroom, you can literally feel these eyes on you and all this hate...."
- Junior Alyssa Galindo ironically has heard she's a "privileged little white girl." A Cuban-American like her grandparents who fled Cuba's communism and the Castro regime, she says, "I was also shocked with just the amount of bullying and labeling. I thought that was a political group that's so against that."
- Galindo called the 2016 presidential election "hell on earth." Kaufman, a Republican, said she did not leave her room for days because after Trump won, noting Emerson's president emailed the day after the election that the results were "tectonic" and faces on campus that "betrayed weariness, fatigue and

disillusionment.... Some of us feel as if our identities—our very beings—are under siege—that our virtuous hope for individual dignity and respect has been profoundly diminished and altered by this election." Picone, a Libertarian, said he got a pass from classmates because he didn't vote for Trump.

- Galindo says she believes her grading in a class suffered because she didn't agree with views in a class discussion about professors at a college dressed up for a Cinco De Mayo party, noting she didn't find it offensive and figured most other Hispanics wouldn't either. "I'm like, 'Am I seriously sitting here, a Hispanic, being told by other people what a Hispanic should be offended by?' I'm being told what I should be offended by."

Galindo, and millions of others, don't appreciate the cultural and political indoctrination.

THE INAPPROPRIATENESS OF CULTURAL APPROPRIATION

In 2015, you may recall an incident at Yale around the issue of cultural appropriation (also called misappropriation by some), which is the adoption or use of elements of one culture by members of another culture. If you played "Cowboys and Indians" in your backyard with young friends, some would have called that cultural appropriation, asserting the mere act is insensitive to the struggles Native Americans faced as white people took their lands and relocated them.

Before Halloween, Yale professor Erika Christakis, associate headmaster of the school's Silliman College, emailed the college's members and suggested they shouldn't be overly sensitive about Halloween costumes. She encouraged students to tolerate them and avoid censorship of expression.

"Is there no room anymore for a child or young person to be a little bit obnoxious... a little bit inappropriate or provocative or, yes, offensive?" she wrote. "American universities were once a safe space not only for maturation but also for a certain regressive, or even transgressive, experience; increasingly, it seems, they have become places of censure and prohibition."

Immediately, some students felt they had been triggered. Outraged, they called for the resignations of Christakis and her husband Nicholas, Silliman's headmaster. Black students and others said the couple's promotion of intolerance made it dangerous for students of color to have a safe experience.

When the headmaster met with students on campus, a tense encounter escalated, caught on video. They accused him of creating "an unsafe space." Here's how it went from there:

"I did not…" Christakis starts before being cut off.

"Be quiet!" a female black student yells. "[In] your position as headmaster, it is your job to create a place of comfort and home for the students who live in Silliman."

"No, I don't agree with that," he said, which was met with a backlash of shrieks.

"Then why the f*** did you accept the position? Who the f*** hired you? You should step down! If that is what you think of being headmaster, you should step down! It is not about creating an intellectual space! It is not!"

"You're supposed to be our advocate!" says a black male.

The attack continues, as she asserts students will transfer because of the failure to provide a "safe space."

"You should not sleep at night! You're disgusting!" as she ends her tirade and the crowd disperses.

Such "safe space" nonsense must be confronted early and swiftly, which occurred at Northern Arizona University in March 2017. During a forum, NAU sophomore Breanna Kramer asked President Rita Cheng about "situations of injustice, such as, last week, when we had the preacher on campus and he was promoting hate speech against marginalized students? As well as, not speaking out against racist incidents like blackface two months ago by student workers followed by no reform and no repercussions?"

Cheng's response was civil, measured and firm: "As a university professor, I'm not sure I have any support at all for safe space. I think that you as a student have to develop the skills to be successful in this world and that we need to provide you with the opportunity for discourse and debate and dialogue and academic inquiry, and I'm not sure that that is correlated with the notion of safe space…"

A few dozen students, mostly members of the NAU Student Action Coalition, walked out, demanded their safe space and called for Cheng's firing.

Wisely, Cheng did not retreat. Later, her spokesperson affirmed: "NAU is safe. Creating segregated spaces for different groups on our campus only [leads] to misunderstanding, distrust and [reduces] the opportunity for discussion and engagement and education around diversity. Our classrooms and our campus is a place for engagement and respect—a place to learn from each other. NAU is committed to an atmosphere that is conducive to teaching and learning."

As good as this response was, universities should be more proactive and less reactive to students behaving like this. One opportunity is to offer and even require freshmen to take courses in civil discourse. These already exist at some schools, but all universities should consider expanding offerings, given the growing calls for safe spaces, charges of faux racism and sexism (amid real racism and sexism), and cultural appropriation.

Though not a freshman, I learned a lot at Lipscomb University's "Politics, Morality and Civility" forum based on the great essay from Czechoslovakian President Václav Havel in 1991.

We discussed how Havel worked in theater before becoming an outspoken dissident against communism. He was arrested four times and spent four years in jail, refusing a government offer to emigrate to the United States. He knew *how* to protest for human rights and social justice. After the communist fall in 1989, he was elected the country's first president. He spoke to Congress in 1990 and warned our nation about complacency and the dangers of new technology.

At Australia's National Press Club in 1995, he warned against "putting our faith in the essentially atheistic technological civilization of today." Instead, he observed, "Our present civilization, having lost the awareness the world has a spirit, believes that anything is permitted."

A believer in God and a great friend of the Dalai Lama, he said, "Humankind, having lost its respect for a higher authority, has inevitably lost respect for earthly authority as well. Consequently, people also lose respect for their fellow humans and eventually even for themselves."

In his 1991 essay, Havel observed, "They say a nation gets the politicians it deserves. In some senses, this is true: politicians are indeed a mirror of their society, and a kind of embodiment of its potential. At the same time, the opposite is true: society is a mirror of its politicians."

Imagine a freshman debating such topics, in the context of tweets he's seeing from the president, or maybe those of his classmates or his own. Imagine a course with writings from Havel and Alexis de Tocqueville, and Thomas Jefferson's letter on church and state, all of which are read and debated, applied in context to today's controversies.

Contrast this opportunity with what some students are experiencing in their classes. Like at Bethel University in Minnesota, where a professor repeatedly confronted a student publicly for wearing a Chicago Blackhawks hockey sweatshirt to class. The student is from Chicago. But it gets worse.

The professor, whose class "Social Perspectives, Human Worth and Social Action" delves into themes of culture, power and oppression in America, confronted the Chicagoan, Cody Albrecht, who offered to turn it inside out "after becoming aware of the unease in his classroom because of his sweatshirt," according to the *Clarion* student newspaper. Still upset, instructor James "Jim Bear" Jacobs took to Facebook to vent his frustration.

"So your college professor is a Native American. A Native American who has spoken multiple times about the offensiveness of Indian Mascots. Yet you come to class with an Indian mascot sprawled across your shirt...Bold move sir."

A week later, after talking with administration officials, Albrecht issued a formal apology to the class. Jacobs called it a teachable moment: "I'm glad to say that this became an incredible learning opportunity for the student [sic] we had a lengthy conversation about it and the student really listened to why those images are offensive and hurtful," posted Jacobs.

A Bethel University campus spokesperson avoided a media inquiry, citing "respect of the privacy of the individuals involved and their ongoing reconciliation." Several students called out the incident for what it was: public shaming.

"It was not necessary to get the head of his major's department involved," said one student. "They were using intimidation tactics."

Said another: "The professor needs to start teaching his students how to think instead of force-feeding them his fringe opinion."

"Is this satire?" asked another.

Another used humor: "This seems pretty ridiculous. Although, as a [Minnesota] Wild fan I am pretty triggered by the Blackhawks."

In June 2017, the U.S. Supreme Court considered a case, *Matal v. Tam*, which speaks to incidents like at Bethel. In an 8 – 0 decision, the high court ruled against the U.S. Patent and Trademark Office's decision that an Asian-American band's use of the term "Slants" for its rock band was a violation of the "disparagement clause."

Justice Samuel Alito wrote for the court: "This provision violates the Free Speech Clause of the First Amendment. It offends a bedrock First Amendment principle: Speech may not be banned on the ground that it expresses ideas that offend." Liberal justices Ruth Bader Ginsburg, Stephen Breyer, Sonia Sotomayor and Elena Kagan also see what's going on and are having none of it. This is great news for free speech.

The cultural appropriation war and whining about mascots like the Cleveland Indians' Chief Wahoo and the name of Washington Redskins is backfiring, in our courts though not in our classrooms. Similarly, in 2014 the trademark office ruled the Redskins violated its "disparagement" clause. In 2016, the *Washington Post* polled Native Americans' feelings about the Redskins logo. The percentage offended? 9%.

MISSISSIPPI BURNING

I recently re-watched the movie *Mississippi Burning*, with Gene Hackman and Willem Dafoe. In one of the opening scenes, a young black man drinks water from a fountain with a sign that says, "Colored," next to another fountain that says, "Whites."

We've come a long way since 1964, but some on college campuses don't seem to remember history well. Separation and segregation, exactly what Dr. King opposed vigorously, are on the rise. In 2017:

- One hundred black Harvard graduate students held their own ceremony separate from the university.
- The University of Colorado Boulder announced the creation of a new residence hall called the "Living Learning Community" for "black-identified students and their allies" to provide a "supportive, social and communal space for students" who identify with "elements of the African & Black Diaspora."
- A coalition of student groups called "UChicago United" gave that university's administration a list of 50 demands, including creation of a "Race and Ethnic Studies Department," a "Black

Studies Academic Department," an "African Studies Department," a "Caribbean Studies Department," an "Asian American Studies Program," a "Center for African and Caribbean Studies" and a "Latinx Affairs Office."

- At Evergreen State College in Washington state, black and white students threatened biology professor Bret Weinstein with violence for refusing to leave campus during a so-called "Day of Absence," during which whites are supposed to stay off campus so students of color can have a safe space to meet and commiserate. Police told Weinstein to stay off campus because they did not believe they could protect him, while campus officials promised to work with activists "to address their issues."

- Schools are separating their students by race in various workshops and classes. Kennesaw State University held a workshop on privilege and interracial relations and asked "those who identify as white" to go to one room and "those who identify as people of color" to go to another. According to Heatstreet, the University of Wisconsin-Madison, the University of Michigan and Concordia University also faced accusations of segregation after holding events divided by race or focused on one particular racial group.

These actions and demands, along with an increase in the number of "hate hoaxes," are counterproductive and undermine what should be done to counter the real xenophobia and sexism that exist in our society. One such swindle occurred at St. Olaf College in 2017, when Samantha Wells, a black female student, claimed to have found a typewritten note on her car that used the n-word. Wells posted the note on Facebook:

"I am so glad that you are leaving soon. One less [n-word] that this school has to deal with. You have spoken up too much. You will change nothing. Shut up or I will shut you up."

After Wells' claim, angry students blocked entrances to the college cafeteria and situated on the student commons demanding retribution. The school canceled classes to allow demonstrators to protest and hold a daylong sit-in. Protesters posted signs like "I'm sick of white tears" and "F*** your white complacency." "

The car note was the latest in a string of alleged racial incidents at the private Lutheran college. Wells had told the local Fox affiliate it was "the third incident this week." The school's president told Minnesota Public Radio there had been nine recently reported incidents. When evidence couldn't point to specific perpetrators, administrators grew wary.

Later, Wells asked that the incident not be investigated and backed off earlier charges: "I will be saying it was a hoax. I don't care....I did not have to admit anything because there is nothing to admit."

There was no apparent disciplinary action against Wells. Other recent hate hoaxes occurred at the University of Southern California, where a black student posted a "no black people allowed" sign outside of a residence hall; at Indiana State University, where a professor was arrested for "reporting phony anti-Islamic threats; at the University of Michigan, where a young woman revealed that she had lied about a pro-Trump hate crime and made up an attack on herself; and at Capital University, where a student admitted to fabricating a hate-filled note posted on his door.

At Chico State University in California, Lindsay Briggs, a white human sexuality professor, went to social media to attack a student of color for a column in the student newspaper, *The Orion*, and then the paper and its editor as well. Undergraduate Roberto Fonseca's had questioned data from the school's Gender and Sexuality Equity Center that one in five college women will be raped as well as the existence of "systemic racism." Briggs put Fonseca, a registered Democrat whose parents emigrated from Nicaragua, in the crosshairs. Said Briggs:

"What in the everloving f*** The Orion? F*** you, Roberto Fonseca. This is garbage....GAHHHHH, SO ENRAGED."

Rage on our campuses is one problem. Another is complacency and tolerance of the intolerant, like at Evergreen State, which went under the national spotlight after a series of bizarre incidents. The school's board waited nearly two months after Professor Weinstein's "Day of Absence" protest to post on its website that it is "deeply committed to ensuring that Evergreen provides a civil, safe campus environment for all" and "the conduct of a small percentage of Evergreen's community members exhibited unacceptable behavior that is completely contrary to Evergreen's values." There was no mention of punishment or suspension of any offending students, but the trustees added, "The tumultuous events...have revealed the need to delve further into issues of diversity and equity at Evergreen. Going forward, the college will take a measured approach, which is crucial to ensure that we respond appropriately, rather than reactively."

They might as well have issued wrestling suits to students. Here's what happened at Evergreen between mid-April and mid-June 2017.

A video of students berating the school's president, George Bridges, surfaced. Students said:

—"F*** you, and f*** the police!"

—"Whiteness is the most violent f***** system to ever breathe!"

—"These white-a** faculty members need to be holding him…and all these people accountable!"

—"F*** you, George, we don't wanna listen to a g***** thing you have to say! No, you shut the f*** up!"

After students learned the video was in the public realm, the activists said the video "created for Day of Absence and Day of Presence that was stolen by white supremacists and edited to expose and ridicule the students [be] taken down by the administration by this Friday." Further, they promised to "seek criminal charges against the individual in consultation with the Attorney General."

They had many demands. Here are a few to which Bridges timidly responded in the *Cooper Point Journal*:

"We demand that no changes to the student code of conduct be made without democratic student consent."

Bridges: "As of today, we're not contemplating any action associated with the demonstrations of the last two weeks, but we can't control what complaints we might receive. If we receive complaints, we'll need to follow up on them.… The current code of conduct remains in place until a revised code is developed. With this timeline in place, a revised code would be submitted that adheres to state law and our campus needs by winter 2018.

"We demand [firing of several university personnel]."

"We demand Bret Weinstein be suspended immediately without pay but all students receive full credit."

Bridges: "We do not and will not fire any employees in response to a request. We do take complaints seriously. We have a college non-discrimination policy which applies to all members of our community.... We must increase our capacity to investigate instances of alleged discrimination. Therefore, we have decided to increase the college's Affirmative Action and Equal Opportunity Officer to full time today."

"We demand the immediate disarming of police services and no expansion of police facilities or services at any point in the future."

Bridges: "The Police Services Community Review Board will review police response to calls and complaints received on May 14 and May 16. A timeline for this review will be finalized by the end of next week. As you know, the Review Board doesn't include individuals from the President's Office or Police Services. Many of whom on the board are people of color.... We intend to retain a campus police force that understands and is responsive to the unique needs of our college campus."

"We demand the creation of an equity center."

Bridges: "Today we commit to establishing a new and expanded equity and multicultural center with design plans finalized for student review by the beginning of fall quarter this year. You will have the space that you seek and deserve."

At least 71 faculty members supported the students' wish list. They sent a letter to Bridges calling for none of the students to be disciplined under "the misguided language of the current Student Conduct Code" and "actions to counter 'alt-right narratives that are demonizing Evergreen and Day of Absence specifically.'" The saved the worst for last, saying Bridges must "demonstrate accountability by pursuing a disciplinary investigation against Bret Weinstein according to guidelines in the Social Contract and Faculty Handbook. Weinstein has endangered faculty, staff, and students, making them targets of white supremacist backlash by promulgating misinformation in public emails, on national television, in news outlets, and on social media."

Bridges' and the board's tepid and ill-advised actions will only enable more ridiculous demands and disorderly behavior. Only protection of the three administrators' jobs, which Bridges should have assertively stated, made sense. The rest of the responses might as well have said: "You, the mob, are in charge. Our code of conduct and free speech mean nothing, like my words, so let's head in the other direction."

This series of events, obviously, is one of the more extreme of what's happening across the country. It invites the question: What are many universities really in the business of—teaching our students the liberal arts, life's complexities, the beauty of learning everything we can about these challenges and preparing them for careers? Or is it holding their hands and enabling radical and sometimes dangerous behavior?

Administrators at the University of Hawaii also seem fine with bizarre assertions from faculty. There, Piper Harron, an assistant professor at the University of Hawaii, with a doctorate degree in mathematics from Princeton University, called on white men to "Get Out The Way" in a disconcerting blog post.

"Not to alarm you, but I probably want you to quit your job, or at least take a demotion," she wrote. "Statistically speaking, you are probably taking up room that should go to someone else. If you are a white cis man (meaning you identify as male and you were assigned male at birth) you almost certainly should resign from your position of power.... What can universities do? Well, that's easier. Stop hiring white cismen (except as needed to get/retain people who are not white cis men) until the problem goes away. If you think this is a bad or un-serious idea, your sexism/racism/transphobia is showing."

Worse than tolerating obvious racism, schools are promoting it. A college guidebook co-published by Haverford, Swarthmore and Bryn

Mawr colleges claims blacks are incapable of being racist, and that racism is a one-way street.

"Reverse racism does not actually exist, because racism is a structure, and people of color do not structurally oppress white people," the online guide states. "Most social justice activists agree that 'Reverse Racism' doesn't make sense."

I totally disagree with that, but if a university wanted to have a fair, protected classroom discussion about it, let the debate begin. Allowed to continue, much of higher education will go into lower and lower depths.

Another example of cultural appropriation gone wild occurred after a basketball game between hometown Hampshire College in Amherst, Massachusetts and Central Maine Community College in March 2017. This time the trigger was braided hair.

After the game, Carmen Figueroa, a 20-year-old Hampshire student, approached members of Central Maine's team and said one of the team's players, a white woman with braided hair, had to remove the braids. She declined, setting off Figueroa, who yelled racial slurs amid charges of cultural appropriation. Players attempted to intervene, but not before Figueroa "grabbed [the player] by the head and threw her to the ground."

Figueroa may have been just as angry by the final score, a 91 – 39 victory by Central Maine. Nonetheless, she pleaded not guilty to charges of disorderly conduct, assault and battery, and assault and battery with a dangerous weapon.

The philosophy of cultural appropriation and these excessive reactions diminish the real racism that remains on college campuses and should be exposed. I can recall several instances at my alma mater, Vanderbilt University, in the 1980s.

One in particular during my Greek life experience will stay with me forever: A fraternity brother who was openly prejudiced refused to allow the first African-American into our fraternity. With his solitary racist vote, we lost an opportunity to break down another barrier and share brotherhood with a vibrant young man with whom we shared values of service and respect.

Don't think this kind of thing doesn't still go on. I hear it from my children and their friends, especially from students attending some southern schools. Racism is very real in our culture. It must be exposed and rejected whenever we see it.

The hyperventilating behavior at Maine and Yale is emblematic of a trend that's not helping, if true tolerance and openness to each other's ideas, assimilations and customs are the shared goals. And they have to be if we are to navigate difficult, complex issues. Consensus doesn't mean acquiescing or rolling over, nor does it mean the domination attempts and even condescension we're seeing from various factions within our culture.

President Obama said as much at a Des Moines town hall in September 2015: "I've heard of some college campuses where they don't want to have a guest speaker who is too conservative, or they don't want to read a book if it had language that is offensive to African Americans or somehow sends a demeaning signal towards women.... I've got to tell you, I don't agree with that either—that when you become students at colleges, you have to be coddled and protected from different points of view. Anybody who comes to speak to you and you disagree with, you should have an argument with them, but you shouldn't silence them by saying you can't come because I'm too sensitive to hear what you have to say."

ALT-RIGHT AIN'T RIGHT, EITHER

The alt-right isn't helping the situation at all.

These uber-provocateurs, backed by well-funded conservative groups, are throwing out a rope that the post-modern left is grabbing quickly, thus "triggering" escalating campus tug-of-wars. Further proliferation of these wars should be of great concern to all who want our higher education system and liberal arts culture to flourish.

One such group is the Young America's Foundation (YAF), whose mission is unabashedly "to restore sanity at your school." It is well funded and organized. Stephen Miller, a White House adviser, is an alumnus.

The foundation, according to the *New York Times*, "teaches essentials such as when it is legal to record a conversation with a college administrator; how to press schools to cover some of the security costs; regulations on sidewalk chalking, fliers and other forms of promotion and whether they can be challenged; and when to call the foundation's legal staff for help." Nothing wrong there, as that's essential homework. But the tactical provoking isn't helping matters on campuses.

YAF also provides "conservative swag" such as instructions for staging a funeral for the death of Halloween, a swipe at efforts like at Yale University to discourage offensive costumes, and "posters to distribute on Sept. 11 featuring vivid depictions of the World Trade Center attacks and terrorist beheadings."

Hmmm. Is that necessary?

That's part of what went down at the University of Buffalo on May 1, 2017. Nearly 200 angry students drowned out the evening's featured speaker, Robert Spencer, a conservative author and blogger who espouses a dark view of Islam. Spencer appeared at the invitation of a conservative student club, one of 250 college and high school chapters across the country funded by YAF. I support Spencer's right to speak, the club's right to organize and YAF's right to fund it all. Radical leftist George Soros is running the same gig on campuses and elsewhere.

But I would argue that's not all that's going on here. YAF President Ron Robinson said the group's goal is simply "to increase appreciation and support of conservative ideas, not to stir up leftists or Muslims." However, says Robinson, "If you disagree with [Mr.] Spencer... don't come to his lecture, don't call attention to him."

So which is it? Are they seeking to restore sanity by engaging the alt-left, as they obviously did in Buffalo, or are they pulling out their gospel and reading to each other? Those meetings would be quite small at most colleges today.

Don't Spencer's words also sound similarly defensive and dismissive, like the Colorado professors who won't allow dissenting views in their climate change class? Along with YAF's recruitment rhetoric to restore campus sanity, it would appear part of the goal is to drop some bombs and then leave in a huff. That's how one professor at the University of Missouri, Craig Roberts, received it when Ben Shapiro, supported by YAF, spoke at his school in 2015.

Roberts agreed with some of Shapiro's points, characterizing his rhetoric as "very eloquent and energetic.... But I would say energetic to the point of inflammatory—militant.

"It's not the kind of speech where we're trying to come together and figure this out."

In 2016 at the University of Michigan, YAF-backed speaker David Horowitz called Black Lives Matter the "most vicious racist movement this country has seen since the Ku Klux Klan at its heyday." Many Americans, myself included, certainly question some (not all) tactics of Black Lives Matter, but "the KKK at its heyday?" Extreme, meet extreme.

Back in Buffalo, Pasha Syed, an imam from a local mosque, and Robert Spencer sparred in vigorous debate over religion-backed violence. Spencer read from the Quran, arguing it says "jihad is obligatory for everyone able to perform it, male and female." Countering, Syed cited a New Testament passage about killing one's enemies. The club's outnumbered conservative students, who stood up front near Spencer, scoffed at their fellow classmates, who jeered back.

"The forces you are enabling are going to come back to haunt you," Spencer warned. One could argue Spencer was both correct about his adversaries' assertions *and his own.*

It would seem this meeting wasn't about a fair exchange of what truths might exist, but something much darker. Shame fights shame, and blame battles blame, with little room for understanding of alternative viewpoints or an attempt to find some common ground, as Roberts observed in Missouri. Enlightenment wasn't making an appearance in Buffalo or Missouri; fear and shame were. That, in a nutshell, is the growing danger on too many college campuses.

A dear friend in academia emailed me observations, with a proposed solution, in early 2017: "Some people on the right deliberately are trying to provoke the unacceptable behavior of some people on the left. If protesting leftists were smarter, they would organize counter-rallies at separate venues rather than immorally seeking to abridge the free speech rights of their opponents. Nothing would demoralize [YAF and its followers and funders] more than a recurrence of half-empty lecture halls."

"All this furor is exactly what [the alt right] is aiming to create. The sad part is, the extremists on both sides feed each other, and the overall culture undergoes a further infusion of polarization and hate."

The tonic is simple. We must rise above all brands of radicalism. Concerned alumni and communities must engage university administrations to take control of these situations and encourage campus activists and leaders to protest in ways that maintain the *peaceful* constitutional rights we share. Ridiculing and intimidating our fellow man is not acceptable, and not liberal arts in its true sense.

Let's look more closely at what's driving the fearful response from the alt-right and what we should do about it.

BAD TEQUILA IN MAINE

There is commonsense among us. People like novelist Lionel Shriver, an American living in London, are exposing nonsense through persuasive arguments and even a little humor.

At the 2016 Brisbane Literary Festival in Australia, Shriver gave a keynote speech "Fiction and Identity Politics," arguing that accusations of cultural appropriation threaten authors' rights to write fiction at all.

"I am hopeful that the concept of 'cultural appropriation' is a passing fad," he said. "People with different backgrounds rubbing up against each other and exchanging ideas and practices is self-evidently one of the most productive, fascinating aspects of modern urban life. But this latest and little absurd no-no is part of a larger climate of super-sensitivity, giving rise to proliferating prohibitions supposedly in the interest of social justice that constrain fiction writers and prospectively makes our work impossible."

Shriver then recounted a prime example, a recent "tempest-in-a-teacup" at Bowdoin College in Brunswick, Maine. There, two students who were members of student government threw a tequila-themed birthday party and provided "attendees with miniature sombreros, which—the horror—numerous partygoers wore," she explained.

After photos of the party circulated on social media, disgust and outrage ensued. Explained Shriver:

> *Administrators sent multiple emails to the "culprits" threatening an investigation into an "act of ethnic stereotyping." Partygoers were placed on "social probation," while the two hosts were ejected from their dorm and later impeached. Bowdoin's student newspaper decried the attendees' lack of "basic empathy."*
>
> *The student government issued a "statement of solidarity" with "all the students who were injured and affected by the incident," and demanded that administrators "create a safe space for those students who have been or feel specifically targeted." The tequila party, the statement specified, was just the sort of occasion that "creates an environment where students of color, particularly Latino, and especially Mexican, feel unsafe." In sum,*

the party-favor hats constituted—wait for it—"cultural appropriation."

Curiously, across my country, Mexican restaurants, often owned and run by Mexicans, are festooned with sombreros—if perhaps not for long. At the U.K.'s University of East Anglia, the student union has banned a Mexican restaurant from giving out sombreros, deemed once more an act of "cultural appropriation" that was also racist.

After noting many books that never would have been written or shelved at campus libraries under the current policing of thought amid tequila-infused revelry, Shriver noted other examples of misplaced cultural modifiers.

- At the 2013 American Music Awards 2013, Katy Perry, dressed like a geisha, was dressed down by Arab-American writer Randa Jarrar for practicing belly dancing for its "white appropriation of Eastern dance."
- The *Daily Beast* accused Iggy Azalea for committing "cultural crimes" by imitating African rap and speaking in a "blaccent."
- A yoga teacher at the University of Ottawa in Canada was shamed into suspending her class, "because yoga originally comes from India." She offered to rename the course, "Mindful Stretching." I would have suggested, "Stretching Small Minds."
- Students at Oberlin College in Ohio, led by supporters like cultural fire-alarm puller Lena Dunham, protested 'culturally appropriated food' like sushi in their dining hall,...whose inauthenticity is "insensitive" to the Japanese.

Cultural appropriation is everywhere, even on campuses in the Deep South. In 2015, Clemson University officially apologized for a Mexican-themed dorm cafeteria food night. Sound familiar? The school also paid nearly $30,000 to an outside vendor to produce online diversity training materials that in part instructed professors that it is wrong to expect students to be on time.

One person's "cultural perspective regarding time is neither more nor less valid than any other," materials advise taxpayer-funded professors. If you own a business, you know one of the greatest challenges is finding trainable, qualified workers. One soft skill is being on time. At Clemson, this soft skill is being taught as racist. This is a disservice to the taxpayer and especially the student who is learning such rubbish.

According to Campus Reform, one slide tells Clemson's faculty that "freedom of speech and academic freedom are not limitless," adding this Orwellian threat: "Language that is derogatory with regard to race, sex, or other protected or emerging forms of diversity does not belong in a university that values inclusion."

This sensitivity may feel good to some, but is it legal? Does the school understand that the Civil Rights Act of 1964 and other laws speak—or do not speak—on such matters? What is case law, nationally and in South Carolina? Is a make it up as we go approach the right and legal way to determine diversity issues? And what does "emerging forms of diversity" mean?

"I PLEDGE ALLEGIANCE . . . TO THE UNIVERSITY"

Universities are adopting their own tactics to advance—and enforce—such theories and approaches.

First, hiring practices at some schools clearly show a preference to include more educators who are center-left, left or alt-left.

There are few Republican faculty members on our campuses, especially in journalism, psychology, English, and sociology departments. Some polls show the ratio of Democrat to Republican teachers as five-to-one and as high as 20-to-1 at some schools. At certain schools, nearly 100% of political campaign contributions from liberal arts faculty go to Democrats. At Cornell University, 97% of faculty contributions to politicians went to Democrats. At Georgetown University, it's 96%.

Ironically, schools that preach diversity don't have much political diversity in their faculties. Their one-sided workforces don't look much like most workforces off campuses, which often have a broad mix of Democrats, Republicans, Independents, Libertarians and others. The true victims are their students, who too often leave their safe spaces and like-minded worlds, and find great difficulty adjusting to complex realities, thoughts and speech that conflict with what they've been hearing for years.

Second, more universities are requiring professors to pledge allegiance—often illegally—to advance their agendas. Some of the conformity push is soft, like at Clemson. At other schools, it's much harder.

The University of California at San Diego, for instance, has the following on their website:

> *Since 2010, UC San Diego has required that faculty candidates submit a statement on their past contributions to diversity or equity and future plans for continuing this effort as part of their application for an academic appointment. In addition to research, teaching, and general professional and public service, service contributions that promote diversity and equal opportunity are encouraged and given recognition in the evaluation of the candidate's qualifications.*

This goes far beyond what should be required of faculty members. It is a different standard of hiring that is illegal or extra-legal. As citizens—and employers and employees—we are required to follow our laws, which include protections for all citizens. The vast majority of us were not recruited to state our past contributions to diversity as a prerequisite for hiring. We were hired to do a specific job!

When we're hired, we acknowledge the equal opportunity clauses in our laws without a loyalty oath or recount of our actions to promote diversity. When our job performance is reviewed, we're rated on how well we met our individual goals that contributed to company or organizational success. We're rated often on our competence and performance, as well as on teamwork, adaptability and work ethic.

It's the same on the other side of our country. Virginia Tech says in its hiring process "[that] candidates should include a list of activities that promote or contribute to inclusive teaching, research, outreach, and service." In fact, there are at least 20 other schools that already have diversity pledges, according to a 2017 report by the Oregon Association of Scholars (OAS). They include Carnegie-Mellon University, the University of Oregon, Oregon Health & Science University, Oregon

State University, and Portland State University. Since 2005, the University of California system has required mandatory diversity statements for all new faculty hires.

Dr. Bruce Gilley is president of OAS and a professor of Political Science at Portland State. His report has several key takeaways.

- "…Mandatory 'diversity statement' threatens to become a 'fifth document' in faculty hiring and promotion at many universities (in addition to cover letter, curriculum vitae, research statement, and teaching statement)."
- "Diversity statements are only a small part of the attempt to reconfigure higher education based on a partisan ideology of social engineering…. [They] represent a clear and imminent threat to academic freedom and research excellence, although the more corrosive and insidious effects of the broader diversity agenda should not be ignored."
- "…Classical liberal approaches, that emphasize the pluralism of a free society, the universalism of human experiences, and the importance of equality before the law, have been regarded as invalid…. More broadly, the idea of a university as a place where leading scholars are protected from any ideological imposition is also rejected."

Concludes Gilley: "Diversity statements are *de facto* [tools] to weed out non-left wing scholars."

George Leef with the James G. Martin Center for Academic Renewal says, "College diversity agendas are little more than a call for ideological conformity…. The last thing that diversity hustlers want is diversity in ideas." He compares these pledges to the persistent demands in the 1940s and 1950s for national loyalty oaths. "In those days, people were expected to declare their support for the U.S. and if they didn't, they could be blackballed, expelled, or otherwise punished."

He suggests "diversity statements can be challenged on First Amendment grounds. In a famous rebuke to ideology intruding on education, the Supreme Court held in the 1943 case *West Virginia Board of Education v. Barnette* that the state could not penalize Jehovah's Witness students for failure to recite the Pledge of Allegiance.

Justice Jackson's majority opinion speaks to the same issues raised by mandatory diversity statements.

Penned Jackson, "Struggles to coerce uniformity of sentiment in support of some end thought essential to their time and country have been waged by many good, as well as evil men...It seems trite but necessary to say that the First Amendment to our Constitution was designed to avoid these ends by avoiding these beginnings...If there is any fixed star in our constitutional constellation, it is that no official, high or petty, can prescribe what shall be orthodox in politics, nationalism, religion, or other matters of opinion, or force citizens to confess by word or act their faith therein."

It is worth noting the U.S. Supreme Court struck down loyalty oaths as a condition of employment in 1964. It found laws in the state of Washington requiring state employees to take loyalty oaths to be invalid. The case involved more than 60 faculty members, staff and students of the University of Washington, and was organized by the Washington chapter of the American Civil Liberties Union (ACLU) and the UW chapter of the American Association of University Professors. The court ruled that both a 1955 statute requiring all state employees to swear they are not "subversive persons" and a 1931 statute requiring teachers to swear to promote respect for government institutions are unconstitutionally vague and violate due process."

Loyalty oaths were omnipresent during the Cold War. Between 1947 and 1956, 42 states and more than 2,000 local jurisdictions adopted laws requiring such oaths from public employees. Today, university diversity statements look eerily like the loyalty oaths of yesteryear.

Legislation may be another avenue for a fix, says Leef. The Higher Education Act could be amended with suggestions from the National Association of Scholars, including amending "Title IV to say that no school that receives federal funds may require any current or prospective faculty member to declare his or her position on or actions regarding any political or social issue."

In 2014, Benno Schmidt returned to deliver a talk at Yale's commencement. Titled "Governance for a New Era" and subtitled "A Blueprint for Higher Education Trustees," Schmidt challenged leaders in higher education to increase academic standards and a culture of independence.

*Trustees should adopt policies that maintain institu-
tional neutrality and distance from political fashion
and pressure. They should take note of and endorse
the principles of the report issued by the Kalven Committee of the University of Chicago, outlining the university's proper role in political and social action: 'To
perform its mission in the society, a university must
sustain an extraordinary environment of freedom of
inquiry and maintain an independence from political
fashions, passions and pressures.' The 'instrument of
dissent and criticism is the individual faculty member
or the individual student. The university is the home
and sponsor of critics; it is not itself the critic. It
is... a community of scholars.' The Kalven Committee
observed that the 'neutrality of the university... arises
out of a respect for free inquiry and the obligation to
cherish a diversity of viewpoints.'*

*The bottom line: With the future of higher education
'in jeopardy,' you, the trustees, need to take charge.*

What do you think about Schmidt's advice? What does your seatmate think about it?

If you and he believe any university should be "the home and
sponsor of critics" and show "respect for free inquiry and the obligation to cherish a diversity of viewpoints," we have work to do.

Here's how we can join Schmidt, President Obama, Van Jones,
Professor Gilley, President Cheng, and other leaders.

CRITICAL POINT:

Free speech on many college campuses is under direct threat through diversity statements, use of safe spaces and cultural appropriation.

ACTION STEP:

Colleges and universities should:

- Establish or maintain basic protections and procedures for anyone who wants to speak and be heard on their campuses.
- Invite and protect speakers with diverse views.
- Remove disorderly or violent people immediately.
- Penalize students for violating school codes of conduct and rules that guarantee civic gatherings. This should include warnings, suspensions and expulsion, on an escalating scale, along with financial penalties and/or withholding scholarship monies.
- Offer, if not require, first-year courses on the importance of civil discourse and free speech.
- Eliminate diversity pledges and safe spaces and teach about the danger of cultural appropriation as threats to free speech.
- Require faculty to use the balance of class time on approved course topics, not as a platform to espouse personal political or social views.

Their boards of directors should:

- Support the above requirements and objectives.
- Hold school officials accountable by being proactive in protecting all speakers and free speech. Administrators who ignore their role to promote and protect freedom of speech should be warned and then fired. Contracts should be drafted to reflect the importance of this part of their job description.

Alumni should:
- Support the above requirements and objectives.
- Stop writing checks until their alma mater shows a commitment to free, protected speech.
- Speak out publicly and not send their children to schools with intolerant policies.

State governments should:
- Support the above requirements and objectives.
- Withhold public funds for extreme abuses of free speech and runaway political correctness that violates the constitutional rights of others.

RESOURCES:

Visit the website for Foundation for Individual Rights in Education (FIRE) and find where your school is on free speech protections, then engage.

https://www.thefire.org
www.EndingOurUncivilWar.com

CONTEMPLATION:

"If your ego is still in charge, you will find a disposable person or group on which to project your problems."
—RICHARD ROHR, JESUS REVEALS THE LIE OF SCAPEGOATING," 2016

WHY WE NEED GOVERNMENT GUARDRAILS

"There are men of principle in both parties in America,
but there is no party of principle."
—ALEXIS DE TOCQUEVILLE, DEMOCRACY IN AMERICA, 1835

Five years after America's bloody Civil War, Tennesseans were reeling.
If the loss of life and property weren't enough to deal with, state affairs had become very untidy under the regime of Governor William Brownlow. The Republican chief executive had directed county election commissioners to block Confederate supporters and sympathizers from voting. Brownlow also made efforts to enfranchise blacks across the state, fueling the ire of resentful Democrats who stayed loyal to the spirit of the Confederacy. Not surprisingly, the Ku Klux Klan began to grow.

Under Brownlow and a dysfunctional Legislature made up of many radicals, state debt soared. Railroad bonds that had matured in 1867 and 1868 went unpaid. People had endured a great Civil War, but, with disagreements over voting rights, racial tensions, mounting debts and government's growing inability to solve problems or even meets its requirements. They were now locked in uncivil combat.

You might say not much has changed. Political and spiritual peril isn't a new threat to our union.

When Tennessee's General Assembly chose Brownlow in 1869 to serve in the U.S. Senate, the more moderate Lt. Gov. Dewitt Senter stepped in as governor. Senter worked to restore the vote to ex-Confederate leaders and soldiers, while energy for a constitutional convention grew. The people wanted systemic reforms to end the heavy-handedness, misrepresentation and corruption in their government.

At Tennessee's Convention of 1870, held at the Davidson County Courthouse in January of that year, profound changes were proposed to limit inattentive, poorly functioning government and provide individuals with certain unalienable rights.

Some proposals mirrored the federal charter. Freedom of speech and religion, along with rights to a fair trial and free assembly would be guaranteed, while unreasonable search and seizures would be banned, among many protections. Political tests for office were outlawed. White and black males over the age of 21 would be allowed to vote, though a racist poll tax was attached along with requiring blacks and whites to be in separate schools. Changes to those sexist and oppressive proposals would come later, over the next century.

Several reforms limiting power and government's authority were proposed. The governor would be required to state reasons for any special session. Credit limits would be established for the state and counties. Legislative pay would be limited to 75 days a year. Many other restraints and specific duties to executive, judicial and legislative authority were discussed and added to the proposal.

The new Constitution, imperfect yet improving, was approved in March 1870, 98,128 to 33,972.

Buried in the transformative state document was a stellar reform called that the "single subject requirement." The requirement says each bill must contain only one subject in its title and substance. It has stood the test of time, and kept administrations and legislatures, regardless of party affiliation, on a disciplined course to debate each issue, one bill at a time. It's a major change we need in Congress.

The requirement is a beneficial guardrail in many states. In short, *it keeps legislators from all parties in check and allows citizens to participate directly and transparently in legislative debates.*

I hope you read that sentence again. People don't like to lose, but they especially don't like to lose when they are surprised by the outcome or they feel like they've been lied to or tricked. Those who win through the current process of combining multiple subjects feel very differently, similar to when legislative leaders use gimmicks to bypass committees altogether. Both undermine civil, transparent and constructive debate.

Debating one bill with one substantive subject matter at a time is commonsense, but anathema to some of the careerists who are running our federal government as they see fit. Their antithetical approach to the matter, as well as unbalanced budgets, enabling regulatory over-reach and dismissing term limits, is fueling a rancorous fire of growing entrenchment, resentment and gridlock that has engulfed our Land of the Free. Over the last few decades, acceptable levels of partisanship have devolved into extreme political polarization and dysfunction.

The single subject requirement is one of several critically needed federal reforms we must pursue to stop a government gone wild. It won't end polarization in our nation, but it will help temper the unnerving uncivil war spreading across our great land.

Your help is needed. And guess what, you almost assuredly agree with your seatmate.

WHY YOUR INVOLVEMENT MATTERS

On November 7, 2016, one day before the surprising election of Donald Trump, respected Democrat pollster Patrick Caddell released an attention-grabbing poll that showed a divided country united in its displeasure with all politicians, asserting there is a rapidly growing "revolt against the political class and the financial elites in America."

> It is a revolt with historic parallels, most closely
> resembling the Jacksonian revolution of the 1820s. It
> is an uprising. It is a peaceful uprising of a people who
> see a country in decline and see nothing but failure
> in the performance of their leadership institutions.
> And they have signaled their intent to take back their
> country and to reclaim their sovereignty.

Caddell's analysis and polling shed light on the strength and energy in the populist rises of two unorthodox candidates, Donald Trump and Bernie Sanders. Consider:

- 87% of Americans agree the power of ordinary people to control our country is getting weaker every day, as political leaders on both sides fight to protect their own power and privilege, at the expense of the nation's well-being, and that we need to restore what we really believe in—real democracy by the people and real free enterprise.
- 87% agree the country is run by an alliance of incumbent politicians, media pundits, lobbyists and other powerful money interests for their own gain at the expense of the American people.
- 69% disagree that most politicians really care about "people like me."
- 81% say powerful interests from Wall Street banks to corporations, unions and political interest groups have used campaign and lobbying money to rig the system for them and that "they are looting the national treasury of billions of dollars at the expense of every man, woman and child."
- 81% agree the U.S. has a two-track economy where most Americans struggle every day, where good jobs are hard to find, where huge corporations get all the rewards and that we need fundamental changes to fix the inequity in our economic system.
- 86% say political leaders are more interested in protecting their power and privilege than doing what is right for the American people.
- 76% say the two main political parties are too beholden to special and corporate interest to create any meaningful change.

These polling results are in line with other polls today that show 70% of Americans either are concerned about the direction of the country or believe quality of life will be worse for their children.

Whatever you think of Trump and Sanders, millions showed up to vote for the bombastic businessman, who gave voice to those who felt like they weren't being heard, or the persistent socialist upstart, who spoke for many who view the system as rigged by greedy people. Both made fair points.

While the revolt against the political elite is a positive development in the electorate, it's unsettling to watch how it continues to unfold. Voters increasingly are gravitating to authoritarian figures and solutions. Whether you liked or disliked President Obama and his policies, it is difficult to argue that his excessive use of executive authority, along with Congress's inability to check much of it, has weakened our legislative processes. Most of our major issues are now settled in our courts, or remain unsettled.

Congress is our voice, but it is not speaking well or often enough. Unsettling rhetoric is filling the power vacuum. Some leaders seem to have no other purpose than to outshout the other side. Many special interests, probably some of your favorites, are fine with the current system. They've figured out how to get things done, sliding their needs into massive omnibus bills that few read, or have time to read. It is government by the few—not of, by or for the people.

My invitation to you is to work together on a new path. Ask yourself and your seatmate, are you OK with authoritarianism of any kind going forward, or would you like to see both sides work together better?

Our task, if you're onboard, is to install new constitutional and legislative guardrails, many of which exist in our states' constitutions. The blueprints in our states limit damage any political party in charge can do, which protects future generations, our freedoms and our way of life. This grassroots push, designed to inspire more at our level and more political and civic leaders at "the grasstops," must be consistent, persistent and insistent. It must be free of unbridled partisanship, inclusive and flexible. Caddell's poll showed we're all feeling the same things, so what are we going to do about it?

I argue it will take the collective efforts of most everyone on this unusual but illuminating plane ride. We can use legislative and constitutional techniques that have been given to us in our founding state documents, just as Tennesseans did in 1870, and federal charter. We can join several reform efforts well under way that are well under the radar of most Americans, at least as of today.

Call it what you will—"drain the swamp," "a political revolution," whatever. We will make it happen, mindful that promises from candidates often fall short or fail. This new coalition, too, will be uniquely historical in its makeup.

Democrats and Republicans
Libertarians and Independents
All ethnicities
Urban and rural Americans
Every friend you and I can muster
Every one of theirs

Expect big distractions from the noisy crowd, the folks who are creating the ground turbulence you're away from right now.

Mainstream media.
Fox News and MSNBC.

Internet news aggregates.
HuffPost and Drudge.

Special interest groups—all of them, including your favorites.

Hardcore partisans.
Especially finger-waggers.

Political parties and your "favorite" politicians
I said this won't be easy!

Though you often may agree with powerful players from your preferred political party, many aren't going to be overly open to systemic reforms until they feel unbearable pressure. Especially when it comes from a diverse group like ours.

We're seeking key bipartisan changes that will help center our politics, focus energy on productive debates, and temper personal attacks. We're signing off on that dirty word "compromise" that will help reform unsustainable practices and policies that threaten our republic.

We have a lot in common. We love our kids and grandkids. We understand previous generations made great sacrifices. We have Caddell's poll that captures what we're about. It's our turn to take a crack at the mess.

None of this is personal. There are many good people among the power class, on both sides of the aisle, despite the dehumanizing comments you read on Facebook. They, however, need to see our train has steam. Until then, many will scoff at the items on our to-do list.

Things like the single-subject requirement, our first action item.

ONE BILL AT A TIME—
THE SINGLE-SUBJECT REQUIREMENT

"I'm just a bill, yes I'm only a bill, and I'm standing
here on Capitol Hill."
                              —ABC'S **SCHOOLHOUSE ROCK**, 1970'S

"No bill shall become a law which embraces more than
one subject, that subject to be expressed in the title.
All acts which repeal, revive or amend former laws,
shall recite in their caption, or otherwise, the title or
substance of the law repealed, revived or amended."
          —TENNESSEE CONSTITUTION OF 1870, ARTICLE II, SECTION 17

Federal legislators from both major political parties are rightly
accused of operating in gridlock. In several ways, some obvious and
some less so, they have abdicated their responsibilities to be directly
accountable to the electorate.

One of them, well under the radar of most Americans, is the
growing use of omnibus bills.

This practice, under which leaders in both parties combine the most incongruous subjects in one massive bill, has caused great damage to our representative democracy. By avoiding separate debates on each issue, leaders in both parties have sheltered their caucus members from voting on individual matters that could lead to trouble in getting reelected. Hence, some of these non-related issues are combined into omnibus legislation, showing up late in the process in 2,000-page bills, never heard in one of the 12 committees in each chamber, with senators and representatives only having 48 hours to read.

Omnibus spending bills have become more widespread since the 1980s because "party and committee leaders can package or bury controversial provisions in one massive bill to be voted up or down," according to Walter Oleszek, a political science professor and senior specialist at the Congressional Research Service, the research arm of Congress. They can be used to protect or pass measures a president might veto if they were standalone. They often contain massive pork spending and earmarks—payoffs to special interests, big donors or active political constituencies back home.

This dysfunctional approach generates significant problems. The most obvious is not allowing the electorate to participate in the process through their elected officials. In addition, it concentrates power to a handful of people among the Washington elite—the leaders in both parties and their staffs and well-moneyed special interests that hover patiently and quietly, away from media scrutiny, to insert their wants into these bills.

These interests are not necessarily evil; they have learned and adjusted to work within a fallacious system. Instead of getting caught up and angered at them, we just need to work under the car hood and make some adjustments to a sputtering federal engine.

There are other reasons to tune up a car that has missed many 30,000-mile inspections. The current approach continues to empower what has become our fourth branch of government—federal agencies whose bureaucrats are unelected and accountable to no one—to implement rules that often look more like legislation, rather than intended support or clarity for legislative intent.

In short, it's not about you. It's about them. While omnibus practices certainly streamline affairs for the power class and temper serious scrutiny, they are destructive to a system that is in dire need of transparency, accountability and fairness.

Lo and behold, right after the Civil War, this missing functionality was a major contention of many Tennesseans, who pressured their delegates to restore it at the Davidson County Courthouse that cold January in 1870.

Wisely so. To this day, every Tennessee legislator must trudge with his or her bill to committees whose hearings are open to the public and streamed live on the Internet. That's exactly what State Representative Beth Harwell did year after year, upon being elected in 1989. Harwell, now Speaker of the House, would appear in committee each year with legislation that proposed to phase out the state's estate tax, which some call the "death tax." Tennessee's death tax was a sizeable levy on an estate at a certain threshold, starting at 5.5% and topping out at 9.5%. It was due a mere six months after a decedent's passing.

Harwell never had the votes when her party was in the minority. The majority party defeated the legislation every year, arguing the $90 million in annual revenue would have to be replaced. But she stayed with it. Gradually, political power shifted in Tennessee. Once in the majority, Harwell asked a caucus member to run the standalone bill again. The effort picked up steam. Interested groups harnessed grassroots and began to rally their members to contact their legislators. The press ran stories. People participated.

A compromise was struck in 2012, with a phase-out of the tax through 2016. More farmers would now be able to avoid selling property to pay the tax, good for the environment and a check on development. More multi-generation family-run small businesses would stay in the hands of the children of owners, which was good for communities. More money would stay in locales.

It took Beth Harwell 27 years, from start to finish, to kill the tax. Even if you opposed the legislation, you knew the bill was debated fairly and standalone. Lawmakers knew what they were voting on, and so did their constituents. The process worked, and Harwell finally won. So did the electorate. The system worked just as well when her bill failed. The playing field was level every year for every debate, whatever your position on this issue and any other.

Forty-one states have versions of single-subject constitutional mandates. Legislators, accountable to the electorate, are always on the record in committees and on the floor of their chambers for how they voted. There is no way to sneak, no place to hide and no way to delay with filibusters, which is a huge weight around the process in the U.S. Senate.

Healthy tension. Accountable. Transparent.

Single subject requirements are one very important reason why most states operate more efficiently than our federal counterpart. It is why we need to borrow productive guardrails from 50 state laboratories.

Congresswoman Mia Love and Senator Mike Lee, both from Utah, have brought similar arguments to our nation's capital. In January 2016, Love introduced "The One Subject at a Time Act."

"I continually hear from constituents about their frustration over the multi-rider, large, must-pass-at-the-11th hour bills Washington is so fond of," Love said. "Each bill should stand or fall on its own merits."

She pointed out that both sides of the political aisle are complicit.

"Members of both parties have made a habit of passing complex, 1,000-page bills without hearings, amendments or debate. That process and the collusion that goes with it are why we are ($20 trillion) in debt and why the American people have lost trust in elected officials."

Love's bill would do what 41 states do, as she articulated in a press release:

- Require that each bill enacted by Congress be limited to only one subject.
- End the practice of attaching controversial legislation to unrelated, must-pass bills.
- Require the subject of a bill to be clearly stated in its title.
- Make void in appropriations bills, general legislation that does not pertain to the underlying bill.
- Make the legislative process more transparent to the public.

"Let's bring a little bit of what works in Utah to Washington," said Love. Yes, and 40 other states that know a thing or two about open debate.

Love astutely noted said she expected opposition from those who benefit from backroom deals and who say it would take more time to pass legislation. That's just the start of where good reforms go off track.

Once a minority party returns to power as Republicans did after the 2016 elections, enthusiasm for reform wanes. Then it's back to the old way.

In early May 2017, Congress passed yet another omnibus spending bill with goodies for all, with no debate on their individual merits.

"Overall," *Bloomberg* reported, "[this] compromise resembles more of an Obama administration-era spending bill than a Trump one." Meet the new boss, same as the old boss, like Caddell captured in his poll.

Senator Rand Paul from Kentucky didn't mince words about the $1 trillion government funding deal, calling it "the Status Quo Protection Act" that "tosses out campaign promises as it continues to fund the military industrial complex and the welfare state." It not only rejected President Trump's call for cuts to many agencies, but also increased their funding and again incentivized those agencies to engage in more 'use it or lose it' spending before the September 30 deadline. The deficit would remain well over $500 billion.

It rewarded government mismanagement and corruption, bailing out bankrupt Puerto Rico with $296 million of additional "fungible" Medicaid funds for the first six months of 2018. Fungible means Puerto Rico can spend the money on Medicaid *and* whatever else it wants, which is like giving the keys of a car to a drunkard, rather than establish an accountability plan to help that country recover for the long haul.

The special interests kept their power, too. Funding to certain defense contractors who are friends of politicians grew. Monies went to sanctuary cities and other groups that Republicans had said would lose monies. Some winked and nodded, then went back to expressing disgust with the process.

The U.S. Senate is dealing with gridlock, much of it its own making. Any senator or group of senators can the previously mentioned filibuster, a Senate rule that allows him/her/them to stand on the floor for as long as it takes, sometimes days, to talk a bill to death.

The filibuster has been around since 1806, but was strengthened in in the 1970s. Under Senate rules, the delay can go on until "three-fifths of the Senators duly chosen and sworn" vote to end the "debate" by invoking cloture under Senate Rule 22 (changed in 1975). That's usually 60 of 100 senators, which is difficult to achieve in hyper-polarized times.

George F. Will notes the Senate created a "two-track" system in 1970, "whereby the Senate, by unanimous consent or the consent of the minority leader, can set aside a filibustered bill and move on to other matters."

"Post-1970 filibusters...are used to prevent debate," says Will. Before then, "filibustering senators had to hold the floor, testing their stamina and inconveniencing everyone else to encourage the majority to compromise. In the 52 years after 1917, there were only 58 cloture motions filed; in the 47 years since 1970, there have been 1,716."

Proponents call removing or limiting a filibuster "the constitutional option," while opponents call it the "nuclear option." Both sides have used it. On November 21, 2013, the Senate under Democratic leadership voted 52-48 to require only a majority vote to end a filibuster of executive and judicial nominees, excluding Supreme Court nominees. On April 6, 2017, the Senate under Republican leadership voted 52 – 48 to require a majority vote to end a filibuster of Supreme Court nominees. Thus, Justice Neil Gorsuch was confirmed.

Today, legislation in the Senate still requires a three-fifths vote to end a filibuster. It's important to note the House of Representatives had something similar in place in the 19th Century, but ended the filibuster option. It's also worth noting only 13 states allow some form of a filibuster, concluding that the pluses don't outweigh the minuses.

Let's look at how the filibuster has impacted the discussion on an important topic to all—healthcare reform. Our healthcare system is broken. Our safety net for the poor, Medicaid, is riddled with inefficiency, has fewer available doctors as the rolls have expanded, poor turnaround time for payments, and lack of incentives for better health decisions. That said, it has saved millions of lives and helped many who need it. We simply must preserve it and hopefully improve it, polls show. But how can we, under the current system?

Elsewhere, the private insurance market, in particular the small group and individual sector, has been a nightmare for participants. Costs have soared and access has declined. The Obamacare exchanges have performed poorly overall. Specifically:

- In May 2017, the Department of Health and Human Services (HHS) reported individual health insurance premiums doubled under Obamacare. On average, Americans were paying almost $3,000 more for health insurance—from

$2,784 per year in 2013 to $5,712 on Healthcare.gov in 2017, a 105% increase.

- Premiums had doubled in two-thirds of states. In three states—Alaska, Alabama and Oklahoma—they tripled.
- In 2016, Tennessee's Insurance Commissioner approved increases for three main insurers of an ankle-grabbing *62, 46 and 11%*. Many policyholders reported experiencing *a combined 98%* increase in 2015 and 2016. Some small business owners and their employees started calling health insurance "affordable havoc."
- Competition for business continues to crumble. Before Obamacare, states like Maine and Alabama had one insurance company that were virtual monopolies. In 2017, 36% of exchange market rating regions in the United States in 2017 had *just one* health insurance carrier and 55% had two or fewer carriers. Seven states—Alaska, Alabama, Kansas, North Carolina, Oklahoma, South Carolina, and Wyoming—have *only one* health insurance carrier per rating region in 2017.

Health insurance doesn't remotely resemble what insurance is supposed to be—underwriting actual risk. Because of "guaranteed issue" and "community rating," market competition doesn't really exist in healthcare. Guaranteed issue mandates everyone who applies must be accepted. Community rating forbids insurance pricing from being influenced by risk assessment, which takes the insurance out of insurance. Also, essential benefit mandates require coverage like umm, pre-natal care *for men* and prostate screenings *for women*. No other insurance market operates like this, to my knowledge.

Democrats have a good point about covering as many people as possible. How can one be against that? Some want universal health care, while others want Medicaid expansion, even if they know Medicaid needs lots of work. They are compassionate and looking to help their brother and sister. It's humane and compelling.

Market competition is how healthcare's soaring costs can be controlled unless you believe in rationing care (like universal healthcare). Today, we're stuck in the middle. We watched Democrats fumble an opportunity to reform the system. Republicans can't seem to get their arms around it either.

Now back to a very important thing—the process. In June 2017, Republicans made clear their intention to use the process of "budget reconciliation" to repeal and replace parts of Obamacare. Reconciliation is a procedure to allow passage of a budget bill without being subject to a filibuster; the debate cannot exceed 20 hours. Senate Republican leadership said the bill would not be heard in the HELP (Health, Education, Labor & Pensions) Committee because hearing all the amendments that would fail would be a waste of time. Democrats were outraged.

Let's reflect on how states debate healthcare. In most states, Medicaid expansion bills went through the committee process, often through many committees, as standalone bills. The debates were streamed live, and people attended and testified. Amendments passed and failed. The debate was raucous but transparent.

Let's look at the D.C.-Beltway way. In the summer of 2017, a group of 13 Republican senators crafted a bill that would never be heard in committee. Senators would be given a few days to read, without much information and real feedback from constituents, just nasty emails from both sides. This put many senators who wanted a compromise or earlier input in a nearly impossible place.

Senate rules must change, if we are to find common ground on tough issues like healthcare reform. Common ground, not perfect ground, must be our goal, because perfect doesn't exist, especially in lawmaking.

Both sides have used and will continue to use the nuclear option, so they need our help. The filibuster is not in our Constitution nor should it be. Senators should have ample time in committee and on the floor to debate, but a filibuster and associated tactics are poisoning the debates. Let's end some procedural gridlock that is fueling nastiness and distrust in that chamber and our country.

It's past time to require single-subject bills, which always go through every committee, and which cannot be filibustered.

Here's our first important political activity once our plane returns to the gate.

CRITICAL POINT:

Omnibus spending and multiple-subject bills are a huge problem in our system. They allow special interests and a few leaders to control much of the debate. The filibuster is a Senate rule that has added greatly to gridlock.

ACTION STEP:

Write your congressman and two senators immediately and demand Congress ban the use of omnibus bills, require single subject bills and eliminate the filibuster. Visit https://www.usa.gov/elected-officials/ to send drafted letters easily, and access and call their phone numbers. Share the link with your friends on social media and otherwise. Commit to talking about this reform, rather than grumbling about it.

RESOURCES:

https://www.usa.gov/elected-officials/
www.EndingOurUncivilWar.com

DEBT—A GREATER THREAT THAN ANY TERRORIST

"I would argue that the most serious threat to the United States is not someone hiding in a cave in Afghanistan or Pakistan but our own fiscal irresponsibility."

—FORMER U.S. COMPTROLLER GENERAL DAVID WALKER

"I've said many times that I believe the single, biggest threat to our national security is our debt."

—FORMER CHAIRMAN OF THE JOINT CHIEFS OF STAFF, NAVY ADMIRAL MIKE MULLEN

Our national debt is currently a staggering $20 trillion.

Sitting at our figurative kitchen table, here's a breakdown of how much you and I owe and our collective leverage. We're all in this together, regardless of your political preference.

- Debt per citizen is $61,000.
- Debt per taxpayer is $166,000.

- Only 10 countries out of world's 193 have a higher total debt to G.D.P. (national economic output) ratio than the U.S. (107%). Countries like Greece, which has been in a financial crisis for a decade.
- Annual tax revenue is $3.3 trillion, six times' annual receipts. If you make $70,000 a year, that's the equivalent of having $420,000 on your credit card.

As soon as you're born, your part of the debt is $61,000! Because our population is aging and because nearly one in five Americans either is unemployed, underemployed or no longer looking for work, we have fewer people generating income or paying taxes. Nearly 100 million Americans are not in the workforce. With output declining and promises to keep, and more promises to be made, we are on a path to fiscal ruin.

No sound banker, no responsible parent and few creditors would allow such a thing. But national Republicans and Democrats are acting irresponsibly, borrowing without abandon and ignoring simple economics. The interest on the debt soon will overwhelm any realistic chance to pay back principal. Politicians are afraid to stop because they know their careers would be over if they did, and too many Americans are addicted or beholden to the dollars coming from government's open fire hydrant.

But it's much worse. The astounding $20 trillion number doesn't include unfunded liabilities like the "untouchables"—Medicare Parts A, B and D, the soon-to-be-broke Social Security trust fund, and federal pensions for employee and veterans. Unfunded liabilities can be described as "the difference between the net present value of expected future government spending and the net present value of projected future tax revenue, particularly those associated with Social Security and Medicare." Federal unfunded liabilities, according to usdebtclock. org, are estimated at near $104 trillion, which is $873,000 per taxpayer. Sobering to say the least!

Programs like Social Security need a bipartisan overhaul before it's too late. How? Would you be OK with raising the social security tax rate, while increasing the eligibility age three or four years, in order to ensure the system is solvent and people will be paid? The alternative is what Kentucky is facing—an insolvent pension system in four years. Congress won't address this reform because it isn't required and is too difficult today politically. It knows kicking the can down the road is easier.

Congress also has not passed, nor has the president signed, a budget bill since 2007. That's a decade's worth of omnibus spending bills and continuing resolutions to keep the government and all of its programs funded, along with numerous debt-ceiling increases. It is important to note that the House of Representatives passed a balanced budget in 2017, but the Senate remains at a standstill.

Also worth noting, Congress has flirted closely with passing a constitutional amendment to mandate balancing the federal budget. It came especially close in 1982 and 1995, when populist pressure moved the football to the goal line. But special interests and heavy spenders dug in and made shoestring tackles on fourth down. In 1995, the Senate came within one vote of a fiscally responsible touchdown.

Once again, we must look at the states' playbooks.

Forty-one states have some sort of balanced budget requirement. Thirty-three states are constitutionally required to balance their budgets. It doesn't matter who's on these state teams in most states, because these leaders have their hands tied in a good way. Most can't swipe our collective credit card or use accounting gimmicks to hide any misappropriating.

Most states are in decent or good shape with their fiscal rudder amidships. Currently, eleven are under "chronic fiscal stress," according to *The Fiscal Times*. The three most problematic, with federal symptoms like heavy tax burdens, unfunded pensions and bloated entitlement programs, are Kentucky, New Jersey and Illinois. Illinois, which often issues IOU's to creditors, may be the first state to declare bankruptcy since Arkansas in 1933. Using gimmicks to balance the books only lasts so long. Our nation is heading in that direction.

As an advocate for small business in Tennessee the last 12 years, I have seen how both Democrat and Republican administrations and legislatures must make difficult decisions during lean revenue years. They must decide whether to cut spending or raise revenues via tax increases. Most states operate similarly.

These processes aren't necessarily enjoyable. They can be conten-

tious. Many people weigh in. Tough choices are made. Not all leave
state capitols especially happy. In good years, the arguments are over
where to "invest" or spend the additional revenues, what taxes might
be cut and how much is put away in a rainy day fund. Either way, the
books are balanced that year, new projections are made for the following
year and healthy tension begins anew.

In 2014, I became part of an ongoing advocacy effort that is seeking to require Congress to do what most states do—balance the federal
budget. This state-led initiative, granted through powers in Article V
of the U.S. Constitution, has picked up grassroots momentum the last
10 years as our federal debt has exploded. It's Item No. 2 on our agenda to end our uncivil war and restore political functionality.

Article V is clear on what states are empowered to do (italics mine):

> *The Congress, whenever two thirds of both houses
> shall deem it necessary, shall propose amendments
> to this Constitution, **or, on the application of the
> legislatures of two thirds of the several states,**
> shall call a convention for proposing amendments,
> which, in either case, shall be valid to all intents and
> purposes, as part of this Constitution, when ratified
> by the legislatures of three fourths of the several states,
> or by conventions in three fourths thereof, as the one
> or the other mode of ratification may be proposed by
> the Congress; provided that no amendment which
> may be made prior to the year one thousand eight
> hundred and eight shall in any manner affect the first
> and fourth clauses in the ninth section of the first
> article; and that no state, without its consent, shall be
> deprived of its equal suffrage in the Senate.*

As noted above, amendments may be proposed either by Congress with a two-thirds vote in both the House of Representatives
and Senate OR BY A CONVENTION OF THE STATES called for by
two-thirds of state legislatures, then ratified by three-fourths of their
legislatures. Under Article V, the Constitution has been altered 27
times in our history, seventeen times since the Bill of Rights. In each

instance, Congress made the changes. Some amendments wound up occurring because states were moving in that direction, but Congress stepped in to finish the job.

States used to be much more active with their Article V power. They convened as many as 30 conventions up until 1861, the last of which dealt with slavery. Several initiatives to convene the states are underway at the moment. One effort would enact term limits, while another would repeal the controversial U.S. Supreme Court decision *Citizens United*.

But none is further along than states pushing to require Congress to balance the budget. Remember Congress failed several times, despite its best efforts. Congressman Ken Buck from Colorado's 4th District explains that "with a balanced budget amendment in place, it would be illegal for the federal government to run an annual budget deficit, except in extreme cases of war or national emergency, and then only with the approval of a supermajority in Congress. The president could not propose it, the House could not offer to do it, and the Senate could not approve it."

Buck outlines key benefits for all Americans. It would:

- Restrict the ability of congressional leaders to manipulate the budget process for personal and political gain.
- Lower the national debt.
- Attract investment by improving America's bond rating.
- Bolster the American dollar.
- Free up credit, otherwise taken up by government borrowing, for job-creating private investment.
- Stop the immoral burdening of our grandchildren with debt.
- Force Congress to make the tough, but necessary, budget decisions it has been putting off for far too long—$20 trillion too long.

He adds, "A balanced budget amendment would force Congress to finally do its job of actually taking responsibility for the nation's finances. Agencies would come under closer scrutiny, because every dollar would matter. Government would be more responsible because it would be on a financial leash, and ineffective, wasteful, and unaffordable programs would have to go."

It's important to note that today the various state-led Article V movements are well off the radar of the mainstream media, special interest groups and others in the power elite. The controlling class doesn't feel threatened just yet, but that day is not far off. You can have a substantive role in this effort and other fiscal reforms.

In the spring of 2014, Tennessee became the 22nd state to call for a convention of the states that would mandate Congress to balance the federal ledger. It was a professional honor to provide favorable testimony in committees in 2014, especially when the resolution passed with overwhelming bipartisan support. In the House of Representatives, 89 of 99 legislators voted yes, and only two voted no. In the Senate, 28 of 33 senators voted yes, and none opposed. As of this writing, 27 states have passed similar resolutions, so only six more are needed to convene the first convention of the states since before the Civil War.

Most Democrats in the Tennessee General Assembly joined nearly every Republican, a true bipartisan vote. Some states with strong Democratic majorities are less supportive, but it's important to note 74% of Americans support a balanced budget amendment, according to a poll conducted for CNN by ORC International. Ask your seatmate how she feels about it. Don't we do this at the kitchen table every month? What happens if we don't?

That poll result is noteworthy for breadth of national support. Many Democrats in Tennessee who voted for the resolution told me they preferred tax increases to spending cuts, which wasn't a surprise and will actually be necessary quite frankly. The resolution didn't specify how to balance the budget, just that it be so. In that same 2011 poll, 64% said they would prefer to trim the deficit by both spending cuts and tax increases, while a *Washington Post*-ABC News poll put that proportion at 62%. As you look around the plane, know there's a good chance you, your seatmate and others are in accord.

Congress's only role in any Article V convention of the states is to choose its time and place. The states, as they approach the necessary magic number of 34, are seeking to make the job easy for Congress through a planning convention in the fall 2017 by establishing the rules and perhaps proposing where to have the first real convention of the states since 1861. It's been awhile, but this mission is historic.

This state-level energy and organization has been sparked because of one four-letter word—our exploding national *debt*.

Another damaging fiscal practice is the use of aforementioned "continuing resolutions" and placeholder bills to fund initiatives, especially in the Senate.

In late September 2016, the Senate actually voted to proceed to a continuing resolution that would allegedly fund the government until Dec. 9. But there was one problem. There was no bill! There was no text! It was a placeholder that passed 89-7. Funding for very controversial measures would be inserted later, without individual debate—Planned Parenthood receiving funding for the Zika virus, Export-Import Bank funding for Boeing deals with Iran, decisions on who controls the Internet, and much more.

These are the special interest projects—for liberals and conservatives—that I mentioned we're going to have to set aside for a spell. If we don't, spokes in the wheel of our movement will break and special interests will win—again. Many of these bills belong as standalone legislation, covered previously. Ask this important question: Are the future and well being of our children and grandchildren and our country more important than continuing funding of pet projects in this dysfunctional way?

Senate leaders scoffed that the September bill wasn't transparent or necessary. They called it a process vote when in fact the Senate had proceeded with a very substantive action. The complicit media, more concerned with Donald Trump's early morning tweets, the status of Hillary Clinton's emails or whatever Kanye or a Kardashian were doing, reported the vote was simply on a "shell bill."

The deals would be struck later, behind closed doors, out of the sight of committees where people could attend, testify or watch on the Internet. All 89 senators who voted to proceed essentially abdicated their authority to have input or influence the outcome of a major funding bill.

Oklahoma Senator James Lankford, one of the seven no votes, told *Congressional Quarterly*, "It's important that we [have the text now], and we do know the direction that it's going when we get to that spot." Lankford and the other six senators who jumped ship sometimes are disciplined when doing so. They may not receive the best committee assignments or even may lose a spot.

Like polling shows, we're miffed, but often don't know why. We know government isn't working, but aren't sure how to fix it. These broken fiscal processes require our bipartisan attention.

CRITICAL POINT:

A balanced budget amendment to the Constitution is a bipartisan fix that will save America from economic ruin and will become reality with more grassroots involvement at the state level. The filibuster must be banned, along with continuing resolutions.

ACTION STEP:

Find our where your state is at http://bba4usa.org and contact your state legislators immediately. Tell them to support a balanced budget amendment resolution, and share the link with your friends. Tell your U.S. senators to end the filibuster and continuing resolutions, and pass balanced budgets, and make it high priority in who you support, and don't. Commit to talking about these reforms, rather than grumbling that nothing changes.

RESOURCES:

www.usdebtclock.org
http://bba4usa.org
https://www.usa.gov/elected-officials/
www.EndingOurUncivilWar.com

BREAKING THE REGULATORY TSUNAMI

"He has erected a multitude of New Offices, and sent hither swarms of Officers to harass our people, and eat out their substance."
—DECLARATION OF INDEPENDENCE, 1776, THOMAS JEFFERSON

We love rules and regulations in this country, way too much.

Under Presidents Bush and Obama, our expanding regulatory code slowed hiring and investment, dampening economic output. Nearly 48,000 new rules—half of all rules in our nation's history—have been issued since 2001 with an estimated economic cost of $174 billion. Near the end of President Obama's administration, the nation's courts were filled with lawsuits contesting many significant proposed rules.

The gigantic federal tax code needs a giant shrinking. In 1913, it was a mere 400 pages. Twenty-six years later, it was only 504 pages. It has since exploded to 16,000 in 1969 to 26,000 in 1984 to 97,000 at the close of 2016. Complying with tax law is nearly impossible, costing businesses and individuals valuable time and resources.

Federal agencies like the IRS, which are empowered to enforce the laws, have a near-impossible job, too. The system is bloated and slow, and bureaucrats at federal agencies are making inconsistent interpretations and are increasingly susceptible to corruption.

Congress isn't making many laws these days. The agencies are, through rulemaking. The executive branch knows that Congress can't or won't do much these days to stop the tsunami of red tape.

President Trump has made regulatory reform a priority, but the problem is he's doing it by reversing some rules. Until Congress really reforms our regulatory system and provides direct oversight, any president with a pen and a phone, Republican or Democrat, has much more power.

The impact of overregulation on people and communities is real.

Mike Wetherington is a successful small business owner in Fayetteville, Tennessee, a small town of 7,000 just north of the Alabama border. Mike owns American Development Corporation, a wastewater and water treatment company just west of town on a small hill. Along with 25 employees, Mike helps companies comply with federal regulations and keep the public safe.

In 2010, one of the company's vendors arrived to deliver the chemicals the company needs to fulfill its customers' needs. Unfortunately, the vendor's delivery went awry. Hundreds of gallons leaked from the truck, cascading down the hill, a potential threat to adjacent property and farmland.

As entrepreneurs do, Mike immediately halted plant operations, put his team to work to contain the spill, and called local authorities to bring in the equipment and personnel needed to help the effort. The coordination went well, and apparently nothing leaked into the surrounding fields.

Four hours after the spill, Mike called the Environmental Protection Agency to report it. Soon thereafter, EPA officials in Atlanta levied a $75,000 fine on Mike's business for not reporting the leak "immediately."

Soil samples were taken. No contamination was found. This didn't appease the EPA, which ignored the heroic teamwork and effort from Mike's company and his close-knit community. The bureaucrats wanted their money, and they had the authority to get it. After six months of conference calls with officials, Mike was told the EPA would reduce the fine to $25,000, a large sum of money to remove from the sleepy southern town. Perhaps those dollars would have helped Mike add another worker or enabled a capital investment benefitting a local vendor. The cost of time away from growing the business was likely much larger than the fine. Money left a community and went to the ever-expanding bureaucracy.

The powerful agency could have issued warnings and praised the company for averting a potential environmental disaster. Instead, it chose to punish. It had its money, extortion complete, all in the name of protecting the environment. Oddly, that's the very thing Mike and his friends had done quite well without waiting too long to be told what to do.

The EPA responds very differently when it's culpable.

In August 2015, a federal cleanup crew headed to the town of Durango, Colorado, to the suspended Gold King Mine, which was slated for treatment. According to CNN, "Instead of entering the mine and beginning the process of pumping and treating the contaminated water inside as planned, the team accidentally caused it to flow into the nearby Animas River."

An estimated three million gallons of contaminants cascaded into a creek and headed for the Animas. A toxic cocktail of lead, arsenic, beryllium, cadmium and mercury swirled into the river's pristine waters. In the immediate aftermath, one water sample showed the level of lead in the Animas River was 12,000 times higher than normal.

Fish, turtles and aquatic creatures perished. Animals that rely on the river scattered for new sources of fresh water across the arid land. Locals that depended on the water for farming and drinking were devastated. Rosemary Hart lives on the Animas River. Her family uses a nearby well to get water. She said the spill has made the water unusable: "We looked at the river, and we cried."

Upon touring the damage and impact, New Mexico Governor Susana Martinez said, "The magnitude of it, you can't even describe it. It's like when I flew over the fires, your mind sees something it's not ready or adjusted to see."

The EPA, which had demanded an immediate response from Mike Wetherington, was very slow to report the spill and alert thousands of people who would be impacted. In a lawsuit filed a year after the spill, the Navajo Nation said they weren't notified until nearly two days after the spill had occurred. The group alleged the agency failed to remediate the disaster properly and compensate thousands of farming families who rely on the San Juan River, which flows from the Animas through New Mexico and Utah, to irrigate their crops and sustain their cattle and sheep. In all, the livelihoods of people in four western states—Arizona, Colorado, New Mexico and Utah—were abruptly altered, with likely long-term health concerns from the environmental disaster.

"After one of the most significant environmental catastrophes in history, the Nation and the Navajo people have yet to have their waterways cleaned, their losses compensated, their health protected or their way of life restored," the complaint stated. "Efforts to be made whole over the past year have been met with resistance, delays, and second-guessing [by the EPA]."

Rather than own their actions from the start and implement an efficient emergency plan, EPA officials attempted to shift the conversation after word about the spill hit the street. They said the Gold King Mine spill was part of a larger problem of contamination, with thousands of mines in 12 western states needing attention. OK, sure, but that's not what the EPA's denial-filled blunder was about.

Later, the EPA asserted that in 2014 it had concluded the floor of the mine was six feet lower than the ground right outside the mine.

It basically guessed the backfilled mine was only half-full and not pressurized, contrary to evidence like available photographs and state documents.

The EPA was charted in 1970 to protect the environment, but has drifted far off course from its original purpose. Let me be clear: I am not in favor of eliminating the EPA, like some on the far right would like to see. The EPA's involvement in a variety of matters has been positive in cleaning up rivers, farmland and inner cities. Its guidance and oversight, and the hammer it brings to repeat offenders, has been positive for the environment.

Today, the EPA too often has become a lever of a radical environmentalist agenda that dictates policy rather than carry out its original purpose to protect human health. Mike Wetherington and many others believe strongly in the EPA's original mission. I do, too, and hope you do as well. Who isn't for clean water and clean air? But we should be more than concerned that common sense has eroded, and the EPA's mission has become more about dictation and control.

Consider two of the EPA's rules in recent years—"Waters of the U.S." and the "Clean Power Plan"—that have triggered expensive lawsuits and created great uncertainty in the business community and slowed growth in our economy. Businesses cannot plan and invest when they don't know the rules or if the rules look like they will be highly unfavorable.

Let me be clear again before proceeding. I believe strongly in protecting our land and water and punishing those who egregiously violate federal, state and local protections. We have come a long way over the last 40 years when it comes to improving environmental protections. We still have a ways to go. I am an avid hiker, outdoorsman and dedicated conservationist, and want our lands to be as clean as possible for future generations. I am opposed, however, to proposals with miniscule benefits, unconstitutional restrictions, and/or egregiously high financial costs. We can and must update our environmental laws by following our legislative process, where the people's will is understood and drives meaningful protections. Acting through executive fiat or unlawful rulemaking adds to the polarization and breakdown of opportunities for incremental improvements.

The EPA's attempt to "enact" the Waters of the U.S. rule was patently outrageous. The EPA went well beyond its statutory authority in an attempt to box out states and achieve a regulatory land grab. Specifically, the agency attempted to radically redefine the term "navigable waters" from the Clean Water Act that had been in place since the Nixon administration, seeking oversight over much smaller bodies of water, including farmers' ponds, irrigation ditches, local creeks and streams and even land that is dry most of the year.

The effort was also unconstitutional, violating the 10th Amendment. States clearly have and should always have this authority. Nearly 30 state attorneys general sued, and many business groups formed a coalition to sue as well.

The EPA says the rule was necessary to protect local drinking water. However, the EPA already imposes stringent regulatory standards designed to protect drinking water. Moreover, the waters that EPA now sought to regulate are already heavily regulated at the state and local levels. It's specious rationale to argue the "Washington bureaucrats and environmental activists have a stronger interest in protecting our drinking water than do the people who actually drink it," I argued in a joint press release calling for Tennessee's attorney general to join the lawsuit. He later did.

The whole thing created a mess for homebuilders, contractors, farmers, and others. Pulling a permit from the EPA, rather than your state or local regulator, feels like pulling teeth. It's also much more expensive. Also under the rule, if you failed to pull a permit through the EPA, for say digging a ditch on your farm, you could have been fined up to $37,500 per day!

That's what Thomas Jefferson would call harassing the people and eating out their substance. Fortunately, the courts applied the brakes to the rule in August 2015. The Trump administration also has been grappling with rewriting or scaling back the rule.

The Clean Power Plan rule wasn't much better. In essence, it was designed as a massive tax on electricity, with very limited health benefits for the country. The rule would have hit some states harder than others.

Tennessee would have felt the impact because coal-fired power plants generate 41% of the state's electricity; natural gas, another fossil fuel that would be affected by the EPA's rule, generates another 6%. Wind, solar and other alternative sources of energy either aren't readily available or would be too expensive to make up the difference.

The Heritage Foundation estimated the rule's annual cost to the U.S. economy at $150 billion a year, or $1,700 a year for a family of four, including already-struggling poor families. The government's own estimate pegged job losses at nearly 500,000 a year by the late 2020s.

None of this stopped the EPA or the activists who drafted much of the rule. Thankfully, the Supreme Court did in February 2016.

Another proposed regulation, the "overtime rule," caused quite a ruckus, as well as more court action. Under the drafted rule, the income threshold under which workers would be eligible for overtime was essentially doubled from $23,000 a year to $47,000 a year. Unquestionably, it would be very good for some workers. Many more, however, would have had significant life-changing experiences (no more flexible work schedules and going on the clock), as well as reductions in pay and benefits.

One of the government's own studies estimated nearly five million workers would see a decline in pay or benefits. Who in particular would be hurt? Mid-level managers at nonprofits, schools and government, as well as aspiring managers at restaurants and retail stores, would be impacted.

The rule caused more than 50 business groups and 21 states to sue. Businesses were worried not only about the difficulty complying with the rule in a very short time period but also the economic impact on their operations *and their employees!* Their lawsuits were predicated on several assertions, including that the Department of Labor failed to conduct a required review analyzing the potential economic impact on small business. In late November 2016, a Texas judge issued a stay.

It is important to look at the level of, and, more importantly, the reasons for, the dysfunction in this evolution, so we can talk about some fixes that will help stop future facsimiles. What could or should have happened before this administration tried to jam through yet another harmful rule?

President Obama had a good point. The threshold needed to be updated. He could have asked Democrat leaders in Congress to craft a bill with Republicans, who could have gone to business groups and other constituencies for guidance on a more reasonable adjustment to the threshold that hadn't been updated since 2004. What could work without causing adverse impact or unintended consequences for approximately five million lower- and mid-level managers?

A compromise could have helped more workers get time-and-a-half pay through a more modest increase (not indexed to inflation and possibly phased in) that businesses, non-profits and governments could afford and implement more easily. Instead, Obama loaned his famous pen to his labor department, whose rule if approved would have done the following:

- Layoffs, more part-time workers, outsourcing, reduced benefits, and delayed hiring
- The end of flexible work schedules for many salaried managers, who would soon go on the clock and resent the "demotion." "What, I can't go to my son's game and make up the time later?" "No, I'm sorry."

- Lawsuits for unprepared or mistake-prone entities already dealing with massive red tape. Job security and greater profitability for law firms and CPAs.
- Small businesses scrambling to make the rule work.
- Another increase in the wage gap that politicians talk about fixing, but actually make worse through such regulation.

Yes, some workers would benefit, but see above. Some labor experts believe the rule actually is not well intended because it would undermine existing flexibility in many workplaces. Some business groups say the real reason for the rule is to give unions another tool to push for organizing disgruntled workers. Just like another agency edict called the "walk-around" rule that would let union organizers follow OSHA inspectors around a business, even if the workplace isn't unionized. That rule (that should have been a bill going nowhere) also was stopped in court.

This is the executive-fiat push, the regulation tsunami, the government-gone-wild mess that the executive branch has been unleashing for several decades, increasingly so over the past 16 years, under both the Bush and Obama administrations. Who suffers? Hard-working millennials, moms returning to the workforce, families needing flexibility...Who wins? Special interest groups advancing their agendas and some lucky workers at the top end of the mandate.

The "Dodd-Frank" law is another example of government creating new problems when it is trying to solve old ones, and some of them of its own making. Significant red tape on smaller banks continues to hold back the economy.

First, there appear to be positives from the law, such as requiring "stress testing," a process to assess whether banks are adequately capitalized and have robust risk management capabilities. Big banks don't seem to mind. The system appears to be more ready when the economy turns dramatically again.

But the law goes too far. The law empowered a few regulators and new commissions that are issuing a massive set of rules that continue to this day. Smaller banks and their customers have been hurt the most.

One can argue government helped create the Great Recession of 2008 in the first place. James Rickards, a hedge fund manager in New

York City, argued in *U.S. News & World Report* that the financial mess of 2008 would never have occurred if lawmakers hadn't repealed a very effective law since the Great Depression.

"In 1933, Congress passed [the Glass-Steagall Act] in response to [several] abuses. Banks would be allowed to take deposits and make loans. Brokers would be allowed to underwrite and sell securities. But no firm could do both due to conflicts of interest and risks to insured deposits. From 1933 to 1999, there were very few large bank failures and no financial panics comparable to the Panic of 2008. The law worked exactly as intended."

Rickards continued: "In 1999, Democrats led by President Bill Clinton and Republicans led by Sen. Phil Gramm joined forces to repeal Glass-Steagall at the behest of the big banks. What happened over the next eight years was an almost exact replay of the Roaring Twenties. Once again, banks originated fraudulent loans and once again they sold them to their customers in the form of securities. The bubble peaked in 2007 and collapsed in 2008. The hard-earned knowledge of 1933 had been lost in the arrogance of 1999."

Congress and the president pointed out the bad actors, like Lehman Brothers, that they themselves had enabled in 1999. In addition, the government's implicit backing of Freddie Mac and Fannie Mae, two powerful quasi-government mortgage agencies, fueled home-buying and a lending craze that was clearly unsound and unsustainable.

The Dodd-Frank Wall Street Reform and Consumer Protection Act, named after Connecticut Senator Christopher Dodd and Massachusetts Representative Barney Frank, seeks to protect consumers with rules that would prevent abusive lending and mortgage practices. Does it? Yes, probably in some ways, but definitely not in others.

A few years after the enactment of Dodd-Frank, which has 24,000 pages of rules and counting, I attended a federal oversight hearing on the campus of Middle Tennessee State University in Murfreesboro. One small, independent banker a few miles down the road in Shelbyville told attendees that he had 15 officers at his bank—seven loan officers and *eight* compliance officers. He had more people keeping up with largely meaningless paperwork exercises that drove up costs for the bank and their customers. He had to have them on staff to keep up with the tsunami of requirements that could lead to massive government fines and penalties or even serious trouble with federal inspectors. This community banker had very little or nothing to do with the financial crisis, but he and his customers were paying a big price for others' misdeeds.

Government did "create" some jobs through the law—thousands of in-house and contract attorneys who read federal code and review paperwork. Dodd-Frank, however, has killed many more thousands of jobs and slowed hiring and investment, especially in smaller communities served by independent banks. It is no small coincidence people in rural areas revolted the last election. Dodd-Frank, Obamacare, Waters of the U.S. and the Clean Power Plan are just a few of many federal laws and proposed rules that lit a fire under the rural electorate, small business owners and others weary of a suffocating and expanding federal bureaucracy.

In June 2017, along party lines, the House of Representatives passed the Financial Choice Act to address the most harmful components of Dodd-Frank. The bill would give the president authority to fire the heads of the Consumer Financial Protection Bureau (CFPB), which had been granted extraordinary powers with no checks and balances, and the Federal Housing Finance Agency, which oversees government-backed mortgage giants Fannie Mae and Freddie Mac. Congress also would oversee the CFPB's budget, and stop the Federal Deposit Insurance Corp's (FDIC) oversight of a requirement of banks to draw plans of how they would operate during a major crisis.

The stories of Mike Wetherington, the Navajo Nation, and small community bankers are not an anomaly, by any means. The EPA, CFPB, IRS and other agencies are harassing millions of other businesses and individuals. Powerful unelected bureaucrats are targeting businesses and individuals, using too much authority or seeking to expand it through new rules, rulings, court actions and enforcements.

Some of these cases are make or break. Most are smaller, but they add up. In my daily role as an advocate, I've heard many business owners tell me that they told an inspector they will go buy a required wrench immediately to avoid a fine, even though the tank or machine they're using is properly calibrated. Many inspectors, looking to achieve quotas rather than compliance in the field, show no mercy or leeway. Just as Mike Wetherington experienced, the argument over the amount of the penalty or fine begins. Many just write a check to stop the endless back-and-forth.

"Absent substantial [regulatory] reform, economic growth and individual freedom in America will continue to suffer," wrote James L. Gattuso and Diane Katz of the Washington, D.C.-based Heritage Foundation in a 2016 report, which noted a $22 billion economic impact from 43 major rules in that year alone.

It's not just the economic impact that Gatuso, Katz and others have cataloged that should concern us, but the cautionary tales of excessiveness that are in our backyard every day. It might be something as small as the stories of regulators shutting down a lemonade stand that children have set up on the neighborhood corner. Or perhaps it's something more troubling, like an instance in my hometown of Nashville that I highlighted in a column in *The Tennessean* in 2013.

In East Nashville, Family Wash, a reputable 11-year business with apparently no history of citations, was raided by 12 local and state officials at 10 p.m. on a Friday evening, their busiest time of the week. Some of the bureaucrats were armed, wearing bullet-proof vests. Witnesses, including owner Jamie Rubin, said the inspectors behaved like bullies.

Their official purpose was to ensure Mr. Rubin was licensed properly to sell, drumroll please, *high-gravity beer*. Twelve bureaucrats, many armed and all protected with bulletproof vests... that's worth a repeat to comprehend the outlandishness.

Family Wash had the appropriate license, but was it necessary to storm the business, scare and scatter Mr. Rubin's customers, and make it appear he was in the wrong and cost him significant revenue on a busy night? Of course not.

I made calls to Mayor Karl Dean's office and to state leaders, calling for a review of Metro Nashville's mysterious Environmental Task Force that acted similarly at other businesses before the raid in East Nashville, and to review state funding of Metro's Health Department. Mayor Dean, to his credit, handled the matter behind closed doors and reined in the nonsense.

In June 2017, in Baltimore, Maryland, police shut down several young black children in school uniforms for selling snow cones without a permit. A week later on the Mall near the Smithsonian Institute in our nation's capital, several black teenagers *were led away in handcuffs for selling bottled water* to hot tourists. What kind of message are we sending to budding entrepreneurs who are in struggling inner-city

communities? That crime is easier or better than getting out and working to make life better?

The chilling effect of overreach cannot be understated. No business understands this better than Nashville-based Gibson Guitars,
which was raided in 2011 by federal agents for allegedly using overseas
wood to make their guitars. The company spent $2.5 million in legal
fees and lost a month of business during a long recovery process.

In 1833, Alexis de Tocqueville expressed his admiration of our free
society and limited, targeted regulation in "Democracy in America," but
not without warnings.

America must avoid, he wrote, becoming "an immense tutelary
power...absolute, detailed, regular...with a network of small, com-
plicated, painstaking, uniform rules through which the most original
minds and the most vigorous souls cannot clear a way."

Overregulation, he continued, "hinders, compromises, enervates,
extinguishes, dazes, and finally reduces [the] nation to being nothing
more than a herd of timid and industrious animals of which the government is the shepherd."

With the authority they've been granted, bureaucrats have an immense
responsibility to strike the right balance when protecting us from harm, and
most necessarily understand the harm they themselves can create.

Shall we wait for Congress to rein in the fourth branch of government that has continually been enabled and not checked? Will a new
president, who promised to "drain the swamp" and pledged repeal of
Dodd-Frank on the campaign trail, achieve this?

We've explored the necessary guardrails to protect us from
fiscal calamity—the balanced budget amendment and single-subject
requirements.

We have a similar opportunity to implement regulatory guardrails.
Several efforts that would bear fruit are underway and would help. The
most important is another effort to amend the Constitution—the Regulation Freedom Amendment. Other efforts are important and worth
noting as part of a playbook that would decentralize power, restore fair
processes, and help end our uncivil war.

REGULATION FREEDOM AMENDMENT

> "Whenever one quarter of the Members of the U.S.
> House or the U.S. Senate transmit to the President
> their written declaration of opposition to a proposed
> federal regulation, it shall require a majority vote of
> the House and Senate to adopt that regulation."
> —REGULATION FREEDOM AMENDMENT TO THE
> U.S. CONSTITUTION, AS PROPOSED

In early 2015, Tennessee Senate Majority Leader Mark Norris summoned several business association leaders into a conference room at the State Legislative Plaza in downtown Nashville. Norris, a constitutionalist from Collierville, a suburb east of Memphis, was planning to run a resolution authorizing Tennessee to participate in an Article V constitution of the states to propose the Regulation Freedom Amendment (RFA). After he outlined his reasons for running the resolution, he wanted to know if the business groups would be able to support the RFA. Several said yes, they would help the leader from West Tennessee.

Simply stated, the amendment would enable Congress to check any regulation it deemed as radical or unconstitutional. Norris and other proponents believe the RFA would be a valuable front-line protection for groups weary of having to march off to court for relief and a powerful new legislative tool that would root out radical, costly federal proposals that were hurting states, too.

Norris's proposal passed the Tennessee Senate overwhelmingly that year. The House concurred in 2016. As of June 2017, support for the RFA was strong and growing. Ten states—Georgia, Indiana, Kansas, Montana, North Dakota, South Dakota, Tennessee, Utah, West Virginia and Wyoming—have fully authorized participation in a convention. That's quite a bit fewer, currently, than the balanced budget amendment movement, but other states look poised to join on the way to the necessary 34 to call the convention of the states.

Polling shows voters favor the Regulation Freedom Amendment by a 2 – 1 margin. The issue unites friends of limited government and attracts Republicans, Independents and Democrats. Former presidential candidates conservative Ted Cruz and moderate John Kasich have endorsed the amendment, as have six governors, dozens of associations, and many other leaders.

Let's rewind a few years and say the RFA was already in place, when the EPA dropped its Waters of the U.S. rule. Clearly, most people without an extreme agenda would agree a ditch isn't "navigable water" and that fines of $37,500 a day are excessive. Congress would have had the necessary 25% in favor of reviewing the rule, and likely the required 50% to ditch the EPA's rule to regulate ditches, well before any coalition lawsuit would be filed, well before shocking any farmer or homebuilder, and well before creating tremendous uncertainty in the economy. If nothing else, the American people would have had the opportunity to weigh in, through their congressmen, rather than be brushed off again during the required rule review by unelected bureaucrats.

Another benefit of the RFA would be to cause future federal agency leaders to pause before promulgating an extreme or unconstitutional rule. Today, an agency leader may be required to testify before an oversight committee, but those hearings are for show. If you've watched C-SPAN, you know the scene—a congressman scolding an agency head, expressing the same outrage he's hearing back in his district. Alas, when the cameras are off, nothing has changed, except more phone calls to both sides' lawyers. Reviewing a controversial regulation on the Senate floor would be more sharpening to an agency director than having to endure a 90-minute grilling in an oversight committee.

What kind of rules could be stopped and put back to the purview of Congress? Here's a sampling from the last few years, besides Waters of the U.S. and Clean Power Plan:

- An IRS fine of $100 per day per worker, *up to $36,500 a year per employee*, on small businesses that reimburse or directly pay their employees for health care costs. Very few businesses even knew about this rule and were at great financial risk for trying to do the right thing—help their workers get healthcare coverage!
- OSHA's "walk around" rule in 2013 that allows union officials to serve as third-party participants on OSHA inspection teams, including inspections *even at non-unionized businesses*.

- The NLRB's "joint-employer" definition, which said businesses that "use facilities staffed by third-party agencies" may find themselves being "liable for employee actions" and "brought to the bargaining table as joint employers to negotiate union contracts." The rule "would make small businesses liable for unlawful labor practices committed by entities completely outside of their control."
- The Department of Labor's aforementioned "Overtime Rule," which doubled the eligibility threshold for employees receiving overtime pay for working more than 40 hours a week.

The last three rules triggered costly, time-consuming lawsuits, and have either been halted or are under further appeal. Congress, after nearly two years of delay, gridlock and uncertainty for millions of employers and employees, finally fixed the IRS rule that had millions of hard-working people in limbo because their access to affordable healthcare was greatly compromised. The RFA likely would have nipped all four in the bud.

Other reform efforts are worth mentioning, and deserving of your contemplation for support and grassroots energy:

REVISIT THE CHEVRON DOCTRINE

Agencies' interpretative powers to make rules regarding legislation passed by Congress grew significantly through a damaging Supreme Court decision *Chevron, U.S.A., Inc. v. Natural Resources Defense Council, Inc.* In his opinion, Justice John Paul Stevens explained that (italics mine) "the power of an administrative agency to administer a congressionally created program necessarily requires the formulation of policy and the making of rules *to fill any gap left, implicitly or explicitly, by Congress.*"

The plaintiff, Chevron, was challenging the Environmental Protection Agency's interpretation of "stationary sources" in the Clean Air Act. The Court found their challenge "must fail" when it "really centers on the wisdom of the agency's policy, rather than whether it is a reasonable choice within a gap left open by Congress." The Court then asked "whether Congress has directly spoken to the precise question at issue," concluding if it was silent or ambiguous on the matter, the court should uphold the agency's interpretation as long as it is a reasonable or permissible reading of the statute.

Elizabeth Slattery, a Legal Fellow and Appellate Advocacy Program Manager with the Meese Center for Legal and Judicial Studies, says the Chevron doctrine has been described as the "counter-Marbury for the administrative state" and that it is (italics mine)*"emphatically the province and duty of the administrative department to say what the law is."*

Justices past and present have said much about *Chevron*:

- Justice Antonin Scalia: "Too many important decisions of the Federal Government are made nowadays by unelected agency officials…rather than by the people's representatives in Congress."
- Justice Stephen Breyer: "[T]he public now relies more heavily on courts to ensure the fairness and rationality of agency decisions."
- Justice Samuel Alito bemoans the "aggrandizement of the power of administrative agencies" because of *Chevron*.
- Justice Clarence Thomas: "This line of precedents undermines our obligation to provide a judicial check on the other branches, and it subjects regulated parties to precisely the abuses that the Framers sought to prevent."

Slattery concludes the new Court (italics mine)"should reconsider when and how much deference is owed to administrative agencies, given the inconsistent application of *Chevron* deference as well as broader concerns about the judicial branch's duty to act as a check on abuses by the political branches in appropriate cases or controversies. *Courts should exercise independent judgment rather than simply accept an agency's "reasonable" interpretation of the law. Many of the justices have expressed concerns about unchecked agencies, and in the appropriate case, they could revisit Chevron deference."*

Recently appointed Justice Neal Gorsuch has said *Chevron* is "a judge-made doctrine for the abdication of the judicial duty." He also believes judicial deference to agencies allows them to "reverse its current view 180 degrees anytime based merely on the shift of political winds and still prevail [in court]."

Ilya Somin, a law professor at George Mason University, agrees, noting "a major part of the purpose of separation of powers is to ensure that the branch that enforces the law is separate from the one that has the final say over its interpretation. That is what enables the judiciary to serve as an effective check on the power of the other branches of government." He wisely warns liberals who have supported agency activism in recent years to be wary of *Chevron*, as well:

"If you believe—as I do—that Trump is a dangerous menace to liberal values," Somin said, "then you have an additional reason to want judges who won't defer to executive agencies' interpretations of the law. Under Trump, those agencies will mostly be headed by people who support his agenda. You have even more reason to reject Chevron if you think the problem is not limited to Trump, and that the GOP as a whole is untrustworthy."

It goes both ways. The Courts must be in the middle, keeping check of the other branches but never assuming their roles, whichever party controls Congress and whoever is in power in the White House.

Chevron should be reversed when the right case comes along, and future justices should be asked about it during confirmation hearings.

THE **REINS** ACT

The "Regulations from the Executive in Need of Scrutiny Act" (REINS) would require Congress and the President to affirm major federal rules with an economic impact of $100 million or more before they could be enforced. Donald Trump has said he supports the legislation, which passed the House several years ago but stalled in the Senate under first Democrat and then Republican leadership.

Cameron Smith, the national director of the Liberty Foundation of America who worked on the REINS Act as a congressional staffer, says the law would establish greater accountability in the regulatory system. He says in 2014 alone "the House and Senate would have been forced to vote on fewer than the 84 major rules that [took] effect last year. Many, if not most, of those rules would quickly move through without controversy. Yet, even with those few votes, Congress would have to answer to the American people for both the laws they pass and the major rules created using the powers they gave away."

Healthy tension has a way of removing greater tension down the road. The earlier we (and thus they) confront problems, the earlier these problems can be addressed, rather than spiral out of control and stoke fires that perpetuate more lawsuits, incivility and entrenchment. In short, you and I will have more of a say.

THE **FINER** ACT

Tennessee Congressman Diane Black says this bill, which she has sponsored, would increase transparency by requiring federal agencies to post online detailed information of the regulatory fines for which they are responsible. Further, agencies would not be allowed to write a fine if that information has not been online for a minimum of 90 days.

Additionally, regulatory fines would be treated like traffic tickets, allowing the fine to be challenged at a Federal Court instead of appealing to the agency that wrote the fine. During this appeal process, the person or entity being fined would not be required to pay until a court renders a final judgment. Agencies would be required to deposit any revenues from fines directly to the Treasury, ensuring that these revenues are not used as supplemental funding for agencies. Finally, if the entity being fined prevails, they could then recover court costs and attorney fees.

Mike Wetherington would have appreciated the FINER Act. The EPA of recent years? Not so much.

SUNSET AND RULE REVIEW

Tennessee and other states have unusually strong and effective accountability processes—sunset and rule review—to rein in runaway agencies.

In 2011, the Tennessee House Government Operations Committee rolled a bill a year that would have reauthorized the Tennessee Wildlife Resources Agency (TWRA) to continue its oversight. The inaction basically put the TWRA into a "wind down" phase, essentially forcing the agency to cease operating.

Tennessee legislators took this action to get the attention of the Wildlife Commission. They were tired of receiving complaints from constituents who felt that had been harassed during routine inspections or allegedly had not had their phone calls returned.

Lo and behold, after some changes in operations and communications, complaints declined and the Government Operations Committee reauthorized the agency for the next period. Sunset reviews in Tennessee typically occur between two to six years, depending on the agency.

The government operations committees also conduct hundreds of "rule reviews" each year, both during and out of the legislative session. Much of the work is mundane, but occasionally there's super-heated oil in the legislative skillet of rule review.

The committees' work caught the attention of *Knoxville News'* columnist Frank Cagle:

> *Conservatives often complain about the U.S. Congress passing laws then letting executive branch bureaucrats promulgate rules, design enforcement and set fees. So the actual effect of new laws is to allow unelected bureaucrats regulate the lives of citizens and businesses. So it shouldn't be surprising that the Republican supermajority in our state Legislature has decided to not follow Washington's lead.*
>
> *State bureaucrats are no longer free to impose draconian regulations, increase fees or make rule changes without first getting a sign-off from the Legislature.*

In the past, rule review in Tennessee was seen as just another tedious exercise. To the credit of Republicans, once they assumed control of the Legislature they used the statutory authority in the Constitution to ask questions, delay votes until answers were provided and even present the possibility of an agency sunset, pulling funding or both.

Bureaucrats in Tennessee are much perkier these days. They work closely with legislators to find common ground and are much more responsive to taxpayers than ever before. Friction and tension exist, but it's healthy. On-the-record conversations are productive and compromises are reached often.

Washington bureaucrats have learned they're not under similar scrutiny. They need to be.

CRITICAL POINT:

Unelected, unchecked federal regulators have expanded their authority and are threatening Americans with greater frequency. Congress grew less effective in checking agency authority and must reassert its authority in various ways.

ACTION STEP:

Activate with the grassroots team (http://www. americanopportunityproject.org/grassroots-team/) to ensure enough states support the Regulation Freedom Amendment. Contact your legislators to support judges who are against the Chevron doc- trine, and for the REINS Act, FINER Act, and sunset and rule review. Share with your friends.

RESOURCES:

http://www.americanopportunityproject.org/ grassroots-team/
https://www.usa.gov/elected-officials/
www.EndingOurUncivilWar.com

TERM LIMITS—SO YOU WANT TO "DRAIN THE SWAMP"?

"In a virtuous government, and more especially in times like these, public offices are what they should be—burdens to those appointed to them which it would be wrong to decline, though foreseen to bring them intense labor and great private loss."
—THOMAS JEFFERSON

"The real destroyer of the liberty of people is he who spreads among them bounties, donations, and benefits."
—PLUTARCH, 1ST CENTURY A.D.

"I think we want to see new voices and new ideas emerge. That's part of the reason why I think term limits are a really useful thing."
—PRESIDENT BARACK OBAMA, AFTER THE 2016 ELECTIONS

Arguably, Congress has never been more impotent and less accountable in our history. As Congress' influence has waned, the executive and judicial branches have filled the vacuum of power, along with the emergence of a fourth branch, our runaway regulatory agencies.

America is still a republic, but its foundations are weakening. Our job is to strengthen the republic's foundations, not abandon them, and install new balustrades.

One of the more important reforms is to enact term limits for members of Congress, just as we do for the president. The more popular term limit movement at the moment is for members of the House to be limited to three terms, or six years, and senators to be limited to two terms, or eight years. I would argue that's too short, based on some experiences here in Tennessee, but more on that later.

The topic is an old one, but never more relevant. Do you recall the "Contract with America" offered by House Republican leaders Newt Gingrich and Dick Armey six weeks before the 1994 midterm elections? The populist Contract, which had some of what Donald Trump was pitching in 2016, had a major effect on the '94 election, helping Republicans regain control of the House with a 54-seat gain. In the Senate, Republicans picked up nine seats.

The Contract included what many of today's reform-minded Americans are calling for, such as constitutional amendments establishing a balanced budget and term limits.

Most of the big stuff in the Contract failed, including a balanced budget amendment. The Fiscal Responsibility Act of 1995 proposed an amendment to the Constitution that would require a balanced budget unless sanctioned by a three-fifths vote in both houses of Congress. The House passed overwhelmingly, 300 – 132, but the Senate rejected it, 65 – 35, falling one vote short of the necessary two-thirds. (Republican Senator Mark Hatfield was the last no vote.) Later, Republican Senator Bob Dole cast a procedural vote to bring up the amendment again in the future, sending any notion of balanced budgets to the congressional graveyard, where many of them wanted it anyway.

Term limits met a similar fate. The Citizen Legislature Act proposed an amendment to the Constitution that would have imposed 12-year term limits on members of Congress: six terms for Representatives and two for Senators. The House soundly rejected the resolution in March 1995, 227 – 204, well short of the necessary two-thirds majority.

To their credit, Republicans put these measures to a vote. To their detriment, they didn't succeed in enacting much that mattered over the long term. These two failures in legislative self-regulation, as well as the current rhetoric from the careerists who have dropped anchor in our nation's capital, give more than fair argument that a different course is needed: direct involvement from individuals and states.

What do the numbers regarding service tenure and patterns of service tell us? According to the Congressional Research Service, which has studied this field since 1789, in the 19th Century the "average service of representatives remained roughly constant, with only 12 Congresses having an average service greater than 3.0 years and just one Congress having an average service of less than 1.5 years." In the next century, average years of service for representatives steadily increased from just over four years in the first two Congresses of the early 1900s to an average of approximately 10 years in the three most recent Congresses.

Prior to the Civil War, it was common for 40% or more of representatives NOT to seek reelection. Prior to 1887, no Congress saw fewer than 25% NOT seeking reelection. Since the 20th Century, it's been much different: The rate at which members have not sought reelection has stayed more or less constant, averaging 11%.

The fact that they stay longer today isn't necessarily the problem. However, the fact that many more are staying for very long periods is. In the 64th Congress (1915 – 1917), only 5% had served more than 16 years; by the 104th Congress (1995 – 1996), 14% had served more than 16 years; in the 114th Congress (2015 – 2017), almost one quarter, 22%, had served more than 16 years. The numbers in the Senate are remarkably similar.

Elected officials used to want to go home. Today, they can't seem to leave easily. There are reasons that make sense. Longevity is a factor; folks are living longer. Transportation improvements have enabled more legislators to be able to more easily return to Washington from their districts. That's good for them and their families, but not good for relationship-building with peers.

Congressmen and friends Joe Barton and Mike Doyle acknowledged much of this after the baseball filed shootings in June 2017.

Said Barton: "I think the Internet and Twitter and all the instantaneous aspect of the news cycle has made it more personal, and members flying back to their district every weekend—very few members live up here. You know, it is a different climate today than it was in 1985 when I first got elected. Part of it is technology and part of it is the way politics have evolved. The attack politics and the 15-second attack ads and things like that. Members are not looked at as people anymore. We're kind looked at as—I won't say targets, but—but people think they can come to our town hall meetings and say just the most obnoxious things and we not feel it personally. I can assure you every member of Congress is a person. He has family, and while we try not to show it, sometimes we do take it personally."

Added Doyle: "I wouldn't think of being harsh to Joe Barton no matter what we may disagree about politically because I feel like he's a family friend, but there's so much pressure on members to get home right after the last vote."

Term limits would help here. Congressmen could move their families to D.C., work hard for several terms and collaborate more with their peers, commute to the District less, and then go home to their districts for good when term-limited.

Consider recent history and the length of service at the very top—Senators Robert Byrd (51 years), Daniel Inouye (49 years), Strom Thurmond (47 years), Ted Kennedy (46 years), Patrick Leahy (42 and counting), Orrin Hatch (40 and counting), and Thad Cochran (38 and counting). That's bipartisan longevity, too—four Democrats and three Republicans. In 2016, 60 of the 100 members of the U.S. Senate had been in office for more than 20 years. Thirty-six had held office for more than 30 years.

Robert Byrd, who chaired the Senate Appropriations Committee, is a case study. Byrd started in the West Virginia House of Delegates in 1946. After two terms and another in the state Senate, he was elected to the U.S. House of Representatives in 1952 for three terms before winning his Senate seat in 1958. He never lost an election in West Virginia.

Byrd was especially adept at bringing home the bacon to his struggling, mostly rural state of West Virginia. He was so revered by legislators that they erected a larger-than-life bronze statue of him, the first and only statue in the halls of their capitol. Upon a pedestal, an inscription boldly reads, "West Virginian of the 20th Century."

According to the *Christian Science Monitor*, "at least 40 contributions bear their benefactor's name, from the Robert C. Byrd Regional Training Center for soldiers at Camp Dawson in Kingwood and Robert C. Byrd High School in Clarksburg, to the 17-mile, four-lane Robert C. Byrd Drive near his hometown of Sophia."

Byrd's behavior isn't exclusive to one party. The proclivity for pork is a bipartisan issue. Republican have had their initiatives, such as Senator Ted Stevens' $223 million "bridge to nowhere" in Alaska, an island with a population of 50. In another, Mississippi shipyards received contracts to build amphibious ships the Navy said it didn't need and the Pentagon said were unnecessary. There are books on this one topic.

As noted in the introduction, government coke is government coke, and too many of us are on it. Many of Byrd's and his friends' projects weren't (and still aren't) debated on merit, and many only go to the states and districts of those who hold the most power, those who have been in Washington longest. Ahh, seniority. It's bipartisan too.

In 2012, Republican Senator Orrin Hatch from Utah pledged to retire. Early in 2017, he backed off that pledge. A survey by the *Salt Lake Tribune* and the Hinckley Institute of Politics, found 58% of Utahans thought Hatch should "definitely not" run for an eighth term, while 20% more said he should "probably not" run. Only 20% backed the most senior Republican senator, aged 82, to run in 2018. By most accounts, Orrin Hatch is a great guy. It's not about him specifically, but how our electoral car is operating. I argue we need to check under the hood again.

The House has a similar problem. Congressmen John Conyers, Charlie Rangel and Don Young tallied a combined 142 years, and counting. That's three men who served for the entire life expectancy of two!

In George F. Will's book *Restoration*, Will argued, "A permanent class of career legislators is inherently inimical to limited government." The author said deliberative democracy is "a disposition to reason about policies on their merits rather than their utility in serving the careerism of legislators" as the ideal to which Congress must return.

Will detailed much of the ridiculous pork-barrel projects from sponsors like Byrd, who once declared *he wanted to be West Virginia's billion-dollar industry*. The author pointed to "the culture of spending" as contributing to public outrage and congressional inefficiency. Will's crystal ball not only was correct, but also continues to glare. Statistically, the growth of bloated government and length of service of legislators continue in the same direction, unhindered.

Term limits are very popular with most of America. Three in four Americans view them as a needed check on power, according to Gallup and other polling. With such overwhelming bipartisan support, you would think our elected officials would go ahead and adopt them. Populist candidates knew this in 1994 and know this now.

During the 2016 presidential campaign, Trump brought up this mainstream idea on the campaign trail, promising a term limits debate to amend the Constitution. Three weeks before the election at a rally in Colorado Springs, he bellowed, "The time for congressional term limits has finally arrived. Not only will it end our government corruption, but we will end the economic stagnation that we're in right now. No growth."

Do you believe him and others on this matter? Here's what Trump said in 2008 to a television crew: "I'm not a believer in term limits. I think a term limit is when you go into a voter booth and if you don't like somebody, you press a button."

Contrast that with what the new president said in October 2016: "When it comes to Washington, D.C., it is time to drain the damn swamp."

Once there, it's hard to leave. Some arrive in Washington as idealistic freshman, intent on changing the system. Soon, they learn how to operate within the system. Over time, they become the system.

Many also get rich in the system. While many senators and representatives on both sides of the aisle have made much of their money in the private sector, many others have used their positions to leverage existing wealth, write books, obtain enormous speaking fees, and cut deals and invest in operations run by some of their wealthiest supporters.

The rich in Congress keep getting richer. A look at the last 12 years shows the average estimated wealth of senators exploded from $1.7 million in 2004 to $2.9 million in 2014. That year, eight members of Congress had an estimated net worth of more than $100 million, including Nancy Pelosi. Vermont Senator Bernie Sanders drew much attention on the campaign trail by blaming the top 1% for many of today's problems. It seems he has point, from his Senate chair.

It hasn't been much different in the people's chamber. House members' wealth rose from $629,000 in 2014 to $860,000 in 2014. Contrast that with the average American citizen's estimated wealth (assets minus liabilities) of $66,000 in 2010 during the Great Recession. In 2010, those with a graduate or professional degree had a median net worth of $245,000, while the median net worth of those with a high-school diploma was $42,000. The Senate is well out of reach of anyone who isn't super-rich, while the House is close to that point.

During the Great Recession, the wealth of members of Congress steadily grew, while the rest of us saw deep declines in our financial portfolios and stagnation for several years. It has been a long, winding road to return to pre-Recession levels, but not for the ruling class, which weathered the storm quite well.

Senator Sanders says the scale is uneven. I believe most people share this sentiment, though their proposed solutions may differ. Many of us are a few paychecks or one bad stock market or plant closure away from financial disaster. We have not saved much for a rainy day, let alone another depression. According to the Economic Policy Institute, the average savings of a family with members between 32-37 years of age is $31,644, and median savings is less than $500. Average savings of families close to retirement between 56-61 is $163,557. The median is $17,000. While mean retirement savings of all families is $95,776, the median for all American families is just $5,000.

It costs unfathomable sums of money for your barber or your neighborhood barista to run for public office, so they don't or don't get any traction. Candidates must have money for necessary airtime, phone banking and get-out-the-vote postcards. Political aspirants in Single-A baseball cannot compete in the Major Leagues. All 450 Senate candidates raised a combined $729 million in 2015-2016, most of it from individuals. All 2,077 House candidates raised a combined $1.02 billion for the same period. The 26 presidential candidates raised $1.31 billion total, almost all of it by Republicans and Democrats. Federal politics has become a game for the wealthy on both sides of the aisle, with some rare exceptions like the Sanders campaign attracting substantial monies from smaller donors.

According to the Federal Election Commission, the *New York Daily News* reports "the average price of winning or holding on to a six-year term in the U.S. Senate averaged $10.5 million in the 2012 election cycle," while a U.S. House of Representatives seat cost an average of $1.7 million. Successful Senate candidates needed to be able to raise an average of $14,351 every day for two years in order to pull off a win, while winning House members had to raise an average $2,315 per day.

"They're spending more of their time fundraising than making actual laws," MapLight President Daniel Newman, whose organization researches money's influence in politics. "They've become high priced telemarketers."

It didn't start out that way. Most of our Founders didn't view their terms in office as careers or platforms to make fortunes. In 1787, only eight of the delegates received a substantial portion of their income from public office. Most of the delegates were in the legal profession (35), merchants (13), land or securities speculators (19), plantation or large farms owners (15), physicians (4), small farmers (2) and scientists (2). As we've seen, up until the late 1800s, many legislators wanted to serve a term or two, and go back home to their farms, families and enterprises.

As of 2016, only 12 of 100 senators have pledged support for a constitutional amendment for the most popular proposal to limit senators to two terms, or 12 years, and representatives to three terms, or six years. So, once again, this important area is in our hands.

Since 75% (Gallup survey) on our plane agree on enacting term limits, there's a decent chance your adjacent adversary is with you on this. Trump says he's for term limits, and so does Mr. Obama. So why don't we work from the same playbook?

Term limits aren't perfect, but they work because they are the better alternative. They are in place with 15 state legislatures, the constitutional officers in 37 states, and eight of the ten largest cities in America for their city councils and/or mayor, according to the grassroots U.S. Term Limits movement.

As noted earlier, I believe the current proposal of three and two terms for the House and Senate, respectively, is too restrictive. A longer duration, perhaps six for representatives (12 years) and three terms for senators (18 years) would have a better effect. I base this belief on our experience in Nashville, Tennessee, where I live. When

Nashville enacted a two-term limit for its councilmembers in 1994, many of us who voted for it patted ourselves on the back. We would be assured the council would always have "fresh blood," corruption would decline, and councilmembers would vote altruistically, knowing their time in service was limited.

While all of that may be true, the two-term limit adoption has created problems in Music City. Three classes would have been better. With three—the rookies, the movers and shakers, and those with institutional knowledge—Nashville would have had easier, less abrupt transitions and eliminated mistakes. Instead, with two classes, the council was weaker, mirroring the two terms Nashville's mayor serves. The mayor's power, in effect, has expanded under our term-limit system, but not glaringly so like at the federal level.

But let's not go for what I think may be better. Let's get onboard with the current movement and give it more steam.

CRITICAL POINT:
Careerism and pork barrel spending are contributing to gridlock and runaway growth in government, and must be addressed.

ACTION STEP:
Activate with the grassroots team at U.S. Term Limits: https://www.termlimits.org and https://www.termlimits.org/u-s-term-limits-amendment/. Share with your friends. Commit to talking about this reform.

RESOURCES:
https://www.termlimits.org
https://www.usa.gov/elected-officials/
www.EndingOurUncivilWar.com

CONTEMPLATION:

"Given the polarizing climate crippling Washington today, there is something to be said about an idea that overwhelmingly unites both parties.
—DAVID PERDUE, U.S. SENATOR FROM GEORGIA, ON TERM LIMITS

REDISTRICTING REFORM

"Part of the problem is not just the rhetoric. It's the fact that we're so polarized in what we've done to each other as parties over the last 30 years in redistricting that it's very, very hard to overcome your own constituencies and move to the middle."

—HOWARD DEAN, FORMER VERMONT GOVERNOR AND
CANDIDATE FOR PRESIDENT

Is it right for legislators to select who their voters will be every 10 years? Or should we be doing that, or have more of a role?

How do we take control to ensure voting districts remain competitive, with fair and balanced representation of an area's population? How do we reverse increasingly rubber-stamp-like elections that increase gridlock?

In early 2017, Tennessee Congressman Jim Cooper issued a press release that said he was reintroducing "two bills that would stop the private practice of gerrymandering and unmask the secretive congressional redistricting process so all Americans can participate."

Hardly anyone noticed, including the media. But Cooper is on to one of the more meaningful systemic government reforms that would drop the temperature and help restore the functionality of Congress, as well as check the power of other branches. The more Congress gets done, the less meddling there can and will be by the other branches.

"Redistricting shouldn't be about protecting the powerful," Cooper said. "Let's bring integrity to a shady process so voters aren't kept in the dark. Sunlight is the best disinfectant."

The congressman from Tennessee's 6th District noted the Cook Political Report's Partisan Voting Index found only 20% of House districts are considered competitive and the number of "swing seats" has dwindled to a record low of 90 out of 435. In 1998, 161 seats, or 37%, were considered competitive.

Almost 60% of House districts are seen as extremely lopsided and partisan, "contributing to the paralysis in Congress in recent years." In Massachusetts, it's 78%. In Texas, it's 86%.

Named for a fellow Tennessee congressman who retired in 2010, Cooper introduced the John Tanner Fairness in Redistricting Act, requiring each state "to establish an independent, bipartisan redistricting commission to redraw congressional district lines once every 10 years that reflect contiguous communities. These communities would replace carved-out, gerrymandered districts that protect extreme political partisans."

Another bill, the Redistricting Transparency Act of 2017, would require states to publicize redistricting information online, including the data used in the process, details of the process, proposed maps and public hearing dates. It also would require that the public be allowed to comment before maps receive final approval.

State legislatures are scheduled to redraw state house and congressional lines again after the general election in 2020. Those lines will be in effect until 2032.

Every 10 years, the U.S. Census Bureau issues its local population data. Shortly thereafter, state legislators (in most states) redraw the lines of its congressional districts.

This will happen again in 2020, and to the victors will go the spoils. The party in charge, in most states, gets to redraw the lines of its congressional districts and state legislative districts, selectively. With computer software and advanced technology, it has become a highly detailed process of cartography. The map-making power brokers in charge carve up which voters go where. Their objective is to gain seats for the party in charge.

In a sense, redistricting, also known as gerrymandering, is like herding sheep or cattle into new pens, based on their voting trends. Afterwards, more sheep look alike in one pen, as well as in the one next to it.

It all started in 1812 when Governor Elbridge Gerry approved legislation that redistricted Massachusetts to favor the Democratic-Republican Party. When mapped, one of the contorted districts around Boston was said to resemble a salamander. The press seized on this, and termed the practice "gerrymandering."

Gerrymandering is good for the parties who win, but often a problem for the rest of us, no matter what party is in charge. While it's important to ensure districts have roughly the same number of people, to keep proportion of one person having one vote for congressional balance. But what has occurred over time is a distortion of this notion.

In a state like Illinois, where Democrats run the show and redistricting is a big issue currently, a district that might have been 52-48 Republican in 2009 might now look 58-42 Democrat in 2010, while an already adjacent Republican district gains many more Republicans.

The issue is well below the radar of most Americans today, but that may change soon. At least three court cases alleging state redistricting abuse are well underway in North Carolina, Virginia and Wisconsin, whose legislatures are controlled by Republicans. The North Carolina case involves federal congressional districts, while the Virginia and Wisconsin cases address state legislative districts. The implications for voters in all states and the country potentially are very consequential.

The North Carolina and Virginia cases involve race. According to *Washington Examiner* editor Michael Barone, who monitors redistricting, both the North Carolina and Virginia cases are responses to a prevailing interpretation of the Voting Rights Act of 1965. "The claim made by [lawyers representing] black voters in both states," the Associated Press said, "is that Republicans created districts with more reliably Democratic black voters than necessary to elect their preferred candidates, making neighboring districts whiter and more Republican."

In May 2017, the Supreme Court struck down two congressional districts in the Tar Heel State, ruling lawmakers violated the Constitution by depending too heavily on race when drawing them. In March 2017, the Court ruled 7-1 in favor of further review of 11 state legislative districts in Virginia because they were designed to ensure 55% of eligible voters were black. Justice Anthony Kennedy opined in the majority, saying the districts can be held unconstitutional "if race for its own sake is the overriding reason for choosing one map over others," even if those districts meet traditional criteria like compactness. The Supreme Court stopped there, sending the case back to the lower court to use different criteria.

The Court is saying clearly there is a problem, but isn't offering remedy, thus far, as it sorts through complexities in these cases. The Wisconsin case, *Gill v. Whitford*, alleges partisan gerrymandering again by Republicans. The highest court will review a federal panel ruling in 2016 that determined state assembly districts are unconstitutional. The final ruling could have significant implications for generations.

Redistricting has had a big impact on the composition of Congress. According to the *Washington Post*, in 2010 there were 50 Blue Dog Democrats, considered the more moderate politicians in their caucus. The Post said in years past "[Blue Dogs] were the most influential voting bloc on Capitol Hill,... [often] pulling their liberal colleagues to a more centrist, fiscally conservative vision on issues such as health care and Wall Street reforms."

Four years later, the *Post* noted "the Blue Dog Coalition is a shell of its former self, shrunken to just 15 members because of political defeat, retirements after redrawn districts left them in enemy territory and just plain exhaustion from the constant battle to stay in office." There are even fewer Blue Dogs today.

As Howard Dean noted, redistricting only has added to our political intransigence and polarization, making it much more difficult for legislators in districts dominated by one party to lead or vote on compromises. He's right: it would be a political death knell for certain legislators who don't want to lose their seats. Gerrymandered districts basically incentivize politicians to eschew compromise and entrench themselves in hardline positions on both sides.

That's bad for many who want Social Security saved from insolvency, or reasonable healthcare reform. Bipartisan compromise bills are nearly impossible to do. Over time, redistricting has put many moderates, often power brokers and swing votes on key bills, out of service.

Perhaps you're seeing a connection between term limits, redistricting and other reforms we've looked at thus far? It's hard to have control, or a reasonable say, in a boat with fewer oars and a short rudder.

There's nothing illegal about the practice of redistricting. If nothing changes in the courts (possible) or legislatively (not likely soon unless we get moving after this plane ride), the year 2020 will be good for Republicans and bad for Democrats. Frankly, it could go the other way the next decade. Wherever you stand politically, the question remains: Is the current practice the right practice? Should we let the people we're going to elect decide who goes where? Or should we be doing this, or have more of a role?

Most of your fellow plane travelers are for a change. The Brennan Center for Justice at the New York University School of Law notes a 2013 poll found 70% of Americans believed that "those who stand to benefit from redrawing congressional districts should not have a say in how they are redrawn."

Right now, the GOP is in charge. After the 2016 elections, Republicans completely controlled 33 state legislatures. Republicans control 67 of the 98 partisan legislative chambers, after winning new majorities by taking control of the Kentucky House, the Iowa Senate and the Minnesota Senate. *Since President Obama took office, Republicans have taken control of staggering 27 state legislative chambers from Democrats. Since President Obama took office in 2008, Democrats lost 1,042 state and federal legislative seats and governorships during Obama's tenure in office.*

Tennessee, where Republicans operate in super-majorities, is a case study in this regard. In the Tennessee Senate, today there are 28 Republicans and only five Democrats, all from inner-city districts. In the Tennessee House, there are 74 Republicans and only 25 Democrats. Fifteen years ago, Democrats ran it all in Tennessee. Today, it's the opposite.

It's like this across much of the country. The national map for state legislatures is widespread red. Democrats only have control of the legislatures and governorships in five states—Hawaii, California, Oregon, Connecticut and Rhode Island. While Democrats made some gains in states like Nevada and New Mexico in 2016, the trend is not their friend. They could lose more seats in Congress in 2020.

As a result, more of the 435 seats in the House likely will look deeper red and deeper blue, not the purple we could use today to solve some problems.

As noted earlier, mostly state legislatures are in charge of choosing new lines for congressional districts. There are several states that have either a citizens' commission or a bipartisan commission, like Arizona, California, Idaho, New Jersey and Washington. One state, Iowa, has a bipartisan panel of citizens that draw the maps that the legislature can adopt without amendment, or not. This is the emphasis of Cooper's Fairness in Redistricting Act.

Our opportunity is to work to establish more commissions and take charge of the redistricting control legislators currently have to pick their voters instead of us picking them. There are some advocacy groups like FairVote worth checking out. But some of their proposals create even splits among the electorate, like replacing the Electoral College, and we're looking to avoid that. We're seeking consensus reforms that have a proven impact and can be done without the legislature's involvement, like state ballots.

The Brennan Center has put forth excellent information and potential solutions on redistricting. Here are some high points of several approaches:

- Put the power of drawing districts into the hands of an independent citizen commission, as California and Arizona have done successfully. The California redistricting commission, for example, is credited with improving representation and competitiveness without compromising the goals of minority empowerment.
- Adopt Iowa's bipartisan panel of citizens that draw the maps the legislature can adopt without amendment, or reject and ask for another plan.
- Use Florida's approach that still allows the legislature to draw maps, but puts in place strong, objective rules on process.
- Adopt Ohio's model, a 2015 constitutional amendment that toughened rules governing redistricting and gave the minority party a greater role, and ensured that a plan not agreed to by both parties would be only temporary.

Will the Supreme Court issue a precedential ruling? Could it be adding up that way, based on other rulings, some by wide margins?

In June 2015, the Brennan Center pointed out "the Supreme Court upheld the constitutionality of the independent redistricting commission Arizona voters created by ballot initiative in 2000. Justice Ruth Bader Ginsburg, writing for the majority, cited John Locke and the Declaration of Independence, and hailed the reform measure as "intended to check legislators' ability to choose the district lines they run in, thereby advancing the prospect that members of Congress will in fact be 'chosen...by the people of the several states.'"

The next month, the Florida Supreme Court used constitutional amendments passed by Florida voters to strike down maps that had been drawn for partisan ends.

Stay tuned.

CRITICAL POINT:

Redistricting essentially allows political parties in charge to choose their voters, not vice versa. Legislators and party leaders often look more intently on the next election rather than what needs to be done now.

ACTION STEP:

Monitor Supreme Court rulings and activate with your state effort to reform how redistricting is done. https://www.brennancenter.org/analysis/democracy-agenda-redistricting Seek ways in your state to remove this authority from the legislature or introduce important checks and balances on their power. Connect and discuss with your friends.

RESOURCES:

https://www.brennancenter.org/analysis/democracy-agenda-redistricting
https://www.usa.gov/elected-officials/
www.EndingOurUncivilWar.com

CONTEMPLATION:

"The difference between try and triumph is a
 little umph."

—UNKNOWN

ISSUES TO KEEP ON OUR RADAR

> "One might plausibly contend that Congress violates the spirit, if not the letter, of the constitutional doctrine of separation of powers when it exonerates itself from the impositions of the laws it obligates people outside the legislature to obey."
>
> —SUPREME COURT JUSTICE RUTH BADER GINSBURG, 1994

Remember that overtime rule we kicked around a few chapters ago?

Democratic Congressman Alcee Hasting from Florida is one of many ardent supporters. At least he was until he realized the likely impact on his hard-working staff.

In the summer of 2016, Hasting told *Bloomberg News*, "We don't have a set-hour kind of situation here; some kids work 12, 14, 16 hours a day, weekends....I don't see how we could pay overtime [for the] 17 or 18 people that each of us is allowed to have—that's problematic for me."

This dismissiveness from a Democrat isn't too dissimilar from Republicans' dismissiveness that passing a shell budget bill without anything in it and without getting committee scrutiny is OK. Is the overtime rule going to apply to everyone, or not?

National Review writer Veronique de Rugy points out the irony
that Hasting and many Democrats who overwhelmingly support the
proposed expansion of overtime pay do so until they realize "they
may also have to live by it.... The newspaper reports that 'Democratic
chiefs of staff are freaking out' about finding room in their budget
for overtime wages" and fear that an overtime mandate will result in
having to send staffers home at 5 p.m.

Noticing the double standard, de Rugy avers, "When employers
say that they would love to pay their employees more but they just
can't afford it, some members of Congress dismiss their comments
and call for government rules to correct these employers' greediness.
But when lawmakers acknowledge budget (provided for by taxpayers'
money) constraints, that's legitimate, loving even."

One of the better laws Congress passed the last 25 years emanated
from the Contract with America. In 1995, President Bill Clinton signed
the Congressional Accountability Act, which required Congress and
all agencies to live under the same laws as the rest of us—the same
civil rights, labor, and workplace safety and health laws that applied
to businesses and the federal government. Previously, agencies in the
legislative branch had been exempt from these laws.

Miss de Rugy points out the 1995 law requires Congress to comply with the overtime-pay standards established under the Fair Labor
Standards Act. But she says that wasn't the case in 2004, the last time
the overtime threshold was updated, noting: "The Board of Directors
for the Office of Compliance (BDOC) must conduct a rulemaking
process, and the final rules proposed...must be adopted by both the
House and the Senate via a resolution. In 1996, all those procedural
boxes were checked. But since 2004, Congress has left the 'adopt'
box unchecked." Congress, she says, never adopted the regulations
proposed by BDOC "to replace the 1996 overtime-pay standards with
the proposed [2004] update. Imagine if private businesses didn't follow
the law or the regulations imposed on them by our giant regulatory
bureaucracy."

That's further irony, but this time compliments of Republicans,
who were in charge in 2004.

The Congressional Accountability Act, which also established a
dispute resolution procedure as an alternative to filing suit in federal

court, has served a purpose. Two positives include the law's impact on accountability and fairness in lawmaking, and the fact that Congress does on occasion act when pressured by an attentive electorate. Fear is a fabulous motivator, in this case the fear of losing office.

But lawmakers and their staffs continue to move the pea under the shell when the stakes are high. The Affordable Care Act of 2010 is another example.

The original legislation did not require members of Congress and their staff to acquire their health insurance from the exchanges that would be built. Republican Senator Charles Grassley from Iowa introduced an amendment that said they must live under the same law as the rest of the country, which included the individual mandate (purchase health insurance or pay a fine) and importantly the employer mandate (in simple terms, businesses with 50 or more employees are required to purchase a certain amount of health insurance or pay a fine). The amendment passed, so legislators and their staffs would have to shift from the generous Federal Employees Health Benefits Program to the exchanges once they were in place.

Here's the catch: Congress is a very large employer, well above the 50-employee threshold. In short, the new law would not allow members and staff to continue receiving a taxpayer contribution of up to $12,000 toward their premiums if they enrolled in the exchanges. The president and leaders in both parties decided they could fix this, considering it one of the oversights that had to be addressed, in this case to avoid what some said would be a "brain drain" with many staffers leaving for greener pastures (and cheaper healthcare).

Under a Freedom of Information Act request, lawyers learned that the House *claimed it only had 45 members and 45 staffers, well under the 435 and thousands, respectively. The Senate did the exact same thing, finagling it only had 45 employees total.* The Office of Personnel Management signed off on the new math, triggering a lawsuit. A Superior Court judge ruled in favor of Congress in February 2015; the issue is currently on hold as the nation grapples with how to amend the act, keep its good parts and fix what many believe has caused much more harm than good.

Senators David Vitter from Louisiana and Rand Paul from Kentucky have made the most noise in recent years to elevate the issue of guaranteed fairness in application of our laws.

Vitter has supported various pieces of legislation to achieve this, while Paul has offered a resolution to establish what would be the 28th Amendment, in line with the others we've covered so far. In 2013, Rand's resolution stated, "Congress shall make no law applicable to a citizen of the United States that is not equally applicable to Congress."

Here's where I'm going to surprise you and others on our plane ride.

Joe Wolverton, an attorney and talk radio host for the New American Review, says it best (italics mine): "I will not contend that such a provision would confer a regulating power; *but it is evident that it would furnish, to men disposed to usurp, a plausible pretense for claiming that power.* They might urge with a semblance of reason, that the Constitution ought not to be charged with the absurdity of providing against the abuse of an authority which was not given... Although Senator Paul's sense of justice is correct and commendable, his choice of a constitutional amendment to accomplish that end is questionable and potentially very problematic."

Wolverton makes other salient points, most of this taken directly from thenewamerican.com:

- Although many... frame any debate on the constitutionality of an issue by arguing that the Constitution doesn't forbid this or that act, that approach is the reverse of that intended by our Founders.
- The Constitution does not catalog restrictions on power. That is to say, the Constitution was not designed to be a list of all the things the federal government cannot do, rather, it was written to contain an exhaustive, all-inclusive list of the authority granted to the federal government by the states that created it. As James Madison explained in *Federalist No. 45*, "The powers delegated by the proposed Constitution to the federal government, are few and defined. Those which are to remain in the State governments are numerous and indefinite."
- So, rather than argue about whether a power is or is not restricted by the Constitution, we should examine the document to discover if a particular power is granted therein.... There is no need to add an amendment to the Constitution forbidding Congress from doing something that it isn't allowed to do in the

first place. Regarding Obamacare, the Constitution gives Congress neither the power to force Americans to purchase health insurance, nor to exempt itself from that mandate. Therefore, the Paul amendment is moot.

I agree with much of this, unless things get wildly out of hand. Let's split the difference on this one. Congress is playing around, or thinking about playing around, but not at a level that needs the attention of other matters we've discussed. But it most certainly needs to stay on our radar.

Just like the next topic, campaign finance reform. Let's explore something that has many "feeling the Bern."

CAMPAIGN FINANCE REFORM

Those, like Bernie Sanders, who argue for further limits on campaign contributions speak often about the *Citizens United vs. the Federal Election Commission* Supreme Court case in 2010.

They believe that ruling enabled further growth of surreptitious Super PACs, and they have a strong case. They run up, however, against a strong case of campaign contributions being a fundamental First Amendment right. So what's all the hubbub about?

In 2008, the conservative non-profit Citizens United sought to air a film critical of Hillary Clinton before the 2008 Democratic primary. This would have violated the also-controversial 2002 Bipartisan Campaign Finance Reform Act, known as McCain-Feingold, which prohibited this kind of special interest broadcast so close to an election (within 30 days of a primary or 60 days of a general election).

In 2010, the highest court reversed the lower court's block of the film, finding its provisions prohibiting corporations and unions in conflict with the U.S. Constitution. The court's ruling did uphold requirements for public disclosure by sponsors of advertisements, but did not affect the federal ban on direct contributions from corporations or unions to candidate campaigns or political parties, which remain illegal. The court essentially prohibited government from restricting independent political expenditures by a nonprofit corporation and extended this right to for-profit corporations, labor unions and other associations.

Critics of the decision, like the Vermont Senator, assert that *Citizens*

United has concentrated power in the hands of a few wealthy people. Sanders rejects "the absurd notion that money is speech, corporations are people, and giving huge piles of undisclosed cash to politicians in exchange for access and influence does not constitute corruption.... Super PACs—a direct outgrowth of the *Citizens United* decision—are enabling the wealthiest people and the largest corporations in this country to contribute unlimited amounts of money to campaigns."

Sanders calls for several solutions: One, to "overturn, through a constitutional amendment, the disastrous *Citizens United* Supreme Court decision...." Two, to "pass legislation to require wealthy individuals and corporations who make large campaign contributions to disclose where their money is going." And three, to "move toward the public funding of elections."

Sanders' argument has merit on one side (the concentrated influence on elections by a few) but not on another (his end game to have elections publicly funded would be subject to corruption and abuse and over time would undermine our society built on free speech and resistance to the concentration of power, exactly what Sanders abhors). Oppression doesn't have exclusivity with any political party or era.

Additionally, if Sanders would call out billionaires on both sides he might win a few more converts. He often mentions the growing influence of the billionaire Koch brothers, who actually are with Sanders on quite a few issues like criminal justice reform, and dozens of other right-leaning wealthy people. That is not what he did on the campaign trail or had on his campaign website. It is hypocritical to call out the Koch brothers when he rarely if ever mentions multi-billionaire George Soros, who is funding the Open Society Foundations, many of them post-modern leftist groups that are espousing violence, riots and other anarchical behavior to undermine protective institutions like the police. One report showed OSF contributed $33 million to fund the looting and mob behavior that tore the city of Ferguson, Missouri even further apart. The Ferguson case involved a police officer allegedly shooting a black man. It did not matter to OSF and Soros that the Department of Justice was investigating the case and later determined no racial hate crime had occurred, months after the cameras were gone and lives and burned-down businesses were being rebuilt. I know some don't agree with that, but that was the government's own finding.

We should tip our hats to Sanders for elevating the issue, but his solutions are dangerous. People who have money have free speech rights. He's right that corporations and unions aren't people, but people count on them and run them. Making these entities disclose their activities makes perfect sense, even with modest blackout periods right before an election. But public funding of elections is yet another way for government to control speech, a very dangerous path that would threaten our representative democracy.

Campaign finance and term limits have a strong correlative relationship. But term limits are the better path. They would temper much of the time and energy legislators spend asking for more money, leaving more time to get work done before they pack up in a few years and head back to their states and districts. Term limits would pull up the roots; campaign finance would be more like trimming their tops.

Let's keep this one on our radar.

SENATE ELECTIONS AND THIRD PARTIES

I'll add another matter to the watch list—consideration to repeal the 17th Amendment. This would return the election of senators to state legislatures, thus making senators more accountable to home states instead of special interests.

The 17th Amendment requires the popular election of senators—eliminating an important check the Founders had placed on the federal government, the representation of state governments in the U.S. Senate. Understandably, many are frustrated with the reduced role of states, which established the federal government long ago. Some argue today state sovereignty exists at the will of the federal government.

This is mostly a Republican idea at the moment, and not a strong one, but I would argue Democrats should have an interest as well. Senator Sanders and many followers talk often about the wealthy having too much power. As we've seen, the Senate is primarily comprised of members who are quite comfortable financially.

Since there isn't much bipartisan energy, however, to move to repeal Old No. 17, let's put it on a back burner as well.

An underlying theme of the 2016 presidential election is many people saying they would have voted for another candidate than Trump or Clinton, if he or she had a chance of winning. One poll found 40% of voters in the 2016 election would have voted for an alternative candidate if they thought that candidate had a chance to win.

In the 2016 presidential election, 135,699,677 votes were cast for the top six tickets, with 94.9% going to Republicans and Democrats. The Libertarian and Green parties made a little more noise than in years past, getting 4.34% of that vote, but most Americans are still uncomfortable with alternative parties, despite growing frustration or disgust with the major parties.

The Libertarian, Green and other parties must create much better infrastructure, and fund and recruit effectively, if they are to be taken more seriously. Millions align with their views, but don't trust being a "wasted vote." Factions of the two main parties are going to have to be more than disgruntled before they bolt for an alternative party. They need to believe any new bloc is viable.

Presidential candidates like Libertarian Gary Johnson also need to know where Aleppo is (Syria, dude). To become relevant, other parties must build from the ground up and not just out West.

Hoping for the next Ross Perot isn't likely to happen for them. Politics isn't played like college football, where the playing field has leveled over the years. Appalachian State might beat Michigan once in a blue moon on the gridiron, but never in the world of politics. Politics today is Alabama vs. Ohio State or Clemson.

The alternative candidates did emerge to have a serious conversation about issues—in particular the Libertarian ticket of Johnson and former Massachusetts Governor Bill Weld, the Green Party's Jill Stein and the Independent duo of Evan McMullin and Mindy Finn. Johnson and Weld, in particular, stood out with their fairly optimistic, positive and more inclusive platform and messaging.

Unsurprisingly, the media essentially ignored the upstarts. In reality, their scarce resources and nearly nonexistent state infrastructures paled in comparison to that of the top two parties. Third parties have a tough road ahead, since gaining ballot access is difficult due to stringent rules created by the two major parties. Independent teams won't compete well with the SEC or Big Ten until they hit the weight room and build better facilities.

The night before the election, Johnson sent a message to supporters claiming victory, whatever the results.

"We smashed fundraising records. We are set to gain ballot access and federal funding for a third party. And we've introduced millions of Americans to an idea that cannot be stopped—we don't have to settle for a lesser of two evils. Don't be impatient. Revolutions take time."

True, but most Americans don't think we have the time to wait for other political parties to get their acts together.

CRITICAL POINT:

Congress living under the same laws as we do and campaign finance reform are relevant issues that need to be monitored and adjusted potentially. Other relevant issues will emerge.

ACTION STEP:

Keep these issues on our watch list, and engage in debates to come. Do not take Nowatchia. Definitely stay on Informmeia.
Monitor www.EndingOurUncivilWar.com for updates.

CONTEMPLATION:

"Don't' find fault. Find a remedy."

—HENRY FORD

"The ones who are crazy enough to think they can change the world are the ones who do."

—STEVE JOBS

NEXT STEPS

We've landed. Our plane is on the ground now.

Maybe you're powering up your smartphone to check your messages or text that you're back safely. Before we deplane and head to baggage claim, and you're back to "business as usual," I'd like to offer a reflection.

Maybe the book resonated, and you're ready to rock and roll in new places.

Maybe some of the book resonated, and you want to get rolling where it did.

Maybe the book didn't resonate at all. Thank you for reading this far, anyway. You have great character!

For those of you moved to follow through on what resonated, the book is a start, not an end. By visiting www.EndingOurUncivilWar.com, you'll find next steps, a Comprehensive Action Plan.

Under the Resources tab, you will find links to reflections of great spiritualists, where your alma mater or prospective university stand on free speech, government reform movements that would welcome your financial and grassroots support, and more.

You can tell friends about the book, where to find book excerpts and how to purchase, and share or follow on social media, too.

You can find out the latest news about the book under In The News. You also can request the author to speak at your civic group, university or elsewhere.

Are you visualizing everyone wearing "End Our Uncivil War" t-shirts at your next holiday gathering? Maybe you would like "End Our Uncivil War" coffee mugs for you and your officemates? You can make it happen by ordering through the website.

It's been an honor to share my personal stories, beliefs and life lessons with you, as well as the stories, beliefs and life lessons of others. I hope you are moved to make the world a better place in ways you hadn't thought of previously. I hope to learn from many of you, too, in the months and years after this publication.

Like Father Charlie Strobel shared so beautifully (paraphrased).

> "Our time on this earth is short. So, what do we do with that time? Do we want to just get all we can while we are here, or do we want to make a difference to others, to leave the world a better place?"

Who's with Charlie?

ACKNOWLEDGEMENTS

Along the way, friends asked, "Who are you writing this for?" I would answer in several ways, including "anyone concerned with the tone and direction of our country" and "anyone who isn't and should be."

Writing my book was more than producing a manuscript, which is a feat unto itself. The process was intimidating at times. Should I self-publish or hire a publisher? How much does that service cost? Who can help me with that? How do I source that properly? Where do I go to find out more?

Thankfully, I met many good people who helped make *Ending Our Uncivil War* a reality. They provided great counsel, services and support. Several people stand out.

Michael Bess, your ongoing feedback the last year was phenomenally valuable. I have learned much from you, not only while writing this book but also through our bonds of raising our children, our Sunday night volunteering, and our vibrant political discussions. You're a dear friend and brother.

To Justin Owen and Grace Lyman, thank you very much for reading the manuscript and challenging me to explain concepts and issues with greater clarity, and to tighten or omit certain sections. Both of you helped to improve the book a great deal.

To my editor, Chris Clancy, you saw my painting and made it wall-worthy. I appreciate you challenging me, especially where I appeared to be too comfortable or needing focus. You are a great editor with a bright mind and keen eye, with wonderful command of overall structure and minute detail.

To Marjorie K. Eastman, your wisdom and selfless lesson sharing in writing *The Frontline Generation: How We Served Post 9/11* was invaluable. I wanted my book to look and feel like yours. I am very grateful for your friendship and your inspiring service. Thank you, John Krenson and Eden Murrie for introducing me to Marjorie.

Thank you, Brian DeMoss, for your exceptional book cover and website designs. Thank you, Doug Cordes, for putting the book together and getting it to production. You are two of the best professionals in the business, and it was a pleasure working with you.

To all the authors I met seeking advice, cheers to each of you for sharing your experiences. Thank you, in particular, to Bob Ravener, Jim Vernon and Andrew Maraniss for your unique examples, encouragement and follow-ups.

To Maureen, thank you for trust and encouragement after my life changed on a dime. Your wisdom has helped me greatly, and now, the book. May our years ahead be as bright as those already shared, with more laughter, fun and service to our loved ones. Thank you for being my best friend.

To my sister, Anne, thank you for sharing great reads like *Quiet* by Susan Cain and *Falling Upward* by Richard Rohr. Your own journey of forgiveness and acceptance has inspired me a great deal. To my father, Jim, thank you for inspiring me by living your life with renewed strength and purpose. To my mother, Rachel, thank you for teaching me about service and loving one another. Thanks to all of you for loving my children. I love you.

Kathryn and Will, again I'm grateful for the time and space to complete this project. You inspire me with your strength, strong friendships and joie de vivre. I bet most children don't have two parents who have written books meant to inspire their children. Your mother's book, *Advice for a Happy Life*, however, would end our uncivil war a lot quicker than mine. I love you dearly and am proud of you.

To spiritual role models, Mark Faulkner and Father Dexter Brewer, thank you for your daily examples of character, presence and love. You are two of the most "awake" people I know.

Last but not least, thank you, dear reader, for purchasing my book. Cheers, until we meet again!

ENDNOTES

INTRODUCTION AND
CHAPTER 1 - SERVICE COMMITMENT

1   CafePress – "Don't believe everything you think." - 10"x3" Rectangle Bumper Sticker Car Decal

2   CNN.com, "GOP House Whip Steve Scalise remains in critical condition after shooting at baseball practice," June 15, 2017

3   *The Daily Caller*, "Shooting At GOP Baseball Practice Latest In Pattern Of Violence Against Republicans," June 14, 2017

4   *Washington Free Beacon*, "30 GOP Congressmen Have Been Attacked or Threatened Since May," June 22, 2017

5   www.huffingtonpost.com (removed by website administrator)

6   *New York Daily News*, "Delta, Bank of America drop sponsorship of Shakespeare in the Park over 'Julius Caesar' stunt that shows Trump assassination," June 11, 2017

7   *Washington Times*, "Trinity College professor calls white people 'inhuman': 'Let them f-ing die,'" June 21, 2017

8   Medium.com, "Let Them F***** Die," June 16, 2017

9   Tennessean.com Facebook page, August 2017

10   WashingtonPost.com, "Mitch McConnell on the health-care legislative process, 2010 vs. 2017," June 19, 2017

11   *To Kill A Mockingbird*, Harper Lee, J. B. Lippincott & Co., 1960

12   *Mere Christianity*, C.S. Lewis, Geoffrey Bles (UK), Macmillan Publishers, Harper-Collins Publishers (US)

13   Bizjournals.com, "3 ways volunteer work will further your career," Dec. 16, 2016

14 *New York Times*, "Obama's Father's Day Remarks," June 15, 2008

15 NashvilleScene.com, "Nashvillian of the Year," Dec. 23, 2004

16 https://www.jimvernonventures.com, "Here to serve blog post," August 2017

17 LeeCompany.com, "Bill Lee is presented volunteer honor by the YMCA," July 12, 2016

18 Vanderbilt Law School website, "Mayor Karl Dean, '81, recounts rewards of 25-year career in public service," Oct. 30, 2007

19 *New York Times*, "Review: U2 Revisits 'The Joshua Tree' in the Here and Now," May 15, 2017

20 www.ONE.org

21 *Irish Mirror*, "U2 frontman Bono BANS President Donald Trump from band's current tour in the US - Irish Mirror Online," May 15, 2017

22 www.TED.com, "Julia Galef: Why you think you're right - TED, Penn State University," February 2016

23 *Business Insider Yahoo Finance*, "Chick-fil-A is beating every competitor by training workers to say 'please' and 'thank you,'" Oct. 3, 2016

24 YahooNews.com, "No Mor Chikin: Johns Hopkins Students Ban Chick-fil-A from Campus," April 23, 2015

25 ABCNews.com, "Chicago Politician Will Ban Chick-fil-A from Opening Restaurant After Anti-Gay Comments," July 25, 2012

26 HuffPost.com, "Chick-Fil-A CEO Dan Cathy Speaks Out On Gay Marriage Controversy," March 17, 2014

27 *Atlanta Journal-Constitution*, July 2012, via HuffPost.com

28 Target.com, "Continuing to Stand for Inclusivity," April 19, 2016

29 FoxNews.com, "'You cannot eat here': Hawaii café riles residents with ban on Trump voters," Dec. 27, 2016

30 *The Frontline Generation: How We Served Post 9/11*, Marjorie K. Eastman, Longbow 6 Publishing, 2016

31 "The Servant Song," Richard Gillard, Scripture in Song/Maranatha! Music (AS-CAP) (admin. by Capital CMG Publishing) © 1977

CHAPTER 2 – SPIRITUAL RENEWAL

32 "Mysterious Ways," album *Achtung Baby*, Lyrics by Bono, Song by U2 (Adam Clayton, Dave Evans, Paul David Hewson, Larry Mullen and Angelique Kidjo, Universal Music Publishing Group, 1991

33 *Truth vs. Falsehood: How to Tell the Difference*, David R. Hawkins, Axial Publishing Company, 2005, p. 170-171

34   "Martin Luther King Jr. and the Global Freedom Struggle," November 17, 1957, "Loving Your Enemies," Sermon Delivered at Dexter Avenue Baptist Church http://kingencyclopedia.stanford.edu/encyclopedia/documentsentry/doc_loving_your_enemies/

35   CBS News, "Trump blasts civil rights icon John Lewis in Twitter attack," Jan. 14, 2017

36   Giving USA, givinginstitute.org, "Giving USA: 2015 Was America's Most-Generous Year Ever," June 13, 2016

37   By permission of Father Peter Wojcik, "The Internet Is My Shepherd," May 2017

38   Wikipedia, Religious Views on Love

39   Wikipedia, Religious Views on Love

40   Wikipedia, Tertullian

41   *USA Today*, "Pastor slammed for Carrie Underwood performance," Jan. 6, 2017

42   "Disciples: Those Who Love Others," Dec. 20, 2016, Adapted from Richard Rohr, "Love Is Not What as Much as How," homily, April 24, 2016, https://cac.org/love-not-much/

43   Resisting Happiness, Beacon Publishing, Matthew Kelly, 2016

44   "Love Never Fails," Dec. 29, 2016, Adapted from Richard Rohr, "The Most Profound Chapter in the Bible," homily, Jan. 31, 2016, https://cac.org/the-most-profound-chapter-in-the-bible/.

45   "Love Never Fails," Dec. 29, 2016, Adapted from Richard Rohr, "The Most Profound Chapter in the Bible," homily, January 31, 2016, https://cac.org/the-most-profound-chapter-in-the-bible/.

46   *The Empire Strikes Back*, Lucasfilm Ltd., 1980

47   "Patrick's Path: A Spiritual Guide," Administrator of Westport Parish, custodian of St. Patrick's oratory, Croagh Patrick, National Shrine

48   *American Gospel: God, The Founding Fathers and the Making of a Nation*, Jon Meacham, Random House, 2006

49   *The Wall Street Journal*, "A President's Credibility: Trump's falsehoods are eroding public trust, at home and abroad," March 21, 2017

50   *Frontline* PBS, "The Choice 2016," Sept. 27, 2016

51   *Quiet: The Power of Introverts in a World That Can't Stop Talking*, Susan Cain, Random House, 2012, 2013,

52   *Liberty Champion*, "Promoting Digital Detox," March 8, 2016

53   The College Fix, "Professor promotes 'Digital Detox,' says she's working to 'preserve humanity,'" June 19, 2017

54   *Falling Upward: A Spirituality of the Two Halves of Life*, Richard Rohr, Published by Jossey-Bass, A Wiley Imprint, Copyright 2011 by Richard Rohr, p. 26

55   *Falling Upward: A Spirituality of the Two Halves of Life*, Richard Rohr, Published by Jossey-Bass, A Wiley Imprint, Copyright 2011 by Richard Rohr, p. 27

56   *Falling Upward: A Spirituality of the Two Halves of Life*, Richard Rohr, Published by Jossey-Bass, A Wiley Imprint, Copyright 2011 by Richard Rohr, p. 28

57   *Falling Upward: A Spirituality of the Two Halves of Life*, Richard Rohr, Published by Jossey-Bass, A Wiley Imprint, Copyright 2011 by Richard Rohr, p. 10

58   *Falling Upward: A Spirituality of the Two Halves of Life*, Richard Rohr, Published by Jossey-Bass, A Wiley Imprint, Copyright 2011 by Richard Rohr, p. 36

59   *Falling Upward: A Spirituality of the Two Halves of Life*, Richard Rohr, Published by Jossey-Bass, A Wiley Imprint, Copyright 2011 by Richard Rohr, p. 37

60   *The Divine Dance: Trinity and Your Transformation*, Richard Rohr, Whitaker House, Copyright by Richard Rohr 2016, p. 141

61   *When Your Ex Doesn't Follow the Rules,: Keep Your Sanity and Raise Happy Healthy Kids*, Maureen Doyle, 2016

62   *American Gospel: God, The Founding Fathers and the Making of a Nation*, Jon Meacham, p. 23, Random House, 2006

63   *American Gospel: God, The Founding Fathers and the Making of a Nation*, Jon Meacham, p. 79, Random House, 2006

64   *Democracy In America*, Chapter XVII, Alexis de Tocqueville

65   *American Gospel: God, The Founding Fathers and the Making of a Nation*, Jon Meacham, p. 5, Random House, 2006

66   *American Gospel: God, The Founding Fathers and the Making of a Nation*, Jon Meacham, p. 262-264, Random House, 2006

67   *Church of the Holy Trinity v. United States*, 143 U.S. 457 (1892)

68   *Everson v. Board of Education*, 330 U.S. 1 (1947)

69   *McCollum v. Board of Education*, 333 U.S. 203 (1948)

70   *Zorach v. Clauson*, 343 U.S. 306 (1952)

71   *The Daily Signal*, "Bakers Accused of Hate Get Emotional Day in Court," March 2, 2017

72   *American Gospel: God, The Founding Fathers and the Making of a Nation*, Jon Meacham, p. 238-239, Random House, 2006

73   American Renewal Project, "Constitution DOES NOT require complete Separation of Church & State," Jan. 19, 2017

74   Gallup.com, "In U.S., Four in 10 Report Attending Church in Last Week," Dec. 24, 2013

75   Adapted from Richard Rohr, *Everything Belongs: The Gift of Contemplative Prayer* (The Crossroad Publishing Company: 2003), 28-29, 149-151.

76   Adapted from Richard Rohr, *Dancing Standing Still: Healing the World from a Place of Prayer* (Paulist Press: 2014), 72-73; and *CONSPIRE 2016: Everything Belongs* (CAC: 2016), sessions 2 and 3 (MP4 video download).

77   Adapted from Richard Rohr, *Dancing Standing Still: Healing the World from a Place of Prayer* (Paulist Press: 2014), 72-73; and *CONSPIRE 2016: Everything Belongs* (CAC: 2016), sessions 2 and 3 (MP4 video download).

78   *American Gospel: God, The Founding Fathers and the Making of a Nation*, Jon Meacham, p. 15-16, Random House, 2006

79   Adapted from Richard Rohr, *A Spring Within Us: A Book of Daily Meditations* (CAC Publishing: 2016), 98-99; *Yes, And . . . : Daily Meditations* (Franciscan Media: 2013), 406; and *The Naked Now: Learning to See as the Mystics See* (The Crossroad Publishing Company: 2009), 34-35.

80   *The New York Times*, "The Year of Conquering Negative Thinking," Jan. 3, 2017

81   *The Daily Caller*, "Samantha Bee To Jake Tapper: No 'Smug Liberal Problem'" April 30, 2017

82   NewsOne.com, "Top 10 Racist Limbaugh Quotes," 2010

83   *The Atlantic*, "How Late-Night Comedy Fueled the Rise of Trump: Sneering hosts have alienated conservatives and made liberals smug," May 2017

84   *The New York Times*, "The Year of Conquering Negative Thinking," Jan. 3, 2017

85   *The New York Times*, "The Year of Conquering Negative Thinking," Jan. 3, 2017

86   Wikipedia, Cognitive behavioral therapy

87   Drwaynedyer.com, "The Power of Intention," July 2017

88   Adapted from Richard Rohr, *Dancing Standing Still: Healing the World from a Place of Prayer* (Paulist Press: 2014), 72-73; and *CONSPIRE 2016: Everything Belongs* (CAC: 2016), sessions 2 and 3 (MP4 video download)

89   "Dirty Laundry," album *I Can't Stand Still*, Asylum, 1982

90   https://daplpipelinefacts.com/, "The Dakota Access Pipeline Will Keep America Moving Efficiently and in an Environmentally Safe Manner"

91   *The New York Times*, "North Dakota Oil Pipeline Battle: Who's Fighting and Why," August 26, 2016

92   NPR.org, "Dakota Pipeline Protesters, Nearby Residents Brace For 2017," Jan. 4, 2017

93   *The New York Times*, "Wall Street Journal Editor Admonishes Reporters Over Trump Coverage," Aug. 23, 2017

94   *The Spectator*, "The law of movies now applies to world politics: nobody knows anything," Nov. 19, 2016

95   Politico.com, "Full transcript: Trump's *Wall Street Journal* interview," Aug. 1, 2017

96   CNN: *Anderson Cooper 360*, "Big Promises: What Coal Country Expects from Trump," Jan. 25, 2017

97   *The Washington Post*, "Audiotape: Katie Couric documentary falsely depicts gun supporters as 'idiots,'" May 25, 2016

98   NPR.org, Opinion: "Manipulative Editing Reflects Poorly on Katie Couric, Gun Documentary," May 26, 2016

99   April 2016 Facebook post by permission of Jim Bryson

100   Adapted from Richard Rohr with John Feister, *Hope Against Darkness: The Transforming Vision of Saint Francis in an Age of Anxiety* (St. Anthony Messenger Press: 2001), 120-121.

CHAPTER 3 – SCHOLASTIC INDEPENDENCE

101   *The New York Times*, "The Dangerous Safety of College," Frank Bruni, March 11, 2017

102   *The New York Times*, "Understanding the Angry Mob at Middlebury That Gave Me a Concussion," Allison Stanger, March 13, 2017

103   *The New York Times*, "The Dangerous Safety of College," Frank Bruni, March 11, 2017

104   *The New York Times*, "The Dangerous Safety of College," Frank Bruni, March 11, 2017

105   *The Boston Globe*, "Middlebury College punishes students who disrupted Charles Murray talk," April 29, 2017

106   *The Washington Post*, "Claremont McKenna College disciplines seven students for blockade that shut down Heather Mac Donald speech," July 17, 2017

107   *The New York Times*, "The Dangerous Safety of College," Frank Bruni, March 11, 2017

108   *The Weekly Standard*, "Bannon: 'The Trump Presidency That We Fought For, and Won, Is Over,'" Aug. 18, 2017

109   CNN.com, "Rep. Wilson shouts, 'You lie' to Obama during speech," Sept. 10, 2009

110   www.FIRE.org, The Foundation for Individual Rights in Education website

111   www.FIRE.org, "Spotlight on Speech Codes 2016"

112   Pew Research Center, "Sharp Partisan Divisions in Views of National Institutions," July 10, 2017

113   "Politics, Morality and Civility," Vaclav Havel, Lipscomb University, Paul Wilson, *Summer Meditations*, Knopf 1992, and The Trinity Forum, 2006

114   www.wlu.edu, Washington & Lee University website, "Our Traditions: The Speaking Tradition"

115   The College Fix, "University distributes seven-page speech guide," Oct. 4, 2016

116   http://www.provost.umd.edu/diversity/grants2012.html, Maryland University website

117   DailyMail.com, "University of Michigan spends $16,000 on campaign telling students to stop using words like 'crazy' and 'ghetto' to avoid hurting others' feelings," Feb. 9, 2015

118   The Cut, "Ratchet: The Rap Insult That Became a Compliment," April 11, 2013

119 The College Fix, "White students undergo weekly 'deconstructing whiteness' program at Northwestern University," Feb. 17, 2016

120 The College Fix, "Princeton HR department: Don't use word 'man,'" Aug. 18, 2016

121 WATE.com, "Lawmakers call for UT chancellor's resignation over inclusive holiday celebration suggestions," Dec. 3, 2015

122 NBCNews.com, "University of Tennessee Shuts Diversity Office After Sex Week, Gender Controversy," May 21, 2016

123 NYPost.com, "Not using transgender pronouns could get you fined," May 19, 2016

124 The Daily Caller, "New York City Lets You Choose From 31 Different Gender Identities," May 24, 2016

125 http://gothamist.com/, "No, NYC Did Not Just Introduce A $250,000 Fine For Any Incorrect Use Of Gender Pronouns," May 19, 2016

126 The Daily Signal, "Canadians Could Be Jailed or Fined for Using Incorrect Gender Pronouns," June 19, 2017

127 FIRE.org, "New Tennessee law is good news for academic freedom," May 15, 2017

128 FIRE.org, "New Tennessee law is good news for academic freedom," May 15, 2017

129 The New York Times, "Climate of Complete Certainty," Opinion, Bret Stephens, April 28, 2017

130 NYPost.com, "Times columnist blasted by 'nasty left' for climate change piece," April 28, 2017

131 Politico.com, "New York Times publisher sends personal appeal to those who canceled over Bret Stephens," May 12, 2017

132 TheHill.com, "'Climate change is a fact,' Obama declares," Jan. 28, 2014

133 Heritage.org, "The Paris Agreement Is a Treaty and Should Be Submitted to the Senate," March 15, 2016

134 Sourcenews.com, "Top 10 Environmental Predictions That Totally Flopped... ," April 27, 2017

135 The Daily Signal, "Here's How Wrong Past Environmental Predictions Have Been," April 27, 2016

136 The Gateway Pundit, "Al Gore Said North Pole Would Be Completely Melted This Year... Guess Not, Huh?" Jan. 13, 2012

137 The College Fix, "Professors tell students: Drop class if you dispute man-made climate change," Aug. 31, 2016

138 The College Fix, "Environmental Justice 101 – Professors argue capitalism abuses poor minorities through pollution," July 18, 2015

139 Politifact.com, "Do scientists disagree about global warming?" Aug. 14, 2011

140   http://www.dailymail.co.uk/, "And now it's global COOLING! Return of Arctic ice cap as it grows by 29% in a year," Sept. 7, 2013

141   *USA Today*, "Study: Ocean acidification stunting growth of coral reefs," Feb. 24, 2016

142   Humphrey on the Hill, "TN meets EPA particle pollution standards statewide," Aug. 31, 2017

143   The Daily Signal, "Five Myths About Extreme Weather and Global Warming," March 31, 2014

144   The College Fix, "Campus flyers touting 'Moral Case for Fossil Fuels' ripped up, covered with pro-socialism posters," March 22, 2016

145   The College Fix, "This commencement speaker nails it: 'Leave your safe spaces,'" May 17, 2017

146   Adapted from Richard Rohr, "Jesus: Forgiving Victim, Transforming Savior," *Richard Rohr on Transformation, Collected Talks, Vol. 1, disc 1* (Franciscan Media: 1997); and Richard Rohr with John Feister, *Hope Against Darkness: The Transforming Vision of Saint Francis in an Age of Anxiety* (Franciscan Media: 2001), 19-20, 22-24.

147   *The Wall Street Journal*, "Universities Must Defend Free Speech," Benno Schmidt, Opinion, May 6, 1991

148   Yale Undergraduate Survey Sponsored By The William F. Buckley, Jr. Program at Yale, April 25, 2017

149   The College Fix, "Right-of-center students at Emerson College, sick and tired of being bullied, demand change," June 6, 2017

150   *The Daily Caller*, "Yale Student Shrieks At Prof For Denying Her 'Safe Space' [VIDEO]," Nov. 6, 2015

151   12news.com Arizona, "NAU students demand president declare safe space or step down," March 31, 2017

152   USChronicle.com, "Student Attempts To Scold University President About Need For "Safe Spaces" – The Student Does Not Like Her Response"

153   Wikipedia, Vaclav Havel, and "Politics, Morality and Civility," Vaclav Havel, Lipscomb University, Paul Wilson, Summer Meditations, Knopf 1992, and The Trinity Forum, 2006

154   The College Fix, "Student apologizes for wearing Chicago Blackhawks sweatshirt to class," May 16, 2017

155   *The Wall Street Journal*, "Saving Chief Wahoo," June 21, 2017

156   https://heatst.com/culture-wars/for-its-workshop-on-privilege-kennesaw-state-university-separates-students-by-race/

157   The College Fix, "CONFIRMED: Racist note that prompted St. Olaf College shut down is hate-crime hoax," May 10, 2017

158 Minnesota NPR, "St. Olaf president says intensive effort underway to find people behind racist messages," May 2, 2017

159 StarTribune.com, "St. Olaf: Report of racist note on black student's windshield was 'fabricated,'" May 11, 2017

160 The College Fix, "Enough with the hate crime hoaxes," Opinion, Daniel Payne, May 17, 2017

161 The Orion, "Debunking GSEC myths," Opinion Robert Fonseca, May 10, 2017, and The College Fix, "Professor publicly slurs student as 'shitty' for questioning alternative gender identities," June 12, 2017

162 The College Fix, "White professor forced to flee campus as police say he's not safe," May 26, 2017; "NEW VIDEO: Madness reigns at Evergreen State College as students 'take over,'" May 28, 2017

163 The Cooper Point Journal, "George Bridges Statement in Response to Student Demands," May 26, 2017

164 JonathanTurley.org, "Evergreen State College Faculty Sign Letter Supporting Students Accused Of Abusing Professor," June 5, 2017

165 https://heatst.com/culture-wars/university-of-hawaii-professor-demands-white-men-quit-their-jobs/

166 The Daily Caller, "College Guide Says That Black People Can't Be Racist," Jan. 31, 2017

167 The Daily Caller, "Fancypants College Student Brutally Attacked White Woman Over BRAIDED HAIR, Cops Say," March 31, 2017

168 The Washington Post, "Obama says liberal college students should not be 'coddled.' Are we really surprised?" Sept. 15, 2015

169 The New York Times, "The Conservative Force Behind Speeches Roiling College Campuses," May 20, 2017

170 The New York Times, "The Conservative Force Behind Speeches Roiling College Campuses," May 20, 2017

171 The New York Times, "The Conservative Force Behind Speeches Roiling College Campuses," May 20, 2017

172 The New York Times, "The Conservative Force Behind Speeches Roiling College Campuses," May 20, 2017

173 The Guardian, "Lionel Shriver's full speech: 'I hope the concept of cultural appropriation is a passing fad,'" Sept. 13, 2016

174 The Daily Caller, "LOCO: Sheltered College Kids Demand Safe Spaces After Party Featuring Tiny Sombreros And Tequila," March 3, 2016, and CampusReform.org, "Bowdoin creates safe spaces for victims of tequila themed party," March 1, 2016

175 The Daily Caller, "Clemson University Apologizes For Offending Mexicans By SERVING TACOS," Oct. 10, 2015

176 The College Fix, "Asking people to show up on time is not inclusive, says Clemson employee training," April 10, 2017

177 The Daily Signal, "The Cancer Eating Away at College Campuses," April 12, 2017

178 UC San-Diego website http://facultydiversity.ucsd.edu/c2d/index.html#Are-there-any-guidelines-for-wr, and The Daily Signal, "The Cancer Eating Away at College Campuses," April 12, 2017

179 "The Imposition of Diversity Statements on Faculty Hiring and Promotion at Oregon Universities: A Report of the Oregon Association of Scholars," Bruce Gilley, March 7, 2017

180 The Daily Signal, "The Cancer Eating Away at College Campuses," April 12, 2017

181 James G. Martin Center for Academic Renewal, "Loyalty Oaths Return with Faculty 'Diversity Statements,'" George Leef, March 29, 2017

182 HistoryLink.org, "U.S. Supreme Court strikes down loyalty oaths for Washington state employees on June 1, 1964," Feb. 13, 2003, and James G. Martin Center for Academic Renewal "Loyalty Oaths Return with Faculty "Diversity Statements," George Leef, March 29, 2017

183 James G. Martin Center for Academic Renewal, "Loyalty Oaths Return with Faculty 'Diversity Statements,'" George Leef, March 29, 2017

184 "Governance for a New Era: A Blueprint for Higher Education Trustees," Benno Schmidt, August 2014

185 Adapted from Richard Rohr, *Dancing Standing Still: Healing the World from a Place of Prayer* (Paulist Press: 2014), 72-73; and *CONSPIRE 2016: Everything Belongs* (CAC: 2016), sessions 2 and 3 (MP4 video download).

CHAPTER 4 – SYSTEMIC GOVERNMENT REFORMS

186 Tennessee Constitutional History, Harry Phillips American Inn of Court, http://harryphillipsaic.com/wp-content/uploads/2013/02/1_TNConstitutionHistory.pdf

187 FoxNews.com, "Patrick Caddell: The real election surprise? The uprising of the American people," Nov. 7, 2016

188 Tom Warburton, and Bob Dorough. *Schoolhouse Rock! USA.*

189 Wikipedia, Single-subject rule

190 Love.house.gov, "New Bill Limits Bills to 'One Subject at a Time,'" Jan. 13, 2016

191 *Deseret News*, "Rep. Mia Love wants to limit congressional bills to one subject at a time," Jan. 21, 2016

192 Bloomberg Politics, "Trump Says He'll Sign Congress Spending Deal That Jettisons His Goals," April 30, 2017

193　Breitbart.com, "Exclusive — Rand Paul on Omnibus Spending Bill: 'President Hillary Clinton Would Have Been Proud of This Bill,'" May 3, 2017

194　*The Washington Post*, "The filibuster isn't what it used to be. It's time to bring the old way back," Opinion, George F. Will, March 29, 2017

195　Wikipedia, Filibuster

196　Breitbart.com, "HHS Report: Average Health Insurance Premiums Doubled Under Obamacare," May 24, 2017

197　*Chattanooga Times-Free Press*, "Tennessee approves costly health exchange price hikes for state's biggest insurers," Aug. 23, 2016

198　*The Washington Free Beacon*, "One-Third of U.S. Will Have Only One Insurer Offering Obamacare Plans in 2017," Aug. 23, 2016

199　Foundation for Economic Freedom, "This Is Why Government Shouldn't Be Involved in Health Care," May 5, 2017

200　*The Tennessean USA Today* Network, "Sen. Lamar Alexander helped shape Obamacare repeal plan, yet bill will bypass his committee," June 22, 2017

201　ABCNews.com, "Former Comptroller General Warns of Greek Scenario in U.S.," March 8, 2012

202　Chattanoogan.com, "Tennessee Passes Application For Federal Balanced Budget Amendment," March 13, 2014

203　http://www.usdebtclock.org

204　*The Fiscal Times*, "Nearly a Dozen States Are Suffering From 'Chronic Budget Stress,'" April 5, 2014

205　Wikipedia, Article Five of the United States Constitution

206　The Daily Signal, "A Constitutional Amendment That Would Drain the Swamp," April 13, 2017

207　Chattanoogan.com, "Tennessee Passes Application For Federal Balanced Budget Amendment," March 13, 2014

208　Accuracy in Media, "CNN Poll: Americans like Balanced Budget Amendment," July 22, 2011

209　The Daily Signal, "Washington at Its Worst: Senate Passes Nonexistent Bill," Sept. 21, 2016

210　NFIB.com, "Infographic: The Great Red Tape Disaster," Oct. 5, 2016

211　*Washington Examiner*, "Look at how many pages are in the federal tax code," April 15, 2016

212　CNN.com, "EPA spill: 'The magnitude of it, you can't even describe it,'" Aug. 10, 2015

213　The Daily Signal, "Exposing the EPA's Gold King Mine Cover-Up," June 14, 2017

214　CNN.com, First on CNN: Navajo Nation sues EPA over toxic mine spill," Aug. 17, 2015

262

215 NFIB.com, "NFIB Applauds AG For Joining Legal Challenge to Onerous 'Waters of the U.S.' Rule," July 23, 2015

216 Humphrey on the Hill, "Business groups urge AG to sue EPA, too," July 14, 2015

217 *Greater Baton Rouge Business Report*, "Baton Rouge business owners highly concerned, confused by new federal overtime rules," July 6, 2016

218 USNews.com, "Repeal of Glass-Steagall Caused the Financial Crisis," Aug. 27, 2012

219 CNBC.com, "Dodd-Frank Act: CNBC Explains," May 11, 2012

220 CNN Money, "House votes to kill Dodd-Frank. Now what? " June 8, 2017

221 The Heritage Foundation, "Red Tape Rising: Six Years of Escalating Regulation Under Obama," May 11, 2015

222 NFIB.com, "COLUMN: Government Intimidation Tactics on Business Must Stop Now," July 2, 2013

223 Foundation for Economic Education, "Without the State, Who Will Handcuff Teens for Selling Water Bottles," June 28, 2017

224 Newsweek.com, "Police in Washington D.C. Arrest Black Teens for Selling Water Bottles, Because 'Safety,'" June 24, 2017

225 NFIB.com, "COLUMN: Government Intimidation Tactics on Business Must Stop Now," July 2, 2013

226 NoRegulationWithoutRepresentation.com, "Update... Regulation Freedom Amendment," June 7, 2017

227 Forbes.com, "Warning: You Could Be Fined $36.5k For Helping Your Employees," Oct. 25, 2016

228 Heritage.org, "Who Will Regulate the Regulators? Administrative Agencies, the Separation of Powers, and Chevron Deference," May 7, 2015

229 DailyCaller.com, "Gorsuch Appears Deeply Concerned With Growth Of Agency Power," Feb. 19, 2017

230 *The Washington Post*, "Gorsuch is right about Chevron deference," March 25, 2017

231 Forbes.com, "The REINS Act: Increasing The Accountability Of Our Elected Officials," Jan. 12, 2015

232 Congressman Diane Black press release

233 Chattanoogan.com, "Legislators Make Good on Threat to Try and Shutdown TWRA," May 11, 2011

234 KnoxNews.com archive, "'Government Ops' serious about work," Frank Cagle, May 18, 2016

235 https://www.termlimits.org/quotes/

236 Wikipedia, Contract with America

237 Congressional Research Service, "Congressional Careers: Service Tenure and Patterns of Member Service, 1789-2017," Jan. 3, 2017

238 Mediaite.com, "'Members Are Not Looked at as People': Managers of Republican, Democratic Baseball Teams Hold Presser," June 14, 2017

239 CSMonitor.com, "Sen. Robert Byrd: King of pork or larger-than-life hero?" June 28, 2010

240 TheHill.com, "Poll: Nearly 80 percent of voters want Hatch to retire," Jan. 26, 2017

241 "RESTORATION: Congress, Term Limits and the Recovery of Deliberative Democracy," George F. Will, Free Press, Aug. 15, 1992, ISBN: 0-02-934437-9

242 *The Washington Post*, "Donald Trump calls for congressional term limits to end 'cycle of corruption,'" Oct. 18, 2016

243 Spectrum News NY1, "In 2008 NY1 Interview, Trump Made Clear He Was Firmly Against Term Limits," Oct. 20, 2016

244 *The Washington Post*, "Donald Trump calls for congressional term limits to end 'cycle of corruption,'" Oct. 18, 2016

245 CNBC.com, "Here's how much the average American family has saved for retirement," Sept. 12, 2016

246 NYDailyNews.com, "U.S. Senate seat now costs $10.5 million to win, on average, while US House seat costs, $1.7 million, new analysis of FEC data shows," March 11, 2013

247 Wikipedia, Founding Fathers of the United States

248 The Daily Signal, "Trump Vows to Back Term Limits. So Do These 48 Lawmakers," Dec. 15, 2016

249 The Daily Signal, "Washington Should Be More Concerned About the Next Generation Than the Next Election," Oct. 26, 2016

250 The Daily Signal, "Washington Should Be More Concerned About the Next Generation Than the Next Election," Oct. 26, 2016

251 Cooper.house.gov, "Cooper Introduces Bills to End Gerrymandering and Reform Redistricting," Jan. 27, 2017

252 NYDailyNews.com, "19th Century Mass. Gov. Elbridge Gerry knew all about gerrymandering of political districts - he invented it!" March 4, 2013

253 Instapundit.com, "MICHAEL BARONE: The Supreme Court — out of the redistricting thicket?" Dec. 6, 2016

254 *The New York Times*, "Justices Reject 2 Gerrymandered North Carolina Districts, Citing Racial Bias," May 22, 2017

255 HuffPost.com, "Supreme Court Agrees To Hear Potentially Monumental Political Gerrymandering Case, The case could dramatically impact the way states draw electoral districts," June 19, 2017

256 WashingtonPost.com, "Blue Dog Democrats, whittled down in number, are trying to regroup," Jan. 15, 2014

257 Brennan Center for Justice at the New York University School of Law "Democracy Agenda: Redistricting," Feb. 4, 2016

258 TheHill.com, "Dems hit new low in state legislatures," Nov. 18, 2016

259 Brennancenter.org

260 Brennan Center for Justice at the New York University School of Law "Democracy Agenda: Redistricting," Feb. 4, 2016

261 *National Review*, "Will Congress Exempt Itself from the Overtime Rule?" June 10, 2016

262 *National Review*, "Will Congress Exempt Itself from the Overtime Rule?" June 10, 2016

263 Forbes.com, "Congress Is Getting A Special Exemption From Obamacare--And No, It's Not Legal," April 15, 2016

264 TheNewAmerican.com, "Sen. Rand Paul's Constitutional Amendment Requires Congress Obey Laws," Oct. 23, 2013

ABOUT THE AUTHOR

Jim Brown was born in Milton, Florida. He spent his childhood in Rhode Island, Connecticut and New York City before moving to Nashville, Tennessee, in 1973. Brown attended Vanderbilt University, earning a bachelor's degree in Communication in 1987, before joining the U.S. Navy, where he served four years as a supply officer. He earned the Navy Achievement Medal for his stellar service aboard the USS Bainbridge (CGN-25), based out of Norfolk, Virginia.

After leaving the military in 1992, Brown worked at Robert Orr Sysco Food Service before joining J.C. Bradford & Co. as an Investment Broker in 1995. In 2000, Brown switched gears into journalism and media relations, working as Business Editor at *The City Paper* and then as Corporate Communications Director for Gaylord Entertainment. He joined the National Federation of Independent Business in 2004 as Senior Media Manager before being promoted in 2007 to his current role of Tennessee State Director.

From 2011-2016, Brown was named to NashvillePost.com's "In Charge" list of 400 influential Middle Tennessee leaders for his role in various reforms that have helped Tennessee become a leader in economic expansion and job growth. He is recognized for his expertise in workers' compensation, unemployment, tax, tort, environmental and regulatory law in Tennessee.

Brown is active with causes dedicated to wiping out cancer, including as Chair-elect of Gilda's Club Middle Tennessee, a cancer support group. He volunteers regularly at Room in the Inn, a support program for Nashville's homeless community. He has served in various roles with Junior Achievement of Middle Tennessee, Prevent Blindness Tennessee and other groups.

He enjoys hiking, biking, traveling, and reading, watching Nashville Predators' hockey, and keeping up with his children, Kathryn and Will.

CPSIA information can be obtained
at www.ICGtesting.com
Printed in the USA
LVOW06*0809121117
555953LV00002B/2/P

9 780999 399903